D0566741

Reconciliation, Healing, *and* Hope

SERMONS FROM WASHINGTON NATIONAL CATHEDRAL

Edited by

JAN NAYLOR COPE

O'Neal Library
50 Oak Street
Mountain Brook, AL 35213

 Morehouse Publishing
NEW YORK

252.009

Copyright © 2022 by Washington National Cathedral

All rights reserved. No part of this book may be reproduced, stored in a retrieval system, or transmitted in any form or by any means, electronic or mechanical, including photocopying, recording, or otherwise, without the written permission of the publisher.

Unless otherwise noted, the Scripture quotations contained herein are from the New Revised Standard Version Bible, copyright © 1989 by the Division of Christian Education of the National Council of Churches of Christ in the U.S.A. Used by permission. All rights reserved.

Scripture quotations marked (NIV) are taken from the Holy Bible, New International Version®, NIV®. Copyright © 1973, 1978, 1984, 2011 by Biblica, Inc.™ Used by permission of Zondervan. All rights reserved worldwide. www.zondervan .com. The "NIV" and "New International Version" are trademarks registered in the United States Patent and Trademark Office by Biblica, Inc.™

Scripture quotations marked (KJV) are taken from the KING JAMES VERSION (KJV): KING JAMES VERSION, public domain.

Reprinted by arrangement with The Heirs to the Estate of Martin Luther King Jr., c/o Writers House as agent for the proprietor New York, NY. "Facing the Challenge of a New Age" Copyright © 1956 by Dr. Martin Luther King, Jr. Renewed © 1984 by Coretta Scott King. "Strength to Love" Copyright © 1963 by Dr. Martin Luther King, Jr. Renewed © 1991 by Coretta Scott King. "I've Been to the Mountaintop" Copyright © 1968 by Dr. Martin Luther King, Jr. Renewed © 1996 by Coretta Scott King.

Morehouse Publishing, 19 East 34th Street, New York, NY 10016
Morehouse Publishing is an imprint of Church Publishing Incorporated.

Cover photo by Danielle E. Thomas, Washington National Cathedral
Cover design by Marc Whitaker, MTWdesign
Typeset by Rose Design

Library of Congress Cataloging-in-Publication Data

Names: Cope, Jan Naylor, editor.
Title: Reconciliation, healing, and hope : sermons from Washington National Cathedral / edited by Jan Naylor Cope.
Description: New York, NY : Morehouse Publishing, [2022]
Identifiers: LCCN 2021041379 (print) | LCCN 2021041380 (ebook) | ISBN 9781640654846 (hardcover) | ISBN 9781640654853 (epub)
Subjects: LCSH: Sermons, American--21st century. | Washington National Cathedral (Washington, D.C.)
Classification: LCC BV4241 .R435 2022 (print) | LCC BV4241 (ebook) | DDC 252.009/05--dc23

LC record available at https://lccn.loc.gov/2021041379
LC ebook record available at https://lccn.loc.gov/2021041380

CONTENTS

FOREWORD

Jon Meacham

n the beginning was a question. In the cool of the evening, in the Garden of Eden, we are told that God is seeking Adam and Eve. "Where are you?" the Lord asks. *Where are you?* As Canon Kelly Brown Douglas preached from the pulpit of Washington National Cathedral in the first weeks of the COVID-19 pandemic, that query echoes through the ages, from antiquity unto this very hour: *Where are we?* And there is, of course, a sequential question—a "follow-up," in the vernacular of the press corps that dominates so much of the life of our capital city: *Where are we going?*

This collection of sermons from a season of plague and of pain hazards a few answers to these elemental puzzles. They are answers grounded in the Christian faith, which is itself formed from two essential sources of life and of light: love and remembrance. The gospel is founded on the injunction to love one another; the tradition that sustains us is summed up in perhaps the most-heeded commandment in all of history, which is to "Do this in remembrance of Me." That gospel and this tradition are under assault in our time, an assault fueled by grievance and exacerbated, in the time of COVID, by disease and distrust.

The words in these pages are addressed to this broken and not-contrite world. As the worst pandemic in American history in a century swept the land, Michael Curry, the primate of the Episcopal Church, noted that the plague went beyond the physical. We faced, he said, "a pandemic of the human spirit, when our lives are focused on ourselves, when the self becomes the center of the world and of the universe. It is a pandemic of self-centeredness. And it may be even more destructive than a virus."

It is surely hardier and more persistent than any medical condition. The sermons here are about the larger pandemic of which Bishop Curry spoke: a pandemic of sin and of selfishness, of self-absorption and the will to power. Such is the lot of a frail and fallen world; and such is the work of the church, to call us to love and to remembrance, for in love and in remembrance lie what Thomas Cranmer called the means of grace and the hope of glory.

Where are we? We are, too often, far from the love and from the call of God. That is in the nature of things; the story the Bible—the story of our lives—is of fall and deliverance, captivity and liberation, exile and return. To everything there is a season, we have been told, and we are only now emerging from a time of trial. What saw us through was grace and science, concern and mindfulness, love and hope.

But our work is not done. It is only beginning, always, at least until the final in-breaking of the Holy Spirit and the arrival of that hour when every tear will be wiped away, and death shall be no more. And that is an hour whose coming we cannot know.

In the meantime—which is where most of life is lived, in the meantime—we are left with the rite of remembrance. I am a historian who tries to make something new and resonant out of the elements of the past. I believe, deeply, that William Faulkner was right when he wrote that the past is never dead; it isn't even past, and that we do in fact live in what G. K. Chesterton called a democracy of the dead. Those who came before us have much to teach us; not everything, perhaps, for history and tradition are not infallible, but we have nowhere else to begin our deliberations about what we should do except with the fact of what we have done.

Remembrance—*history*—lies at the heart of our common ecclesiastical tradition. From the Song of Moses—"Remember the days of old; consider the years of many generations; ask thy father, and he will show thee; thy elders, and they will tell thee"—to the Last Supper, we are commanded to look back in order to summon the strength and the courage to move forward.

A place like Washington National Cathedral dwells in a particular and somewhat precarious place. It is at once sacred and secular; at once out of the world and *of* the world. Its pulpit and its altar are pivot points. Or, to switch the metaphor, gateways—gateways from the visible to the invisible, from the temporal to the eternal. The cathedral's message is clear: For the people of God the most important and indeed radical thing we can do is to love and to *remember*. To keep the feast and say our prayers. To keep the candles lit and the lanterns burning. To read the office and sing the hymns. To preach the word and to heed it. A sacramental tradition will be relevant in direct proportion to how well and how faithfully it is carried forward in the ways it has been through so much storm and strife from Golgotha to twenty-first-century America. And though it may seem conventional, in fact the boldest course we can take is to preach the oldest piece of good news in the Christian story: *He is not here, but is risen. He is not here, but is risen.*

So how do we advertise the truth that shapes our lives? By celebrating the sacraments and by proclaiming the Word. We believe that the world has been transformed by the death and resurrection of the Son of the Living God and that he will come again to judge the quick and the dead and whose kingdom shall have no end. It is the most thrilling of messages, the most improbable of worldviews. And for decade after decade, century after century, and now millennium after millennium, the most enduring act of witness to that enveloping truth has been the act of remembrance. Devout or distracted, ecstatic or gloomy, if we "do this in remembrance of me," we are mysteriously but unmistakably in communion with God the Father through the sacrifice of God the Son by the working of the Holy Ghost. No matter how we feel, no matter what kind of day or week we've had, our thirst is satisfied, and order is restored to a broken world, if only for a moment.

Great preaching can help us in this task. The bishop of Washington, Mariann Edgar Budde, drew on the wisdom of Gandalf in *The Lord of the Rings* to make the point that we cannot choose the times in which we live; we can only choose what to do within those times. "I believe that God wants us to trust that, in the midst of this pandemic and the enormous cost of efforts to slow its spread, there are also forces for good at work now," Bishop Budde preached, "that we are our best selves whenever we join those forces and do our part, tipping the scales ever more slightly toward the good in the midst of trial." The dean of the cathedral, Randolph Hollerith, turned to Isaiah: "You shall be called repairers of the breach, the restorer of streets to live in," the prophet wrote. To Dean Hollerith, "If you pressed me for four words that describe what it means to be part of the Jesus movement, four words that describe what it means to build the kingdom of God, four words that exemplify the Christian life, it would be—'repairers of the breach.'"

Where are we? We are in the wilderness beyond the Garden and short of the kingdom, moving uncertainly through what George Eliot called the "dim lights and tangled circumstance" of the world. But God is calling out, seeking us and ultimately loving us. A plague may be past, but the work of answering Him, of loving one another, knows no season.

INTRODUCTION

On March 12, 2020, we closed the Cathedral's doors. It was a Thursday, cloudy and unremarkable in the way that March often is. We, like many others, had not fully grasped the magnitude of this virus and thought we would be back to "business as usual" in a matter of weeks. Yet we, unlike many others, had cameras and microphones in place, a YouTube channel, and a full-time videographer on staff. As more and more churches across the country also closed their physical doors in the days and weeks that followed, we found ourselves at the threshold of a new, online Cathedral with virtual doors wide enough to welcome worshippers from across the country and around the world.

In those early days of the pandemic, friends and colleagues often asked me what it was like preaching to an empty Cathedral nave, looking out at endless rows of brown leather chairbacks, each word echoing against the bare stone. While it took quite an adjustment to learn to preach to a camera affixed to a stone pillar twenty-six feet from the pulpit, the hardest part was not the empty chairs, but rather not knowing how a sermon was resonating. I could "see" familiar worshippers in my mind's eye and hold their stories in my heart, but I could not "see" how they were reacting to the sermon. Is the pace too slow? Is the message coming through? Are they following me or starting to fidget? Preaching is meant to be an aural and communal experience; this felt like preaching in a vacuum. We all wondered if worshippers would stay with us from week to week in this new virtual reality. The answer came quickly.

The idea for this book came from the hundreds of emails, letters, cards, and calls we received in thanksgiving for our worship services and sermons during the pandemic. Many of these kind messages flowed in immediately, with lifelong churchgoers and clergy alike wrestling with what Holy Week and Easter would look like in the midst of a global pandemic and with no churches to go to. In Christianity's holiest season when we journey together from the cross to Calvary to the empty tomb, what would it mean to not be journeying anywhere—essentially locked behind closed doors in fear like the disciples were two thousand years ago?

When Bishop Mariann Edgar Budde presided at the Easter Sunday service on April 12, 2020, proclaiming the Good News of the resurrected Christ to an empty Cathedral, fifty-five thousand people were watching online. When Presiding Bishop Michael Curry preached during that service, he did so from his North Carolina home 275 miles away. That was when the reality of our new landscape and the responsibility of our reach truly began to take root. A presider and preacher separated by geography, an online congregation united by technology and large enough to fill the nave eighteen times over—the Cathedral's long-held aspiration to be a spiritual home for the nation was on our virtual doorstep.

During the months that followed, the Cathedral community here in Washington was a microcosm of what was happening in the world around us: the pain of the pandemic's deadly toll and economic uncertainty, mounting anxiety, racial injustice, and divisive politics. A beloved member of our Cathedral staff community died of COVID-19 after caring for her mother who had previously contracted the disease. The daughter died; the mother survived. Hers was a heartbreaking story seen so many times across the globe, and the first of what would become many virtual funerals at the Cathedral. We would endure several scares and self-quarantines among our staff over the course of the year.

Closing the Cathedral to worshippers, tourists, event attendees, concertgoers, and public visitors of any kind also meant a total loss of our earned income. Like many businesses and organizations from Main Street to Wall Street, we were forced to make extremely difficult decisions, including staff layoffs, furloughs, and budget cuts. It was unquestionably one of the most painful periods in the Cathedral's history. Only days after sharing this hard news with our staff, George Floyd was murdered. Protesters streamed through downtown Washington, demanding accountability for the racial injustices and social inequities laid bare during the pandemic. The Cathedral provided a safe space for some of the protests on the green space of our west lawn.

And yet, as my dear friend and colleague Rose Duncan says, "Sunday comes."

Week after week, we were blessed to welcome more and more worshippers, each yearning to hear the Good News in a time when good news seemed so hard to come by. We wanted to learn more about these new friends—How did they find us? What were they interested in?—so we sent a brief survey to about one thousand new supporters. Over fifty percent of those surveyed answered "Preaching" to "What aspect of Cathedral online worship services are you most drawn to?" We have always taken our preaching seriously, but the landslide margin of the survey, and the increasing numbers of viewers on YouTube and Facebook, pushed our clergy way beyond humility onto what felt like hallowed ground.

As preachers, our task is to stay engaged with what is happening in our community and the world around us, and to seek understanding and interpretation through the lens of the gospel and biblical narrative. Indeed, theologian Karl Barth is often quoted as saying, ". . . take your Bible and take your newspaper, and read both. But interpret newspapers from your Bible."[1] We look for our story within "The Story." And we hope our words allow listeners to find their story within ours—and God's. That is the preacher's life; our sacred responsibility and privilege.

It is also our task to set aside the noise and chaos of our individual lives and the world around us, to reach down deep to preach whatever we had fervently asked God to give us and received to say. Those are the words we took with us on typed manuscripts or iPads, or no notes in my case, as we ascended the eight steps to the center of the Canterbury Pulpit each Sunday. Words of reconciliation, healing, and hope.

The sermons in this book reflect the uncertainty, pain, and disorientation of the COVID-19 pandemic and the pandemic of systemic racism. They also point us toward the goodness and hope that is always ours if we have eyes to see, ears to hear, and hearts to respond. The preachers are a diverse group by age, gender, race, sexual orientation, denomination, and geographic upbringing to name a few. It is important to remember that all sermons are crafted to be heard. As you read these sermons—imagining the voice of each preacher emanating from the Canterbury Pulpit and reaching through space and time to you—we hope that you will see and hear and feel the richness of God's grace in the diversity of our voices and life experiences. My dear friends and fellow preachers never failed to encourage and spiritually nurture me; it is my sincere hope that their words and presence offer the same to you.

---

1. "Barth in Retirement," *Time*, May 31, 1963. *http://content.time.com/time/subscriber/article/0,33009,896838,00.html.*

This book is organized chronologically and by liturgical season. The sermons often build on one another and reflect what was happening at the time in the world around us. The notable exceptions to chronology are the first two sermons which establish the arc of the book—reconciliation, healing, and hope. In the first, Presiding Bishop Michael Curry names the two pandemics of COVID-19 and systemic racism. He had prepared and pre-recorded an entirely different sermon for Pentecost. Then the murder of George Floyd happened. The world saw the deadly effects of racism with our own eyes, and Bishop Curry knew he needed to preach a very different sermon instead. The second sermon in the book is the first sermon that Dean Randy Hollerith preached at the Cathedral, August 21, 2016. "We are to be healers, reconcilers, peacemakers, seekers of justice, and builders of bridges between people, races, and religions." He called us to be repairers of the breach, and that has been the hallmark of his leadership ever since.

This book begins with Bishop Curry's Pentecost 2020 sermon and concludes with his Pentecost 2021 sermon. He reminds us, "Pentecost is about a revolution. It is not about mere moral reform. It is not about tinkering at the edges. It is about transforming an old order into a new order. . . . This is a revolution. A revolution of love; a revolution of goodness; a revolution of kindness; a revolution of compassion; a revolution that happens when the Spirit gives birth to Jesus in our lives." So much has happened in our lives in the year between Pentecost 2020 and Pentecost 2021, yet we are reminded that the way of Jesus is, and always has been, about transformation.

I want to thank my friends and colleagues whose sermons are included in this book, and our online worshipping community who inspired and challenged us to be our best whenever we stepped up to preach. Our editor Nancy Bryan and Church Publishing were encouraging and wise counsellors from the very beginning. My Cathedral colleagues and friends Diane Ney, Kathy Prendergast, Margaret Rawls, Gabrielle McKenzie, Bonnie Willette, and Margaret Shannon contributed untold hours of editing, copyediting, and footnote chasing to make this book a reality, and the exquisite photography of Danielle Thomas graces the cover of our book. No service at the Cathedral could happen without the collective gifts of our worship, music, communications, and video production teams, tireless sextons, and truly every department of the Cathedral—the dedication and professionalism of our Cathedral staff is an incredible blessing. I also want to thank all the spouses of the contributors who love and support us in the work we feel called to do. It is a gift beyond measure. As editor, I would like to take a moment of personal privilege to thank my husband, John, who is my biggest supporter and beloved life partner in all things.

In the time since March 12, 2020, we have welcomed over three million virtual worshippers. Our online congregation spans all fifty states, several territories, and countries around the world. This book covers but one chapter—about sixteen months long—in the Cathedral's over 125-year history. Washington National Cathedral was created through an Act of Congress on January 6, 1893, over one hundred years after Major Pierre L'Enfant designed the original plans for the city of Washington and in one rendering envisioned "a great church for national purposes." It would take an additional fourteen years before the Cathedral's foundation stone was laid, on September 29, 1907, and President Theodore Roosevelt announced to the crowd of ten thousand, "Godspeed in the work begun this noon." The foundation stone is a solid block of granite embedded with a smaller stone quarried from a field near Bethlehem. The inscription on the Bethlehem stone reads: "The Word was made flesh and dwelt among us" (John 1:14, KJV). This is the Cathedral's bedrock—physically and spiritually. God loved us enough to take on flesh and dwell among us. It is also the sacred responsibility of every subsequent generation to pursue the work God has given us to do: to be reconcilers, healers, and beacons of hope. May it be so for you and for me.

Jan Naylor Cope
Provost, Washington National Cathedral
Pentecost 2021

1

The Pandemic and Our Call to Be Reconcilers

PENTECOST IN A PANDEMIC

THE MOST REV. MICHAEL B. CURRY

The Day of Pentecost, May 31, 2020

A note about A Prayer for the Power of the Spirit among the People of God:

From Pentecost Sunday through the first Sunday in September, Presiding Bishop Michael Curry and his Lutheran counterpart Presiding Bishop Elizabeth Eaton welcome congregations and individuals to regularly pray "A Prayer for the Power of the Spirit among the People of God." This prayer—crafted by a team of Lutheran and Episcopal prayer leaders in light of the COVID pandemic—is meant to unite us in common prayer and revive us for common mission, wherever and however we may be gathered.

A Prayer for the Power of the Spirit among the People of God

God of all power and love, we give thanks for your unfailing presence and the hope you provide in times of uncertainty and loss. Send your Holy Spirit to enkindle in us your holy fire. Revive us to live as Christ's body in the world: a people who pray, worship, learn, break bread, share life, heal neighbors, bear good news, seek justice, rest and grow in the Spirit. Wherever and however we gather, unite us in common prayer and send us in common mission, that we and the whole creation might be restored and renewed, through Jesus Christ our Lord. *Amen.*

Today is the day of Pentecost, sometimes referred to as the birthday of the church, the beginning of the Jesus movement being launched into the world when the Spirit of God, the same spirit that rested upon Jesus, rested upon those first gathered apostles and followers. It was the beginning of what we call the church, this movement of those who follow Jesus. But this year, we observe Pentecost in the midst of a pandemic, and that's what I'd like to talk with you about for a few moments. Pentecost in a pandemic.

For our text, the words of the Apostle Paul in Romans, Chapter Five:

> *"We . . . boast in our sufferings, knowing that suffering produces endurance, and endurance produces character, and character produces hope, and hope does not disappoint us, because God's love has been poured into our hearts through the Holy Spirit [who] has been given to us."* (Rom. 5:3–5)

The old spiritual says it this way:

> If you cannot preach like Peter and you cannot pray like Paul, just tell the love of Jesus how he died to save us all. There is a balm in Gilead to make the wounded whole. There is a balm in Gilead to heal the sin-sick soul.[1]

Pentecost in a pandemic. We really do observe this Pentecost in the midst of a pandemic. The pandemic of COVID-19 is real. It is painful. We pray that scientists and researchers and all of the folk who are working hard will find a way to bring this pandemic to an end.

But there's another pandemic, not of the viral kind, but of the spiritual kind. It is a pandemic of the human spirit, when our lives are focused on ourselves, when the self becomes the center of the world and of the universe. It is a pandemic of self-centeredness. It may be even more destructive than a virus.

This pandemic of self-centeredness, if you will, has been the root cause of every humanly created evil that has ever hurt or harmed any child of God or even the earth itself. James, in the epistle, says, "What causes wars? What causes fightings among you? Is it not the passions that are at war in your own members? You desire and do not have, so you kill. And you covet and cannot obtain, so you fight and wage war" (cf. James 4:1–3). That is the pandemic of selfishness, of self-centeredness. It is the pandemic where I am the center of the universe and if I'm the center of the universe, then everybody else and everything else, including you, is on the periphery.

---

1. "Balm in Gilead," African-American spiritual, public domain.

That pandemic is the root cause of every humanly created evil that has ever been made. Every war that has ever been fought, every bigotry, every injustice, every wrong that has ever been wrought. Anytime a human being has hurt another human child of God directly or indirectly, explicitly or implicitly, at the root cause is me being the center of the world and you on the periphery. Dr. Martin Luther King called this the reverse Copernican Revolution, where not the sun is the center of the universe, but the self. Love is the antidote to that. Love is the cure for that. Love is what can help us remove that way of living and establish a way of life where we find life for us all.

If you cannot preach like Peter,
and you cannot pray like Paul,
just tell the love of Jesus,
how he died to save us all.

There is the balm in Gilead
that can make the wounded whole.
There is the balm in Gilead
that can heal the sin-sick soul.

There is a cure for that pandemic: unselfish sacrificial love. If you listen to the writer of the spiritual, that's what's grasped. Jesus didn't die for himself, he died for others. He died for the good and the well-being of others, not for anything that he could get out of it. It was an unselfish act, if you will, a sacrificial act. It is that way of unselfish, even sacrificial, living that has the innate spiritual capacity to actually save and help us all.

Jesus, following the teachings of Moses, told us long ago, you shall love the Lord your God and your neighbor as yourself. To love God and love the neighbor and genuinely to love the self—not prideful false self-love—but genuinely to love the self. That is the way. That's the way to life, not just for us individually, but for us corporately as a society and us globally as a global human family. Love is the way. It is not a mere utopian dream. It is our hope, our only hope, and it is the cure for this pandemic caused by the human spirit.

But let no one deceive you. This is not cheap grace or sugar-coated religion. It's not easy. It's not easy to live an unselfish life. It's not easy. The truth is, much that we see around us is the fruit of this unhealthy self-centeredness seemingly ruling the day. But again, the spiritual may help us here. The singer said it this way,

> *Sometimes I feel discouraged,*
> *and think my life's in vain,*
> *but then the Holy Spirit*
> *revives my soul again.*
>
> *O, there is a balm in Gilead*
> *to make the wounded whole.*
> *There is a balm in Gilead*
> *to heal the sin-sick soul.*

Love is the way, but we don't always have the power to live that way. But the spirit of the living God does have that power, because I think, if I read my Bible correctly, in 1 John chapter 4, it says, "Beloved, let us love one another, because love is of God and those who love are born of God and know God, because God is love." If God is love, and the Spirit of God is the spirit of God's essence and life and heart, then when that spirit is poured out on us, the very love that is the heart of God is being poured out on us and love becomes possible. But it's hard.

This past week, we have not only had to endure a pandemic occasioned by a virus—a viral pandemic—but we've had to endure and face a spiritual pandemic: the roots of self-centeredness, where one person can look upon another person and despise and reject them, and not even behold them as a fellow child of God. We have seen once again the unthinkable become thinkable. It's caused great pain or better said, increased the great pain that was already there.

In Minnesota, the killing of George Floyd was a violation of basic human decency and dignity and we all saw it. We all saw it. Maybe the deeper pain that comes with that is that that wasn't an isolated incident. It happened to Breonna Taylor on March 13th in Kentucky. It happened to Ahmaud Arbery on February 23rd in Georgia. And need I mention Melissa Ventura, Paul Castaway, Sandra Bland, Eric Garner, Michael Brown, Trayvon Martin? This is a painful path that we have been on for a long time. We've made such progress in our human relationships and in our racial relationships, and yet this seems not to have changed at all.

I'm sixty-seven years old. In the late 1960s and early 70s when I was a teenager, the same thing was going on then. My father, who was an Episcopal priest, rector of St. Philip's in Buffalo, also served not only as a parish priest but as the director of human relations for the city of Buffalo. In that capacity, after riots in the 1960s, he was brought on board and brought others on board to lead sensitivity training sessions for police officers in the Buffalo police force. That was necessary because some of the riots that were occasioned resulted from precisely the same thing that happened just this past week in Minneapolis.

I was a teenager then and it was going on then. I was a teenager when my father warned me when I learned how to drive, that if ever you have encounters with the police: obey; do what they say; do not talk back and watch how you move your hands. I was told that in the 1960s and we're still having to say it today. That's where some of the anger and the frustration that we're seeing on our streets is coming from. It's accumulated hurt and disappointment, not just for those on the streets, but for people of goodwill and human decency of all races, of all stripes, of all religions, of all kinds.

There is a part of us that just wants to throw up our hands, and in the words of the Psalmist cry: How long? How long, O Lord? How long? And yet, we are not victims of fate. We are people of faith. We are not doomed and condemned to continue our past into our present and future. We need not be slaves of fate. We follow in the footsteps of Jesus. This Jesus taught us that love will make a way out of no way. He taught us that sometimes you have to take up the cross and follow in his footsteps and that if you dare to follow his way of love, you will find God's way of life. We will not submit to fate. We must not give in to fate. We must dare to follow Jesus in the way of love that can save us all.

But I don't have the power to do that all the time and, I suspect, neither do you. But God does and that's why the singer of the spiritual had a verse that said,

> *Sometimes I feel discouraged,*
> *and [I] think my life's in vain,*
> *but then [that] Holy Spirit*
> *[It] revives my soul again.*
>
> *There is a balm in Gilead*
> *to make the wounded whole.*
> *There is a balm in Gilead*
> *to heal the sin-sick soul.*

Love is the way. It can save us all. And maybe we've seen a sign of it and maybe we've seen evidence that by the power of the Spirit, we might be able to do it.

Public health officials have told us that we all need to start wearing these when we go out in public—these face masks. It's interesting, when you put the face mask on, it's not fun to wear. They've told us that you're really putting it on not to save yourself. You're not putting it on to protect yourself. The reason for wearing the face mask is so that I don't spread anything to you. I wear it to protect you. It's a small inconvenience, a little sacrifice that actually may be a symbol of what it means to love. The possible miracle could be that if I wear it to protect you from me, and you wear it to protect me from you, or the virus within you, we get protected and we all win—and that is the power of love.

If I make room for you, and you make room for me, and if we will work together to create a society where there is room for all of God's children, where every human being, every one of us is treated as a child of God, created in the image and likeness of God, where everybody is loved, everybody is honored, everybody is respected, everybody is created as a child of God—if we work together to build that kind of society and don't give up, then love can save us all.

> *If you cannot preach like Peter,*
> *and you cannot pray like Paul,*
> *just tell the love of Jesus,*
> *how he died to save us all.*
>
> *There is a balm in Gilead*
> *to make the wounded whole.*
> *There [really] is a balm in Gilead*
> *to heal the sin-sick soul.*

So, walk together children and don't you get weary because there is a great camp meeting in the promised land.

REPAIRERS OF THE BREACH

THE VERY REV. RANDOLPH MARSHALL HOLLERITH
Fourteenth Sunday after Pentecost, August 21, 2016

Good morning! What a joy it is for me to be here with you this morning, my first Sunday, in this storied cathedral. My thanks to everyone who has reached out to welcome us. Thank you for the nice notes, emails, and phone calls. My family and I are so glad to be with you. My wife Melissa and my daughter Eliza are here this morning. Eliza leaves next week to begin her freshman year at the University of the South in Sewanee, Tennessee. Keep her in your prayers. My son Marshall could not be with us today; he is a rising senior at Washington & Lee University and in the middle of two-a-day football practices. God bless him in all this heat. Now, some of you might be wondering if I am nervous standing up here in this famous and imposing Canterbury Pulpit, looking out over this grand nave. Well, I have to admit part of me was hoping that if my first Sunday was in the middle of August and people were on vacation, I might be able to have a soft opening. No such luck! Am I nervous? Yes, I am nervous, but if you think I'm nervous, just imagine what the Search Committee is feeling right about now!

In all honesty, what I am feeling most this morning is grateful. I am grateful to Bishop Mariann, the Chapter, and the Search Committee for the honor of serving amongst you. I feel humbled by the task and blessed by the opportunity.

As we begin this journey together this morning, let's take a look at the words of Isaiah. Isaiah writes, "If you offer your food to the hungry and satisfy the needs of the afflicted, then your light shall rise in the darkness and your gloom be like the noonday . . . Your ancient ruins shall be rebuilt; you shall raise up the foundations of many generations; you shall be called the repairer of the breach, the restorer of streets to live in" (Isa. 58:10, 12). I believe these words touch the heart of the gospel; they point to the essence of what it means to be a faithful Christian. Let me share a story with you that I hope illustrates this truth. In 1987, during my first year at Yale Divinity School, I interned for an unusual woman named Betsy who spent her life doing street ministry. Betsy was an upper middle class White lady in her late sixties. She was happily married, lived in a good neighborhood, and had a bunch of grandchildren. At a time when many people in her situation were playing more golf, growing a garden, or traveling on weekends, Betsy was busy repairing the breach, determined to help the homeless on the streets of New Haven. She spent her days in the alleys and abandoned buildings of the city reaching out to the addicted, the destitute, and the often mentally ill homeless men and women of the city. She was passionate about their welfare. She spent all her money on them and gave them all her time. She was determined to get as many people as possible off the street and into a better life.

I ended up as her intern because her husband and her children were worried about her. They did not want her doing this work. They worried for her safety and as a result they demanded that she not undertake her ministry alone. When she worked on the streets, she had to have someone with her. So, she applied to the Divinity School for an intern assistant and she wound up with me. For a year, I followed behind her in awe, marveling at her faith and her determination, marveling at her willingness to love and to risk for the sake of the gospel. Her family thought she was unnecessarily placing her life in danger. I learned that she was one of those beloved souls St. Paul would proudly call a fool for Christ. I am not sure I was much help during that year, but being a part of her ministry changed my life.

"You shall be called repairers of the breach, the restorer of the streets to live in." If you pressed me for four words that describe what it means to be part of the Jesus movement, four words that describe what it means to build the kingdom of God, four words that exemplify the Christian life, it would be: repairers of the breach. This is what Isaiah makes clear this morning as he speaks to the people of Israel who have just returned from exile. If you want to know what God wants from you, he tells them, then quit your bickering, your finger pointing, your slandering of others, and offer your food to the hungry, satisfy the needs of the afflicted—work to repair that which is broken in your own lives and in the lives of those around you. I believe that this is our calling, and it is the reason I am so excited to share in ministry with you, because this cathedral has been a repairer of the breach for many, many years.

Some of you know this, but as a child growing up in Alexandria, I used to come to the Cathedral to watch the stone carvers work and to attend services. I had three great aunts who lived on 29th Street in Georgetown. Those ladies, along with my mother, grandmother, and godparents, were passionate about this cathedral and its mission to be a house of prayer for all people. For decades they were proud to contribute to the work of the [National Cathedral Association] and to play some small role in the Cathedral's creation. As a result, this place has always been a beacon for me—a cathedral that not only points to the glory of God in its grandeur and beauty, but a community of people dedicated to sharing the love of God within this city and across our nation. Leaders like Bishop Walker inspired me during some very formative years in my life. You have a powerful legacy as repairers of the breach, and I am proud to be a part of this community and its mission.

Yes, this cathedral, like any cathedral, indeed like any Christian community in this day and age of rapid cultural change, has its fair share of challenges—financial and otherwise. But we should never forget that we are also immeasurably blessed. We are blessed with talented and gifted people who are willing to share their gifts and talents here. We are blessed with vibrant ministries and an important mission. We are blessed to worship in this space of unparalleled beauty that touches so many who enter these doors. Yes, we have much work to do, but we should never forget that our God has given us so many good gifts with which to do that work.

Now, in closing, our gospel for this morning reminds us to keep central that which is central, to stay focused on the core of our faith. In our passage from Luke, Jesus is attacked for healing a woman on the Sabbath, a woman crippled for eighteen years. Life has literally bent her over and she is unable to stand upright. Jesus in his compassion lays hands on her and says, "Woman, you are set free from your ailment" (Luke 13:12). However, the leader of the synagogue sees Jesus's act of healing as work, and work was forbidden on the Sabbath. In his zeal for the law, this leader allows legalism to trump grace, tradition to trump love, doctrine to trump compassion. He misses the entire point of God's law, and Jesus calls him on it.

My brothers and sisters, Jesus calls to us today and reminds us to never lose sight of what is central to our faith. He reminds us to never let anything distract us from the healing and reconciling work of God's kingdom. He reminds us to be careful not to let the trappings of our faith divert us from the heart of our faith. As the body of Christ, as the hands and feet of Christ in the world, we are to be repairers of the breach in everything we do. We are to be healers, reconcilers, peacemakers, seekers of justice, and builders of bridges between people, races, and religions. The Washington National Cathedral is perfectly positioned for this kind of work. It is work that has been a powerful part of our history, and God willing it will be a powerful part of our future. Thank you for the opportunity to serve amongst you, to share in this ministry with you. I am honored to be here and excited for the future. Amen.

2

A Lent and Easter Season Like No Other

WHERE ARE YOU?

The Rev. Canon Kelly Brown Douglas
First Sunday in Lent, March 1, 2020

Good morning, Cathedral family! On this first Sunday of our Lenten season, we encounter an all too familiar story from the book of Genesis. This story in a garden with a serpent, temptation, and the eating of forbidden fruit has carried the burden of numerous interpretations, reinterpretations, and misinterpretations for countless generations. In fact, this Genesis story has been used and misused to sow divisions within the family of God as it has been misread and misappropriated to sustain sins of sexism, racism, heterosexist homophobia, and all manner of harm against God's creation. This is a story that in so many ways just won't go away—but that is not really all bad. For it is a story that indeed speaks to us across time—for it is a story reflective of a people trying to figure out their place, if not their purpose, as sacred creatures of God in the world that God has created for them to live in.

In essence, it is a story of an ancient Israelite people trying to discern who it is God has called them into the world to be. It is for this reason that this story compels our attention. It begs us on this day to read it anew, with fresh eyes if we can. So, try to hear what it may be saying to us—in this our time as a people seeking to discern God's call to us. And so, let us look to see how in fact this story told by a people from many ages past is speaking to us today. What are we to learn about who it is God has called us to be in this our world, in this our time?

The key to answering that question, I believe, is found two verses beyond where our first reading ends this morning. For if we read just a little further, verses 3:8–9 (NIV) say this, "Then the man and his wife heard the sound of the Lord God as [God] was walking in the garden

11

in the cool of the day, and they hid from the Lord God among the trees of the garden. But the Lord God called to the man, 'Where are you?'"

"Where are you?" God asked. The drama of this story all comes down to this often-overlooked question that God puts to Adam— "Where are you?" Now in asking this question, God is not asking Adam to make known where amongst the trees he has fled in order to hide his nakedness. This is not a "hide and seek" game and hence a "hide and seek" question. No, this question is about much more than that. Indeed, it is the garden drama itself that reveals the very significance and meaning of this question. And so, let us go back to recapture anew this drama as it is before us this morning.

It begins by telling us that "The Lord God took the man and put him in the garden of Eden to till it and keep it" (Gen. 2:15). Now as an aside, the Hebrew word here that has been translated as man, is *ha adam*—meaning earth creature. At this point, there is no gender attached—that is, this earth creature has not been identified as male or female—indeed the point is not about gender at all, rather it is to show the close relationship that human creatures have to the earth itself, for the Hebrew word for earth is *adama*. So, from *adama* comes Adam— what a wonderful poetic play on words to show the interconnectedness of divine creation. But back to the unfolding drama and our question of what precisely is God asking in the question "Where are you?" The first clue comes in the "commission," if you will, that God gives to the earth creation. Again, we are told that God puts Adam in the garden to "till it and keep it."

In assigning the human creature to till and keep the garden, God has called human beings to care for and to look after the world that God has placed us in. Essentially, God's human creation has been given the responsibility to partner with God in caring for that which God has created. And this, my friends, is essentially what *faith* is all about—for faith is about nothing less than our "yes" to God's invitation to partner with God in doing the work that is required so that our very world reflects the image of its divine creator.

And so, inasmuch as we are a people faith, tilling and keeping the garden of God's world as God has created us to do, then a laissez-faire, laid-back attitude toward the world is not an option for us. Put simply, being faithful to our very divine creation means that no matter how messy, how frustrating and disheartening the world may be, we cannot withdraw from it, or passively exist within it. Rather, we are to take an active role in this our world. Silence, indifference, and apathy are not options—for they are unfaithful to who God has created us to be: tillers and keepers of God's world. Bottom line: we cannot hide from our responsibility as God's human creations. And so it is that God's question "Where are you?" is a question about faithfulness. "Where are you," God asked Adam. Are you being *faithful* to who God has created you to be—a tiller and keeper of the garden?

Now, the story doesn't end here, for the drama continues to unfold—providing us with two defining aspects, if you will, of what it means to be faithful to our divine creation, that is, to till and to keep. What precisely are we being asked to do?

The answer to this again takes us to a part of the drama that is not included in our reading this morning. For a few verses before we enter the story, we are told that God planted many trees in the garden. But at the center of the garden, as if to show their significance in this unfolding drama, are the tree of life and the tree with knowledge of good and evil, also the only two trees named. Now, as we know, the human creature is not to eat from the tree with knowledge of good and evil—which means that the human creature is permitted to eat from any of the other trees, most notably from the tree of life. And herein lies the first aspect of what it means to be faithful to our very creation—it is about tilling the ground for the tree of life, which represents nothing less than the life-giving breath of God.

You will recall that in this Genesis story we are told that when God made the human creature from the dust of the earth, God breathed into the creature's nostrils the very breath of life. For us to till the ground that is the tree of life is for us to respect, foster, and protect the sacred breath of life that is all of ours to breathe and thus to do nothing to creation or to one another that might profane or take that breath away. And I must say, there is nothing that takes my breath away more than seeing another human being humiliated, belittled, put down, degraded, or destroyed in any way, let alone being subjected to the breathtaking realities of inequality or poverty.

To be faithful to our very divine creation is for us to till the ground that is the tree of life and thus to use our sacred breath in a life-giving way, which means protecting the sacred breath of others and thus refusing to be consoled until all of God's creatures can breathe a life-giving breath. "Where are you?" God asked the hiding Adam. Where are you in tilling the ground for the tree that is the breath of life? To be faithful to our divine creation is indeed to partner with God in honoring our sacred breath by respecting the sacred breath of others. But there is another aspect of our created faithfulness that this Genesis story points to.

As the drama unfolds, we find that God has created a helper for the earth creature, *adam*. And so, we now have two human beings, a man and woman, in the garden. As the story goes on, we find the woman in dialogue with the serpent, a dialogue which of course culminates in both the man and woman eating fruit from the forbidden tree—the tree with knowledge of good and evil. It is in the dialogue that we find the final aspect of what it means to be faithful. For you will recall in the dialogue the woman said to the serpent, "We may eat of the fruit of the trees in the garden; but God said, 'You shall not eat of the fruit of the tree that is in the middle of the garden, nor shall you touch it . . .'" (Gen. 3:3). It is interesting to note, however, that God did not say that the humans were not to even touch the prohibited tree. In claiming such a thing, the woman is proffering a justification for breaking God's prohibition as she suggests that God's demands are unreasonable and hence ripe for breaking. With the woman's proclamation, the serpent goes on to suggest that God actually was withholding the real truth from the human beings, by saying, "You will not die; for God knows that when you eat of it your eyes will be opened, and you will be like God, knowing good and evil" (Gen. 3:4–5).

Essentially, both the woman and the serpent have at best misrepresented divine truth by essentially obscuring it with their desires and ambition. Being faithful to our divine creation of tilling and keeping the garden that is God's world means that we are to keep, to steadfastly cling to, the very truth that is God's.

We are living in confounding and complicated times. It is a time in which wrong sometimes looks like right, in which injustice masquerades as justice, and where expediency overwhelms morality. These are times where it is easy to distort the truth that is God's so to satisfy the self-interested and short-sighted desires and ambitions that are ours. To keep the garden as God has commissioned human beings to do, is to keep the truth that is God's. And by the way, that those humans in the garden did in fact eat the fruit from the tree of good and evil, suggests that we as humans cannot hide behind the innocence of not knowing right from wrong, divine truth from human falsehood. Put plainly, we know what is and what is not God's truth. This is a truth that, as Paul tells us, is noble, right, pure, lovely, admirable—and praiseworthy (Phil. 4:8). This is the divine truth we are to dwell on and to keep, regardless of how expedient or popular it may be to not do so. It is for this reason that Jesus proclaimed the truth will set you free—for indeed to keep the truth that is God's is to be free from immoral human mendacities that masquerade as divine truth. And so, when God entered the garden and asked adam, "Where are you?" it was a question about truth. Where are you in being faithful to keeping the truth that is God's?

And so there you have it. When all is said and done, God's question to God's human creature, "Where are you?" is a question about faithfulness—faithfulness to who God has created each of us to be—tillers of the sacred breath of life and keepers of divine truth.

And so back to the beginning. After looking with fresh eyes, how is it that this story of a garden drama told by a people from many ages past speaks to us today? It speaks to us as it has spoken across time. It compels us in this our time to hear the voice of God asking each and every one of us, "Where are you in tilling and keeping the garden that is God's world?" Are we faithful to the tasks of tilling the tree that is the breath of life and keeping the truth that is God's? Each of us must hear this question as it is put to us—and answer it for ourselves. For be clear, it is a personal question in that God is not asking where others are or are not, rather God is asking each of us—where are you?

Church, as I hear this question from God to me, especially on this weekend that marks the end of Black History Month, I think of those who were indeed faithful to their divine creation as they tilled the breath of life by refusing to be content until the breathtaking shackles of slavery were broken, and in so doing, clung to the truth of God that no human being was created to be a slave. And I know it is because of the faithful Harriet Tubmans that have gone before me that I am standing here today in this pulpit as embodied testimony to their faithfulness. And so how could I, in this my time, be any less faithful to whom God has created me to be—a tiller of life, a keeper of truth. And indeed, how can any of us who claim to follow the one who proclaimed, "I am the way, the truth, and the life" (John 14:6) be other than faithful tillers of the breath of life that comes from God and the truth that is God's?

And so, on this first Sunday of Lent, let us leave this Cathedral place, resolved during this Lenten season that is ours in 2020, to hear and to wrestle with this question of God to us. Where are you? Where are you? Where are you? Where are you? Amen.

SEEING WITH NEW EYES

The Rt. Rev. Mariann Edgar Budde
Fourth Sunday in Lent, March 22, 2020

But the Lord said to Samuel, "Do not look on his appearance or on the height of his stature . . . for the Lord does not see as mortals see; they look on the outward appearance, but the Lord looks on the heart." (1 Sam. 16:7)

For once you were darkness, but now in the Lord you are light. Live as children of light—for the fruit of the light is found in all that is good and right and true. (Eph. 5:8-9)

As he walked along, he saw a man blind from birth. His disciples asked him, "Rabbi, who sinned, this man or his parents, that he was born blind?" (John 9:1-2)

Grace to you and peace from God our Creator, and from the Lord Jesus Christ. I'm honored to speak with you today. My prayer, echoing the words of an old hymn, is that God will grant you wisdom and grant you courage for the living of this hour. I pray that God will use this time and my imperfect words to speak in your heart what you most need to hear.

I can't help but think of a line from J. R. R. Tolkien's *Lord of the Rings*, when the reluctant young hero Frodo confesses to his mentor Gandalf, "I wish the Ring had never come to me. I wish none of this had happened." Gandalf replies, "So do all who live to see such times, but that is not for them to decide. All we have to decide is what to do with the time that is given to us." Gandalf goes on, "There are other forces at work in this, Frodo, besides the will of evil."[1]

This is a statement of faith: that there are forces for good at work in the world, even in the darkest hours. I believe that God wants us to trust that amid this pandemic and the enormous cost of efforts to slow its spread, there are also forces for good at work now. God wants us to remember that we are our best selves whenever we join those forces and do our part, tipping the scales ever more slightly toward the good in the face of trial.

Jesus often said to his followers, "Do not be afraid." It's important to remember, however, that he wasn't scolding them for their fear. Fear

---

1. J. R. R. Tolkien, *The Lord of the Rings, The Fellowship of the Ring,* 2nd ed. (Boston: Houghton-Mifflin, 1954), 50.

was an understandable response to the realities they were facing, as it is for us. What he meant then, and what I believe he is saying to us now, is that alongside all there is to legitimately fear, the spirit of wisdom and courage and love is here; that Jesus himself is here. Fear is not a bad thing; yet fear need not be the only lens through which we see, and thus the sole driver of our lives. There are other forces at work for good in the world and in us.

I'm not suggesting that any of this is easy. But we are here for the living through this pandemic whose end we cannot see. Lord knows we wish the virus had not come to us. So do all who live through such times. But that decision was not ours to make. What we can do is decide how we will live now. How we live now will be determined in large measure by what we see—what is revealed to us and what we are willing to face, eyes wide open.

All the scripture passages appointed for this, the fourth Sunday in Lent, are about sight and blindness. In the story of the prophet Samuel's search for the one God has chosen to be Israel's next king, God warns Samuel not to look as mortals do, on physical appearances alone, but to see, as God sees, with eyes of the heart. In the letter to the Ephesians, we hear an exhortation to live as children of the light—light being essential to vision, both physical and inner light. From the Gospel of John, we read the first part of a very long story describing how Jesus healed a man who was blind from birth, while at the same time the opponents of Jesus's day willfully blinded themselves to Jesus's identity.

The theme of the relationship between sight and blindness runs through the entire Bible. The prophets of Israel were those who saw what others refused to see and paid the price for it, yet in the end were those whose sight others came to trust. In the Gospels there are numerous accounts of blind people receiving their sight. I'm reminded of the man Bartimaeus, a blind man who waited on the roadside for Jesus to pass by. "Jesus, have mercy on me!" he cried out. "What do you want me to do for you?" Jesus asked him. "Lord," Bartimaeus answered, "I want to see" (cf. Mark 10:47–51).

If we are to live with strength and courage in this hour, we need to see with as much clarity as God can give us. So, consider with me some of the things that affect our vision, and indeed, how many forms of blindness there are. No one knows this better than the physically blind who must live alongside those of us who are blind in other ways, but with far less awareness than they of what we can and cannot see. There are also gradations of sight and blindness. Ophthalmologists can measure our eyes' varying degrees of blurriness and distortion, some of which can be corrected, and others cannot. But the relative health of our faculties isn't the only thing that affects vision.

Our emotional state influences what we can and cannot see, as can the level of anxiety within and around us. That's why it's helpful to try and bring your anxiety levels down through exercise, meditation, or a good laugh.

Another factor that affects our vision is where we're standing relative to whatever it is we are looking at. Consider how our perspective on the spread of the coronavirus has changed and continues to change according to geography as the virus spreads. Time is another factor: what was unimaginable as little as two weeks ago, we now see all around us, a reality that humbles us as we consider the future. We don't know what the next few weeks will reveal.

Relationships affect vision. We can't see one another clearly if we aren't in right relationship, and as a result we lose the needed perspective that others might have.

Finally, there is the factor of character. In the words of C.S. Lewis, "What you see depends a great deal on where you are standing; it also depends on what sort of person you are."[2]

Sometimes it just happens—our eyes are opened, and we see something we didn't see before. Such eye-opening can be a wonderful experience. Think of people who have known each other for years who one day are given new eyes with which to see, and they fall in love. Or how we can see something breathtakingly beautiful as if for the first time, when in fact, we've walked by it a thousand times. Other times, however, having our eyes opened is jarring, for we now can see a truth that had been hidden or that we had been avoiding.

And sometimes the world simply turns upside down and we see everything through the lens of a new reality. That's what it feels like now.

So, what are we to do?

I suggest that we pay careful attention to what's happening, right now, with all our faculties in play.

---

2. C. S. Lewis, *The Magician's Nephew* (London: The Bodley Head, Penguin Random House, 1955), 135.

Years ago, my husband Paul and I traveled to Ireland and spent a week in the company of the poet David Whyte. On the very first day, as our group arrived exhausted from international travel, instead of encouraging us to go to our rooms, David and his team took us on a long hike. He said to us, "I want you to pay particular attention to what you see right now, for jet lag and physical exhaustion have a way of lowering your natural defenses. You are more vulnerable tonight than you will be tomorrow, and you are more open. Pay attention to what you see tonight, for you won't have these eyes again."

We are not going to see with COVID eyes forever. What do you see now that you didn't see before? What new revelations is God giving us now that we are particularly and uniquely open to receive?

Some of the revelations are hard and frightening, but we have no choice but to face them. It may be that some of the harder revelations will be temporary, for this season only, and will then pass. But others may last a long time. I suspect that we don't see well enough now to distinguish between the two, although some may be instantly clear for you.

Some of the revelations are pure grace, as we're given eyes to see beauty we've missed, experience our own resilience and innate goodness as individuals and community. It turns out that we needn't be as divided as we've allowed ourselves to behave as a nation. We actually can rise above less pressing concerns and foolish polarities when something really big happens. We are capable of greater sacrifice for the common good than we realize.

I believe that God can take even the worst that can happen and bring good from it. That, too, a statement of faith. But why not dare to believe that there are forces for good at work and strive to align with them?

Let me close with this simple exhortation that you be as gentle with yourselves and one another as you can in these vulnerable days, even as you may need to make difficult decisions. Don't rely on your eyes alone—reach out for support and guidance from those you trust and even from those with whom you might otherwise dismiss. Tend to the eyes of your heart. Be sure to focus on something of goodness and grace and lasting truth.

Ask God to open your eyes, so that you might see what you need to see now, in this new reality. Remember that there are forces for good around and within you, within us all.

May God grant you wisdom and grant you courage. Never forget it is for this hour that we are here.

SPIRIT OF HOPE

THE VERY REV. RANDOLPH MARSHALL HOLLERITH
Fifth Sunday in Lent, March 29, 2020

Welcome everyone. Thank you for joining us this morning. I have to admit that it is a little weird standing up here in this great pulpit looking out on an empty Cathedral. Now, I've preached sermons before that fell so flat that it felt like the place was empty, but this is a first. I must admit, it feels a little lonely up here.

I love the story you may have seen in the news of the Italian priest who printed out photos of his parishioners and taped them to the pews in his church. Seeing all his flock gave him comfort while it reminded the community that even though they were physically apart, they were together in Spirit, together as the Body of Christ. The truth is, this Cathedral may be empty this morning, but I have no doubt that this gathering of community across the internet and around the world is as real and as important as if you were all sitting here together today. Because even though we are far apart, we are bound by the Spirit, bound together by a force greater than any distance and stronger than any separation. So, wherever you are, thank you for being with us today and remember, this Cathedral is your Cathedral.

So, how are you doing? I pray that you are well, safe, and sound. How are you holding up during these days of staying at home and social distancing? I heard someone say the other day that we are about three weeks away from knowing everyone's true hair color. I know that during these days at home, I have been eating way too much, changing out of my sweatpants far too infrequently, reading a lot, and watching a ridiculous amount of Netflix and silly dog videos.

Let's be honest. This is a strange time, a stressful time, a frightening time. It's a time of waiting and watching. As the psalmist says this morning—"I wait for the Lord; my soul waits for him . . . My soul waits for the Lord, more than watchmen for the morning, more than watchmen for the morning" (cf. Ps. 130:5–6). Every day on the news we see more people getting the virus, and more people losing their lives to this terrible disease. We hear stories of overcrowded hospitals, people losing their jobs, businesses closing, the economy shrinking. And so, we are forced to wait, forced to stay away from each other, not only to protect ourselves but to protect those most vulnerable. And, in the midst of all of this, we have to cope with the fact that we don't know when this pandemic will come to an end. We know that it will indeed end, but not when. There is no date certain, and so it feels like we are stuck in a kind of limbo—waiting and watching and worrying.

For those of us who call ourselves Christians, we are part of a faith that is all about hope. We are part of a faith that knows the reality of suffering and loss and yet proclaims that even in the midst of the most difficult times, there is always the promise of new life, of life that defeats death, of a love that binds all things together and conquers even our worst fears.

Our readings from Ezekiel (37:1–14) and from John (11:1–45) this morning are both lessons of hope, lessons that point to God's deeper purposes at work during moments of stress, fear, and loss.

At a time when so many of us feel as disconnected and brittle as dry bones, the prophet Ezekiel gives us a vision of a God who not only gives life, but a God who restores it. Writing to the Hebrew people suffering in exile in Babylon six hundred years before Jesus was born, Ezekiel tells his people that they may feel disjointed and far away from home, but God's Spirit will breathe new life into Israel and bring them all together again. They are promised that there is nothing God cannot redeem and the Lord has not forsaken them.

Many of us have heard this reading all our lives and sung more times than we can count the great old spiritual about Ezekiel connecting "dem dry bones." But perhaps today our current situation will enable us to hear Ezekiel's words in a new way, in a very personal way, as we too are disconnected from one another, experiencing our own kind of exile from our normal lives. The good news is that in this present valley of dry bones, God's promise of life restored is as true now as it was all those years ago. Indeed, my friends, the Lord has not forsaken us.

In a similar way, our gospel reading this morning reminds us that as Christians we proclaim a faith that is unique among the vast majority of world religions. That's because we worship a God who is not distant and other worldly, but a God who takes on our flesh and becomes one of us, a God who walks among us and experiences firsthand the joys and the sorrows of this life. Jesus loved Lazarus, and he wept at his friend's death. Because of this, we can take comfort in the fact that Jesus understood and understands our grief, our worry, our sense of loss during these difficult days.

In fact, my friends, I think we are supposed to see ourselves in Lazarus whose name literally means—God helps. As Alyce McKenzie writes, "Lazarus represents all those who Jesus loves, which includes you and me and all humankind. This story is a story about our coming to life from death in this present moment, not just in a future event."[3]

Friends, I hope you realize that the same Spirit that moved over the earth at the instant of creation bringing life out of nothingness, the same Spirit that reanimated Ezekiel's dry bones, the same Spirit that came to rest on Jesus at his baptism, the same Spirit that brought Lazarus up from the grave, this Spirit is present and working amongst us now. We can see it in the sacrifice and service of so many health care professionals and first responders around the world who are freely risking their own lives to care for the sick and those in need. We can see it in the restaurants around the country that are helping to feed children stuck at home who cannot receive the school meals on which their families depend. We can see it in the GoFundMe drives to support hourly workers and to raise money to purchase protective gear for hospitals. We can see this same Spirit at work in the person who after enjoying a $90 meal left more than $9,000 as a tip to help the employees who otherwise would be out of a job. We can see it locally in organizations like Feed the Fight who have partnered with local restaurants funding and delivering more than seven hundred meals to local hospitals. We can even see the Spirit at work when a Cathedral finds more than five thousand protective masks literally hidden away in a crypt space intended for a casket. Masks that can now help to protect doctors and nurses at two of our Washington hospitals.

Friends, in a few days we will be entering into the holiest days of the Christian year. Next Sunday is Palm Sunday and the beginning of Holy Week. These are the days in the life of the church when we are reminded that while suffering and death are real, we worship a God who not only walks with us and suffers with us, but we have a God who loves us enough to always bring us through death into new life. These are the promises that lie at the heart of our faith.

As we move through the last days of Lent, remember that God is not done with us. God's Spirit is at work in our midst. God's promises

---

3. Alyce McKenzie, "Lazarus Is Us: Reflections on John 11:1–45," *Patheos* (blog), April 3, 2011. *https://www.patheos.com/resources/additional-resources/2011/04/lazarus-is-us-alcye-mckenzie-04-04-2011.*

are as real for us this morning as they were for Ezekiel and Lazarus so many years ago.

I wish I could say something to you this morning that would absolutely take away the worry and the fear. But I can't. There are some things we just have to go through. But I do know this—we are all in this together, and we will come through this struggle to see better days. So, say your prayers and keep the faith. Say your prayers and fight the fear. Say your prayers and share God's love wherever and however you can. Amen.

A SEASON OF DISORIENTATION

The Rev. Canon Jan Naylor Cope
Maundy Thursday, April 9, 2020

Having loved his own who were in the world, he loved them to the end. (John 13:1)

Tonight, we remember Jesus's farewell meal, the Last Supper with his disciples. For Jesus knew what was ahead of him. He knew who would betray him, who would deny him, who would desert him. Yet he took this opportunity with his disciples to tell them one last time what he wanted them to remember when he was no longer physically with them. He told them so many things, but the commandment that he gave them was that they love one another as he loved them. It was a self-sacrificing love—deep, radical, never ending. He went on in his conversation with the disciples to tell them that he wouldn't leave them orphaned, that the Father would send another—an Advocate, a Comforter, the Holy Spirit—who would be with them always to abide with them, but also comfort them, encourage, strengthen, and guide them, and that his presence would be with them always.

He went on to wash their feet, modeling for them what servant ministry looks like, that no task is too small or too lowly. He told them that there is no greater love than this, but to lay down one's life for one's friends. You see, he was trying to equip those disciples for what was coming, which they couldn't fully comprehend or understand. Their world as they knew it was about to be turned on its head, and he wanted them to remember that God was with them, that God would abide in them so that they, after the Resurrection, could carry out his work of love and reconciliation; that they would, in fact, transition from being disciples, followers of Jesus, to the apostles, the bearers of the good news of the resurrected Christ. That lesson wasn't just for the disciples two thousand years ago. It is a lesson that is ever urgent for you and me today: loving one another as Jesus loved us in a sacrificial, giving way. Our world needs that sacrificial love, now more than ever.

There are times in our lives when we have cycles and seasons that we go through. In his book, *The Message of the Psalms*,[4] Walter

---

4. Quoted in Denise Dombkowski Hopkins, *Journey Through the Psalms* (Nashville: Chalice Press, 2002), 27–30.

Brueggemann talks about those seasons as beginning with orientation, when things seem as they should be. They're secure, they're stable.
They're somewhat predictable. We can sense God in our very midst
because things are going well, or at least we think so. But then, inevitably, as life goes, something happens that knocks us right out of the
homeostasis into disorientation, which is chaos, not knowing what the
future holds, being terrified of the unknown. The disciples were just
about to enter that season. So, God was equipping them, through Jesus
and his love, to help them come out on the other side to the next season, which Brueggemann calls reorientation, or new orientation, where
you come up out of that pit. By the grace of God, you see the light in
the darkness again, but you are changed from the experience that you
had in that time of disorientation.

I would suggest to you that our global community is very much
embedded in that season of disorientation. Our world has been turned
upside down. We don't know what tomorrow will bring. It's uncertain,
it's frightening, but it's ever more urgent that we remember Jesus's
words that he never would leave us or forsake us and would be with us
always. If we look for signs of that hope and the light out there, we will
see it—that self-sacrificial love in the first responders, the grocery store
workers, the package deliverers, the bus drivers—people who are putting their own lives at risk for you and for me, out of love.

Just last week I saw what Mr. Rogers would have characterized
as one of the helpers. Years ago, he told children that when they were
frightened, if they would just look for the helpers, they would see
them. When you see the helpers, you see hope. This helper came in
the form of a seven-year-old boy living just across the river in Ash-
burn, Virginia: Zohaib Begg. You see, Zohaib spent some of the early
years of his life in the hospital. During that time, he developed a
great affection, respect, and connection with the doctors and nurses
who brought him back to health. When he was reading about the
coronavirus and the fact that so many hospitals weren't equipped
with the personal protection equipment that they needed, he knew
he needed to act.

This seven-year-old helper had the idea of going to hotels in the
area to see if they would donate shower caps. What he discovered in the
process was they not only had shower caps, they had masks and gloves.
So Zohaib set a goal. He wanted to beat the National Cathedral's tally

of five thousand masks that we donated to some local hospitals. And guess what? He not only met that goal, he exceeded it. Zohaib contributed 6,009 articles of PPEs to hospitals in the area. You go, Zohaib! I hope at some point in time, I'll have the opportunity to meet and thank you in person. For when you see the helpers, you see hope.

I know that in this time, one of the greatest pastoral heartbreaks for so many people, due to social distancing and the virus, is not being with their loved ones when they are sick and when they are dying. That is truly heartbreaking. But I want to share a personal experience with you of a way that we must be creative in these times. I share this experience with permission. About two weeks ago, our dearest friends John and Margaret Dalton called on a Sunday afternoon because Margaret's mother, who was in Texas, was close to death and Margaret couldn't be with her. Of course, she was heartbroken. I went over to be with them, and as I was putting on my collar and getting my prayer book, it occurred to me that while we couldn't physically be present, with technology we could at least be connected.

When I arrived at their home and from a safe distance, I asked if they would be open to our praying with Margaret's mother with FaceTime, knowing that their niece Maggie was right there with Margaret's mother, Maggie's grandmother. So, together, with FaceTime, Margaret and John had a chance to tell Carolyn how much they loved her and that they were with her and that God was with her. Then we prayed the prayers that are commonly known as the last rites, committing her to God and blessing her to God's care. Carolyn died the next day. It wasn't the same as being there in person, but it was one way that we could spiritually be connected and to commend her to God for eternity.

These times call for expressing love in so many different new ways for all of us. Last Sunday, Queen Elizabeth said that "better days will return: we will be with our friends again; we will be with our families again; we will meet again."[5] That is true. But my prayer for all of us is that we learn the lessons of this time in disorientation: the things that we have seen with clarity and the things that need to be changed, like the fact that the majority of deaths disproportionately

---

5. BBC America, "Queen Elizabeth II Reassures Public 'Better Days' Will Return in Rare TV Broadcast," April 6, 2020. *https://www.bbcamerica.com/blogs/queen-elizabeth-ii-reassures-public-better-days-will-return-in-rare-tv-broadcast--18220.*

are among people of color in this country. Injustices and inequities are with us, and we must change together, loving one another as Jesus loved us.

I pray that this time of connecting in deeper and different sorts of ways won't give way to considering a relationship being held by email and a text. There's much we have to learn. Jesus shows us the way and gives us a commandment: that we love one another as he has loved us. These times are uncertain, but we know with assurance that God is with us and will see us through this.

I leave you with words that have given me courage and strength throughout my adult life. They were written by my paternal grandfather in his well-worn Bible, and the words are these: "Faith is the ability to be so sure of God that no matter how dark the day, there's no doubt as to the outcome."

May God bless you and keep you this day and always. Amen.

NOT ALL RESURRECTIONS
HAPPEN IN THREE DAYS

THE REV. CANON DANA COLLEY CORSELLO
Good Friday, April 10, 2020

Good afternoon, my dear ones. I want to ask you to get settled, comfortably, wherever you are, presumably in front of a screen. If you can darken your space, pull the curtains, shut your blinds, block out any signs of light or springtime life, all the better.

Scripture tells us that Jesus gave up his spirit at twelve noon, and for the next three hours, darkness fell upon the Earth in what must have felt like a total eclipse of God.

So that we can be together at this moment, our hearts heavy and hurting as one, I plead with you to suspend any Easter morning expectations, if only for the next few hours. There are times, like today, Good Friday, when all of us need to feel what death looks like. We need to sit with Jesus's mother, Mary, and her sister and Mary Magdalene and the Beloved disciple John, who were there when they flogged him, whipped him, and beat him.

They were there when they nailed him to the tree. And they were there when he bowed his head and gave up his spirit. We need to claim their pain as our own, to be permeated by it: "I am poured out like water . . . all my bones are out of joint; my heart within my breast is melting wax" (Ps. 22:14, ESV).

So, stay with me as I ask you to let your guard down, to wallow even, wallow in despair as death breathes down your neck, as your future feels precarious at best, as the plague of COVID-19 keeps you up at night. I believe we owe it to ourselves and to Jesus to name it—to live our faith authentically even when life is unraveling before our eyes.

This Holy Week is singular. We are witnessing history from the entombment of our own homes. Some of you have lost your jobs, your paychecks, your futures. Seventeen million Americans have filed for unemployment. Some of you are numb and disassociated, unable to process the scope of what is happening around you. Some of you are depressed, anxious, lonely, afraid. Some of you are sick. Some of you are saying your final goodbyes through an iPad held up to the deathbed of a loved one by a nurse. Some of you are mourning your dead from a distance, with a grief that finds no purchase.

The purpose of my sermon is not to be macabre or to fetishize your pain, but to name it—to release it. Over these past few weeks, we have seen death exceeding all the boundaries we are normally able to impose upon it. We have our lives stifled, even suffocated, by the masks on our faces and the distance imposed between us.

No doubt many of you want to know if we can rest on our "shiny religious certainties" given the scope of these losses, these uncertainties? I say, "Yes, yes, we can!"[6] Of course I do. But I also say that we cannot take anything for granted—not anymore. God is calling on us to place our trust in the one thing we know for certain—and that is God's merciful, healing love. We are not forsaken. We will never be forsaken. But we are called at this moment to abide in the reality of uncertainty, and in a faith that for now is shrouded in the late afternoon shadows of Golgotha.

Several years ago, I came to the stark conclusion that not all resurrections happen in three days. In my own family the twin curses of alcoholism and depression run deep through the roots of our ancestral family tree. I think of that tree not as a lone freestanding entity but as a grove of aspens with a single, genetically enmeshed root system. What has long been a subterranean and dormant potential has now budded on the branches of my own tree. Prayers and interventions and medications don't immediately resurrect our loved ones to the versions of them we assumed we would be raising or growing old with. I know of friends who have survived bad marriages and are still reeling years later. Just yesterday morning, I received a phone call from a friend who said her son was unravelling, finally, over the death of his father this past October. For the living, not all resurrections happen in three days.

I share these things because this is the reality in which we find ourselves—when what we thought we could count on is lost in the miasma of a pandemic. Our lives and livelihoods are not going to be restored to health from the sting of the coronavirus on Sunday. We're going to have to pray for patience.

But like Mary, her sister, Mary Magdalene, and John, to be present at the foot of the cross and to witness the death of a loved one is something altogether different.

Earlier this week, the CBS reporter David Begnaud interviewed a young woman named Sheryl Pabatao whose parents died last week in the same New Jersey hospital, seven days apart, from complications arising

---

6. Debie Thomas, "A Crucified God," April 5, 2020, *Journey with Jesus* webzine, *www. journeywithjesus.net.*

from coronavirus. Her father died first. Sheryl had to call her mother to tell her before she read it on the family's group chat. Upon hearing the news, her mother couldn't or wouldn't speak. Sheryl, through tears, described how she could hear only the beeping and whirring of the machines in her mother's hospital room. Her mother hung up the phone but called Sheryl back in the afternoon to say that she simply couldn't do it anymore.

Sheryl said her parents were inseparable after forty-four years of marriage. The official cause of her mother's death is complications from the coronavirus, but she knows better. Her mother died of a broken heart. Both of her parents died alone. Sheryl and her family watched from their cars, prayed, and cried through FaceTime as each parent's body was taken into the crematorium.[7]

Yet as surely as I stand here, I know with every fiber of my being that Sheryl's parents did not die alone. Our faith offers us a core truth, a comforting truth, a paradoxical and shocking truth: that our crucified, broken, desolate God, who died on the cross, gave up his spirit so that it could be in those very hospital rooms with her parents and everyone else the world over who dies alone and in agony. This promise leaves no one to die in anonymity or oblivion. There is no death that we can die, big or small, literal or figurative, where Jesus will not hold us in his crucified arms.

You see, our God is not an unfeeling, indifferent heavenly power named "fate," but rather an eternal love who feels and suffers with us. God loves with those who love. God weeps with those who weep.

When Dietrich Bonhoeffer, the theologian of the German resistance movement against Hitler, was imprisoned by the Gestapo in Berlin, he felt a similar assurance. As he wrote in a letter to his best friend, "Only the suffering God can help."[8]

Jesus is revealed on the cross; "only a suffering God can show us the way. Only a suffering God can help us bear our burdens. Only a suffering God, wounded and shamed, can draw us to the light that dwells in darkness, and teach us how to love.[9] Only the suffering God can lead us home.

For those of us left in the wake of death, "I cannot tell you how many sorrows, disappointments, farewells, and endings we will have to endure before resurrection comes home to stay."[10] If anything in the

---

7. CBS This Morning, April 7, 2020, David Begnaud Reporting for CBS News.

8. Dietrich Bonhoeffer, "Letter to Eberhard Bethge," July 16, 1944, page 361.

9. Thomas, "A Crucified God."

10. Ibid. (paraphrase).

Christian story is true, it is that Jesus and all the dead after him are resurrected in three days. But for us, the living, it's more complicated. We
have to take it a day at a time, some of us hour by hour.

There is a poem by Pierre Teilhard de Chardin, the twentieth-
century Jesuit philosopher, theologian, and paleontologist, that I have
kept tucked in my wallet for years. It begins,

> Above all, trust in the slow work of God.
> We are quite naturally impatient in everything to reach the
>   end without delay.
> We should like to skip the intermediate stages.
> We are impatient of being on the way to something unknown,
>   something new.
> And yet it is the law of all progress
> that it is made by passing through some stages of instability—
> and that it may take a very long time.
>
> Only God could say what this new spirit
> gradually forming within you will be.
> Give our Lord the benefit of believing
> that his hand is leading you,
> and accept the anxiety of feeling yourself
> in suspense and incomplete.[11]

My friends, the adventure ahead of us is not dark but light. My
hope for you is that you never give in or allow the dark side of grief,
uncertainty, or fear to define you—but rather allow our crucified Jesus
to carry it for you. The love that emanates from that cross gives us the
courage to accept death without being conquered by it.

The love that emanates from that cross means that even if a virus
can take a life, it cannot destroy the meaning of that life. The love that
emanates from that cross means that hope of new life and a healed
heart are certainties.

Until the day we can walk out of our homes with our faces unmasked
and physically embrace our families, friends, and neighbors, be patient.
Endure, Emmanuel! God is with you. God knows your hurt. God holds
you in the infinite safety of the most sacred tract of his heart. Amen.

---

11. "Patient Trust," by Pierre Teilhard de Chardin, excerpted from *Hearts on Fire: Praying
with Jesuits* by Michael Harter, ©1993. Used with permission of the publisher, Boston College
Institute of Jesuit Sources, Chestnut Hill, MA 02467, *www.jesuitsources.bc.edu*, Institute of
Jesuit Sources, Chestnut Hill, MA.

IT'S EASTER ANYWAY!

THE MOST REV. MICHAEL B. CURRY
Easter Day, April 12, 2020

There is an old Easter hymn that says this:

> *The strife is o'er.*
> *The battle done.*
> *The victory of life is won.*
> *The sound of triumph has begun.*
> *Alleluia!*[12]

The Bible, in John's gospel, chapter 20, verse 1, says this:

> *Early on the first day of the week, while it was still dark, Mary*
> *Magdalene came to the tomb . . .*

It's Easter Sunday.
It doesn't look like it. It doesn't smell like it. It doesn't really feel like it.
But it's Easter anyway.

Churches are empty.
There's no sight or smell of lilies.
No children dressed in new clothes for Easter Day.
When I was a child, I remember that all the women would come to church with hats, white and pink, and flowers and fruit adorning them. None of that today.

When it happened, in those days,
It was Easter.
And we knew it.
And we would sing. *"Jesus Christ is risen today."*
We would sing, *"Hail thee festival day. Blest day that art hallowed forever."*
We would sing, *"Welcome happy morning age to age shall say."*
We would sing, *"Because he lives I can face tomorrow."*

---

12. "The Strife Is O'er, the Battle Done," trans. 1861 by Francis Pott, *The Hymnal 1982* (New York: The Church Pension Fund, 1985), 208.

We would sing, "*The strife is o'er. The battle done. The victory of life is won. The sound of triumph has begun. Alleluia!*"

Oh, we would sing, and we would shout, "Alleluia! Christ is risen! The Lord is risen indeed! Alleluia!"

> It's Easter.
> But it doesn't look like it.
> It doesn't feel like it.
> It doesn't even smell like it.
> But it's Easter anyway!

To be sure, there is no Easter bunny in malls.

To be sure, there are no crosses now adorned with beautiful flowers by children from Sunday school.

There are no crying babies in churches, no wiggling children, no old and young alike packed into seats.

The pews are empty.

The church is quiet.

Even the sounds of trumpets on great organs, even if they sound, they bounce from wall-to-wall, echoing in empty churches.

For there is sickness and hardship in the land, there is death and destruction, there is sadness and fear, anxiety. As the old slaves used to say, there is a weeping and a wailing.

But it's Easter anyway!

Think for a moment. That first Easter. It was Easter, but nobody knew it.

The Bible says, early in the morning, Mary Magdalen got up and went to the tomb while it was still dark. It was dark and she wasn't exactly sure how to get there, but she went anyway. She didn't know for sure that the rumor about soldiers having been posted to guard the tomb, to prevent anyone from doing anything, was true. She knew that there was a stone rolled in front of the entrance of the tomb. She got up and went anyway.

Luke's gospel says that Mary of Magdala and several other women were well-to-do women, who actually helped to finance and pay the bills, if you will, of that Jesus movement. Jesus had touched her, and their lives, and she never forgot. She loved him. They loved him. They were actually living the love that he had taught them because they had heard him. They had heard what he taught.[13]

They had heard him say, "Blessed are the poor and the poor in spirit."

They had heard him say, "Blessed are the peacemakers."

They had listened.

They were listening when he said, "Blessed are those who hunger and thirst, that God's righteous justice might prevail in all the world."

They listened to him when he said, "Do unto others as you would have them do unto you."

They listened when he said, "Love your enemies. Bless those who curse you."

They were listening when he said, "A new commandment I give you, that you love one another."

And Mary and those women followers of Jesus were there when he was dying on the cross and they saw him love, even in death.

They probably heard him say, "Father, forgive them. They don't know what they're doing."

They probably heard him cry out, "My God, my God, why hast thou forsaken me?"

And then they heard him make sure his mother was cared for, "Woman, behold your son, behold your mother."

They had heard him say to that revolutionary thief on the side of him, "Today you'll be with me in paradise."

They had heard him cry, "I thirst. It is finished. Father into thy hands, I commend my spirit."

Oh, they had listened to him.

They learned from him and they saw in him, as that old hymn says, "A love that would not let them go. You shall love the Lord your God, and your neighbor as yourself. This is the way to life."

They had listened. They had taken it in.

So, Mary and those women got up in the dark, not knowing for sure what was going on, just doing what love does. Love can't change the fact of death, but love can live through it and thereby defeat death. So they got up and went to the tomb just to do what love does. They

---

13. Cf. Matt. 5:3–10, 5:44, 27:46; Luke 6:31, 23:34, 23:43–46; and John 13:34, 19:26–30, 19:48 for Bible passages that follow.

didn't understand what was going on. They just did what love does. They went, as folk used to say, to "Make sure Jesus had a proper burial." They went to anoint his body and to make sure that the linen shroud was still clean and to give him a new one if necessary. They went to the tomb that morning, just to do what love does.

They didn't know. They really didn't know that Easter had happened. He had been raised from the dead. He was alive, new, transformed, not walking dead. He was alive, new, the new creation beginning. He was alive, but they didn't know that.

It was Easter, but it didn't look like it.
It didn't smell like it.
It didn't feel like it.
But it was Easter anyway.

Stay with me. The amazing thing was that it really was Easter. Jesus really was alive. God had been somehow behind the scenes all along, working through the chaos. They just didn't know it.

All that Mary knew was that Jesus was dead. She knew where he was buried. She knew the stone was there. She knew there might be guards there. She just knew where he was buried, and she just got up to do what love does. When she got there, she found the tomb was empty. The stone had been rolled away. The soldiers weren't there. What Mary didn't know was that Easter had happened anyway, in spite of what her eyes could see, her ears could hear, her nose could smell, her hands could touch. Easter had happened anyway, and maybe that is the way of God, that somehow behind the scenes, in ways that we may not fully behold at the time, God is there. And not just there, but somehow working in the midst, even of the mess.

The psalmist in the Hebrew Scriptures, Isaiah, says, "Surely, God thou art a God who hidest thyself" (cf. Isa. 45:15).

Eighteenth-century Christian poet and hymn writer William Cowper said it this way:

> God moves in a mysterious way.
> His wonders to perform.
> He plants his footsteps in the sea
> And rides upon the storm.[14]

---

14. William Cowper, "God moves in a mysterious way," *The Hymnal 1982* (New York: Church Hymnal, 1985), hymn 677.

This just seems to be the way of God.

One of my favorite poets from the nineteenth century, James Russell Lowell, who was very much involved in the movement to end chattel slavery and in movements to right grievous wrongs, and who stayed with it even when the odds were against it, wrote a poem in which he said,

> *Truth forever on the scaffold, Wrong forever on the throne*
> *Yet that scaffold sways the future, and, behind the dim unknown,*
> *Standeth God within the shadow, keeping watch above his own.*[15]

Easter had happened. Mary didn't know it, but she did what love does anyway. She got up, went to the tomb to do what love does. And though she and the other women didn't know it at the time, because they were acting on their love for Jesus, their trust in him, even when they didn't understand, they found their lives aligned with the very life of God. The God who the Bible says is love. And in so doing, discovered faith, hope, and eventually Mary would actually see Jesus alive, raised from the dead.

The late Howard Thurman was arguably one of the great spiritual masters, if you will, of the twentieth century. He was a close advisor behind the scenes to Dr. Martin Luther King. And it was greatly Howard Thurman and the late Rabbi Abraham Joshua Heschel who, behind the scenes, were quiet, spiritual counselors to King in some of his darkest moments. Thurman wrote a book entitled, *Jesus and the Disinherited*. Dr. King carried a copy of that book with him wherever he went. In that book, he tells of a time when he was a little boy growing up in segregated Florida, growing up poor in a rural community.

When Halley's Comet had come, people didn't understand what this comet was and what it meant, and people were frightened, anxious, not knowing what to do. The store down the street from where Thurman grew up was selling comet pills that were supposed to immunize you from the comet. But most people were just frightened. Late one night, Thurman was in bed and his mother came and got him out of bed and asked him if he wanted to see the comet in the sky. So he got out of bed and went outside with his mother, looked up to

---

15. "The Present Crisis," poem by James Russell Lowell, 1845, public domain, *https://poets. org/poem/present-crisis*.

the dark sky, saw this comet blazing in the heavens. He said, "Mama, are we going to die?" And she just said, "God will take care of us."[16]

Later he wrote:

O simple-hearted mother of mine, in one glorious moment you put your heart on the ultimate affirmation of the human spirit! Many things have I seen since that night. Times without number I have learned that life is hard, as hard as crucible steel; but as the years have unfolded, the majestic power of my mother's glowing words has come back again and again, beating out its rhythmic chant in my own spirit. Here are the faith and the awareness that overcome fear and transform the fear into the power to strive, to achieve, and not to yield.[17]

It may not look like Easter.
It may not smell like Easter.
It may not even feel like Easter,
But it's Easter anyway.
And trusting that, we can make it.

A little song says it this way.

(*singing*)
He's got the whole world in his hands,
He's got the whole world in his hands,
He's got the whole world in his hands,
He's got the whole world in his hands.[18]

God love you. God bless you. May God hold us all in those almighty hands of love. It's Easter. Amen.

---

16. Howard Thurman, *Jesus and the Disinherited*, copyright 1976 Howard Thurman; reprinted with permission from Beacon Press, Boston, MA.

17. Ibid.

18. "He's Got the Whole World in His Hands," African American spiritual. *https:// hymnary.org/text/hes_got_the_whole_world_in_his_hands.*

CHRIST WALKS WITH US

The Very Rev. Randolph Marshall Hollerith
Third Sunday of Easter, April 26, 2020

Did you know that no one really has any firm idea where the village of Emmaus is? It's ironic because our gospel lesson this morning clearly says that the village of Emmaus is about seven miles from Jerusalem (Luke 24:13–35). The confusion arises because in the earliest known manuscripts of Luke's gospel, some of them say that Emmaus was sixty stadia away from Jerusalem and others say that it was one hundred sixty stadia. A stadia is an ancient Greek unit of measurement equal to about six hundred feet. Now sixty stadia is about seven miles, but one hundred sixty stadia is about eighteen miles. Several places currently claim that they are the site of the ancient Emmaus, but scholars can't be sure. It's ironic because nowhere else in the gospels do we get such seemingly clear directions.

And yet, isn't this kind of fitting? When you think about the deepest meaning of this passage, isn't it better that Emmaus is nowhere specific so that it can be everywhere in general? One of the truths we are invited to see this morning is that Christ will travel wherever his followers are going. I bet you met him, or at least saw him, the last time you went on a walk to get out of the house. You might not have known it, but I bet you did.

The other truth we are invited to see this morning is that Christ will appear wherever his followers gather together to break bread, even here, even now, when we are gathered as a digital community. If we invite him to stay.

"The Road to Emmaus" is my favorite of all the resurrection stories. Cleopas and his friend are getting out of town after the crucifixion. They have seen enough. The dream Jesus promised them that he was the Messiah who would redeem Israel seemed to be destroyed by each nail the soldiers drove into his hands and his feet. The hope that God's kingdom would reign on Earth seemed crushed by the stone rolled in front of the tomb. Sure, there were rumors that Jesus had been seen alive. Some strange story about the women seeing an angel. But, they wondered, who could believe something so outlandish. No, the facts seemed clear—the dream of Jesus was over and done with, and now the only thing left to do was to get out of town.

I think Cleopas and his companion are good stand-ins for you and me. We are just like them and they are just like us. All of us traveling through life in our own little worlds. Thinking about too many things. Worrying about too many things. All of us trapped in our homes, watching the news as more than fifty thousand Americans, and hundreds of thousands of others around the world, lose their lives to this virus. All of us focused on the terrible facts that confront us and perhaps unaware of the deeper mystery that travels with us.

Some years ago, when the world was a very different place, Melissa and I were watching The Tonight Show and an interview with Emma Stone, who was promoting what was then the new Spiderman movie filmed in Manhattan. She related that New Yorkers were so focused on getting where they were going, heads down, minding their own business, heading to work or heading home, that when they were filming the big fight scenes for the movie on the streets of New York City with stuff exploding and cars on fire—New Yorkers would just walk on by. She remarked that the director complained that they actually had to hire extras to react and look surprised.

In a similar way, Cleopas and his friend were so wrapped up in their own little world, so consumed with their grief, that when they were joined by a third traveler, they had no idea who he was. This stranger was wise. He knew his scripture. They felt comforted by his presence. They seemed to understand more than they did before they met him. They felt a little more at peace as he journeyed the road with them. So, when it came time to stop for the evening, they took the risk to invite this stranger to stop with them. They invited him to dinner.

It was a risky thing to invite a stranger on the road to do anything in those days. Too much crime. Much safer to just mind your own business. But they took the risk. And it was at dinner when this stranger took the bread, blessed it, passed it around, and then took the wine, blessed it, and passed it around that they finally saw what they previously could not see. Their eyes were opened. This was no stranger—it was Jesus—alive and well and with them.

Do you realize this passage is the first recorded Eucharist? On Maundy Thursday, we read about Jesus's last supper with his disciples, right before he was arrested. But that's Jesus before the cross. Cleopas and his companion are the first to encounter the *risen* Christ in the bread and the wine. Theirs is the first Eucharist. And what the church has clung to so tightly all these centuries is the promise that what happened to Cleopas and his friend that day was not a one-off, it was not a singular event. It happens again and again each and every time his followers gather together, whether digitally or in person, to share the bread and the cup, if we are paying attention, if our eyes are open, if we invite Christ to come and be our guest.

Dorothy Day, the great Catholic writer and social activist, once said that Christ is disguised in every person we live with and work with, indeed in every person we meet, if we have the eyes to see him.[19] Are we prepared to meet him? Are we open to see him in others, even in the stranger? What would it be like if we dealt with each person we encounter as if we were dealing with Christ? What would it be like if we responded to each person in need as if we were responding to Christ? How different would our world be?

In a similar way—what if each person who shows us kindness, who offers us a comforting word, who goes out of their way to show us hospitality, the people who make us smile, show us love, help us to find some hope in a tough situation—what if each of those people is more than a good human being? What if it is actually Christ in them, through them, who is loving us and caring for us? Can you see Christ in the other? Can you see Christ in yourself?

Years ago, shortly after the birth of our daughter Eliza, my wife Melissa became very ill. This illness came on suddenly, dramatically, mysteriously. Melissa was hospitalized for several weeks, and there were moments in the midst of this terrifying time when I feared we might lose her. Eliza was not even three weeks old, and my son Marshall was just three years old. I was scared and overwhelmed, wanting to be by Melissa's side every second of the day but needing to take significant amounts of time to care for our newborn and our toddler. Melissa was in constant pain, frightened that the doctors could not seem to figure out what was going on with her and grieving that she was separated too soon from her newborn daughter who she longed to hold and nurse. Of course, the members of our parish were incredibly supportive with food and prayers and encouragement, but there were

---

19. Dorothy Day, "Room For Christ," *The Catholic Worker,* December 1945, 2. *https://www.catholicworker.org/dorothyday/articles/416.html.*

many long hours when Melissa was alone in her room. Even now, as we look back at this time, we can clearly see that Christ was present with her in a number of ways, but there was one way in particular that shines out for us still to this day.

One evening, after I had gone home to take care of the children, Melissa was awakened from a fitful morphine-induced sleep to the sounds of someone speaking. Struggling to stay awake, she realized this person was quietly reading psalms to her. It was our friend Tiva, sitting in a chair by her bed reading one psalm after another in a quiet, soothing voice. Tiva was one of the doctors in the hospital. A pediatrician, Tiva was the only pediatric cardiologist on the staff, and he was incredibly busy. But every day, for an hour or more, during whatever time he could get off from the demands of his practice, Tiva would sit in Melissa's room and read her psalms. What was so touching to us was not only the generosity of this wonderful act, but it was the realization that Tiva, a lifelong Buddhist, was ministering to Melissa with the words of her own faith. We didn't share the same religion, Tiva wasn't a Christian, but Christ's presence was made deeply manifest to Melissa during a very difficult time by the ministry of this special man.

My friends, I have no doubt that across this country and around the world Christ is being made manifest to thousands of people who are alone in the hospital, battling this terrible virus. He is being made known through the sacrifice, the devotion, the loving care of doctors, nurses, and medical technicians risking their own lives to care for the sick. I know this because I have experienced it myself. We need not fear, the risen Christ is here.

We are not alone on the journey to Emmaus that we call life. The message of Easter tells us that the risen Christ is as present here with us now as he was with Cleopas all those years ago. He is present with us on the road, present with us on the Zoom call, present with those we love who are alone in the hospital, and present with us at the table. He is present in those around us and present in the bread and the wine. Our job is to greet him, and to welcome him, and to invite him to stay for a while. Amen.

OUR MASTER CLASS ON GRIEF

The Rt. Rev. Mariann Edgar Budde
Fourth Sunday of Easter, May 3, 2020

Jesus said, "Very truly, I tell you, anyone who does not enter the sheepfold by the gate but climbs in by another way is a thief and a bandit. The one who enters by the gate is the shepherd of the sheep. The gatekeeper opens the gate for him, and the sheep hear his voice. He calls his own sheep by name and leads them out. When he has brought out all his own, he goes ahead of them, and the sheep follow him because they know his voice. They will not follow a stranger, but they will run from him because they do not know the voice of strangers." Jesus used this figure of speech with them, but they did not understand what he was saying to them. So again, Jesus said to them, "Very truly, I tell you, I am the gate for the sheep. All who came before me are thieves and bandits; but the sheep did not listen to them. I am the gate. Whoever enters by me will be saved, and will come in and go out and find pasture. The thief comes only to steal and kill and destroy. I came so that they may have life, and have it abundantly." (John 10:1-10)

I begin with a prayer that Dr. Rueben Varghese, director of public health in Arlington County, Virginia, recently shared on social media, originally written by the Atlanta-based pastor Laura Jean Truman.

> O God, keep my anger from becoming meanness.
> Keep my sorrow from collapsing into self-pity.
> Keep my heart soft enough to keep breaking.
> Keep my anger turned toward justice, not cruelty.
> Remind me that all of this, every bit of it, is for love.
> Keep me fiercely kind. Amen.[20]

While we were not strangers to grief before the pandemic, these last weeks have been something of a master class. "Each person's grief is as unique as their fingerprint," writes grief counsellor David Kessler. "But what everyone has in common is that no matter how we grieve, we share a need for the grief to be witnessed."[21]

We are witnesses of one another's grief.

---

20. Posted on the "Sad Jesus" Facebook page, prayer written by Laura Jean Truman. *https://www.facebook.com/thesadjesus*.

21. David Kessler, *Finding Meaning: The Sixth Stage of Grief* (New York: Simon & Schuster, 2019), 29.

In our witness, we must acknowledge that loss is not equally distributed among us. The greatest disparities fall along long-standing inequities and injustices, and they are the direct result of policies and priorities that deem some sectors of the human family expendable. Those of us with privilege have allowed this to happen, and we have much to answer for before God and so much that we must work to change. And we don't have all the time in the world.

For today, I'd like to consider what grief does, which is to break our hearts. I am persuaded that there is more hope for finding common ground and common purpose among us, as a people, in the solidarity of suffering than in proving one another right or wrong.

As the Israeli poet Yehuda Amichai so beautifully reminds us:

From the place where we are right,
Flowers will never grow
In the spring.
The place where we are right
Is hard and trampled
Like a yard.
But doubts and loves [*and I would add grief*]
Dig up the world
Like a mole, a plow.
And a whisper will be heard in the place
Where the ruined
House once stood.[22]

Globally, we are living in a ruined house now. There is a voice whispering. What do you hear?

I hear voices, both human and divine, that point us toward reservoirs of healing and deeper meaning that can emerge from this loss—if we choose to heed them.

I don't mean to gloss over the magnitude of loss. We need never give thanks for it, pretending that it isn't devastating to those touched by it. I'm reminded of what Rabbi Harold Kushner said about how he was changed for the better by the death of his young son. "Yes," he said, "I am a more sensitive person, a more effective pastor than I would have been had my son not died. But I would give up all those gains in a

---

22. Yehuda Amichai, "The Place Where We Are Right," from *The Selected Poetry of Yehuda Amichai* (Berkeley: University of California Press, 1996), 34. Used by permission.

second if I could have my son back. If I could choose, I would forgo it all. But I cannot choose."[23]

None of us can choose the grief we must endure. We can choose, however, to cultivate what lies within us through the mystery of grace and the power of love: our God-given desire to make the world better in the wake of ruined houses, to make meaning from the most painful of losses. It's not the loss itself that becomes meaningful, but how we live and who we become because of it.

In this master class we're in, I've noticed a particular expression of grief that naturally leans us toward this making-better and meaning-making side of ourselves. It's the grief we feel when we cannot spare those we love the suffering they are experiencing.

I hear this empathic grief in parents who can't spare their children the sudden disruption of their lives and the loss of rites of passage for which they have been preparing for years. I hear it in children of elder parents who are sick with worry, and in family members of those deemed essential workers and who, by choice or compulsion, risk their lives each day. I hear it in the business owners doing everything they can to keep employees on the payroll, in teachers, caregivers, advocates, my fellow clergy. I hear it every day in people like you.

This grief propels us like no other to do whatever we can to make things better and to offer hope and meaning for those we love. So, we see spouses standing outside of nursing home windows with signs that say "I love you," and long lines of cars driving by the house of a child celebrating a birthday or graduation. Last night I watched a concert that our unemployed music producer son organized via Instagram so that his fellow musicians could perform live from their homes. The love expressed on the chat bar was palpable.

And then there's the woman in my neighborhood who has been involved for years in the sanctuary movement, an effort to protect undocumented families from being deported. In her heartache for how undocumented families in our region are suffering now—and their suffering is severe, with no safety net to fall back on—she has almost single-handedly formed a volunteer network that provides food and essential supplies for hundreds of households each week. This is grief mobilized for good, helping us all to do something to redeem the time we're in.

---

23. Harold S. Kushner, *When Bad Things Happen to Good People* (New York: First Anchor Books, 1984), 145.

These are the stories we'll remember when the pandemic has passed, for they will tell not only that we got through it, but *how*—how we loved and cared for each other, how our hearts were broken open, and how we resolved to change things. A poet I admire, David Whyte, asked a question last week that I'll pass on to you: How can you live now such that your future self, and all who come after you, will look back with gratitude? How, in other words, can you become now the blessed saint of your future memory?[24]

There's another form this empathic grief can take whenever we monitor or regulate expressions of our personal pain and fear for someone else's sake, particularly those who are looking to us for stability and reassurance. If you have someone coming up behind you or who in any way depends upon you, you know what I mean. This empathic grief requires us to find a place inside to hold our emotions—not deny or bury them, but hold them in such a way that they are available to us but aren't so front and center that we can't be fully present to those looking to us for direction.

Rabbi Edwin Friedman popularized the phrase "being a non-anxious presence," which isn't easy to pull off when you're feeling anxious yourself. But he also said this: "If you can manage to regulate your anxiety enough to keep the outward expression of it just a notch or two below that of the group you're in, you're helping to bring the collective anxiety level down."[25] This is one of the most needed attributes of leadership—for parents and presidents, as Friedman used to say, and it can be learned. We all need to learn and practice it, because we all have someone coming up behind us.

In the fall of 2001, our older son entered eighth grade, which was the highest grade level of his school. So it was a big year for him and his classmates, and they entered it, his teacher later told me, with real apprehension. They kept on looking around, she said, wondering when the real eighth graders would show up, the ones they had always looked up to.

On the morning of 9/11, as the terrible news of that day reached our Minneapolis neighborhood, the parents on our block decided that it was best for our children to go to school. I volunteered to drive. Our

---

24. David Whyte, as part of a three-week online class, "The Courage of Poetry," www.davidwhyte.com. With reference to the poem "Coleman's Bed," found in *River Flow: New & Selected Poems, 1984–2007* (Langley, WA: Many Rivers Press, 2007), 288.

25. Edwin Friedman, *Generation to Generation: Family Process in Church and Synagogue* (New York: Guilford Press, 1985), 27, 208–10.

older son was in the front with me, and in the back sat his younger brother and other boys, all very quiet. I put my arm around our older son's shoulder and said something to the effect of, "Try to be kind to the younger kids today. They'll be looking up to you."

Later I learned that a few of the eighth-grade class went to the principal and asked if they could organize a prayer service. To her eternal credit the principal said yes, and by the end of the day, the entire school was in the chapel, led in prayer by the eighth-grade class. "From that point on," my son's teacher told me, "they never questioned who the real eighth graders were." You see, there's something about acting on behalf of other people that makes the energy of our grief an offering with which God can help create meaning.

In the gospel passage for today, Jesus speaks of himself as a shepherd who calls us each by name and whom we follow because we recognize his voice. He also speaks of himself as a gate through which we enter and find salvation. Here's the line I invite you to dwell upon in the days to come: "Whoever enters by me will be saved . . . I have come that they may have life and have it abundantly" (John 10:9–10).

I wonder where and how do you need to be saved? What would it look like and how would it feel like to experience being saved now?

It's a risky question to ask. But if we don't ask it, how can we enter a conversation with the One who calls himself our good shepherd, and who promises salvation amid our lives as they are and our world as it is?

This is what salvation looks like for me—when Jesus comes to me as the whispering voice, the presence of divine love. And when he encourages me and teaches me in a way of love that is merciful, forgiving, sacrificial, and universal.

I believe that in Jesus's life, his suffering, death, and resurrection, God reveals and invites us all to join in the divine mystery of bringing life out of death and meaning from grief.

I believe that salvation is deeply personal, but not individual. As the great peace activist Daniel Berrigan was known to say, "We will walk in the kingdom of God together, or we won't walk in at all."[26]

Followers of Jesus are not immune to human suffering, nor are we spared anxiety or grief. He never promised us that; in fact, he prepared

---

26. I couldn't find the citation for this line that I have carried with me since I first read it in the mid-1980s. A good source for an overview of Berrigan's work is: Daniel Berrigan, *Essential Writings*, Modern Spiritual Masters Series (Maryknoll, NY: Orbis Books, 2009).

us for the exact opposite—that like him, ours would be the way of the cross, which is the way of salvation through suffering, not around it. In our master class on grief, he is the master teacher.

Here's the point: we are closest to him and most like him in our grief for those we love in their suffering. That's what propelled him to the cross—his love and his grief for us all. This grief propels us to take on, gladly, whatever is needed to make things better, to wrench whatever meaning we can from this ruined house for love's sake.

So listen for his voice. It's the one that rings true—not with false promises of escape but with the real promise to see you through what you did not choose. Lean on him now, because he loves you. He is on the side of making things better, bringing meaning out of this mess we're in. When you, in your love for others, join in that making-better, making-meaning work, you are the embodiment of his love. You are.

There are surely easier ways to live, but there are none more meaningful, and none more needed now.

> May God keep your heart soft enough to keep on breaking
> And your anger turned toward justice.
> May all that you do now be for love.
> And may God keep you fiercely kind. Amen.[27]

---

27. Laura Jean Truman, "Keep Me Fiercely Kind," Twitter post, October 7, 2018, 10:56 p.m., *https://twitter.com/laurajeantruman/status/1049131455778119681?lang=en* (paraphrase).

TO WATCH AND WAIT

JON MEACHAM
Seventh Sunday of Easter, May 24, 2020

It was the most reasonable of questions. After the cataclysm of the Passion, the horrors of Golgotha, and then the wonder of the Resurrection, the disciples were understandably seeking answers. Who wouldn't? In our own time, you and I are impatient about the reopening of barbershops and baseball—imagine how hungry we'd be for clarity on the meaning of a murdered Master. "Lord," the disciples ask in our first lesson, "is this the time when you will restore the kingdom to Israel?" But Jesus, as, alas, was his wont, is maddeningly elusive. "It is not for you to know," he says in reply, "the times or the periods that the Father has set by his own authority" (Acts 1:6–7).

And then he is gone—again. He ascends out of time and history. He leaves his followers in confusion. So what do they do? They pray, they wait, and they wonder.

Which is what you and I are doing now: praying, waiting, and wondering. If you are anything like me—and I suspect you are—the praying is fine. We're used to that. It's the waiting and the wondering that give us pause. The Christian story is at once reassuring and confounding. In the gospel, Jesus tells the Father, "All mine are yours, and yours are mine. . . . Holy Father, protect them . . . so that they may be one, as we are one" (John 17:10–11).

And yet, and yet—so much of our faith is captured in that phrase: *and yet.* We're assured that the world has been put to rights, that Jesus's death and resurrection have restored the order that was shattered in Genesis, that salvation and renewal are ours for the asking.

And yet: Where's the Lord when we need him? We're as enveloped in mystery as human beings have been since the first fist was raised toward the sky, asking *Why?* Why do the innocent suffer and the innocent die? Why are some rich, others poor? Why do some find love while others search fruitlessly? Why are some hearts full and others perpetually broken?

We do not know. The world is a tragic place. Religion offers one set of responses, philosophy still others. It is, however, religion that has most fundamentally shaped the world in which you and I live. "All men," Homer wrote, "have need of the gods," and the persistent role of faith across human experience is testament to its power. And so let us consider for a moment: *Why* does faith endure in the face of disease and death? *Why*, in other words, do we wait and wonder?

Here's my answer: We wait and wonder not in spite of history but *because* of history. Had Jesus simply been a great moral teacher, the most charismatic of rabbis and messianic figures in the teeming world of the first century, you and I would most likely not be living our lives as we do. The great truth at the heart of this complex story is that those disciples who so rarely managed to elicit a straight answer from their Lord genuinely believed that reality had been upended by their lived experience of the ministry, passion, and resurrection of a single man.

Their faith was about making sense of a series of events so singular and so compelling that they were willing to die in defense of their vision of a new truth that came into the world and utterly transformed that world.

The New Testament is very much a product of a particular time and place. It was written by authors who expected Jesus's imminent return to inaugurate the kingdom of God on earth, a new reality of a restored Israel. They waited and wondered, sustained by counsel such as that offered in 1 Peter (8–10): "Like a roaring lion your adversary the devil prowls around, looking for someone to devour. Resist him . . . And after you have suffered for a little while, the God of all grace . . . will himself restore, support, strengthen, and establish you."

So they were ready—ready for the Son of Man to return on clouds of glory; ready to fly to meet Him at the sound of a trumpet; ready for that elusive hour when every tear would be wiped away.

And yet—there it is again—the Lord did not return. It's been more than a little while. We are left, then, with history and with hope. History in the sense that we seek act in love within time and space, and those acts of love sustain us—in the giving and in the receiving—as glimpses of reconciliation and restoration.

Love is difficult. We are commemorating Memorial Day, the annual occasion of honoring those who gave what President Lincoln called the last full measure of devotion. Today's epistle is also part of the Lincoln canon. Though our current translation tells not to be surprised "at the fiery ordeal that is taking place" amongst us (1 Peter 4:12), the King James Version, which Lincoln intimately knew, rendered the passage as "the fiery trial," which Lincoln quoted in late 1861, writing: "Fellow citizens, we cannot escape history. . . . The fiery trial through which we pass, will light us down, in honor or dishonor, to the latest generation."

We face those trials which unfold within history with an abiding sense of hope—hope that the promises of the Passion will come to pass at an hour and in a place veiled from our eyes and beyond our understanding.

One can, of course, dismiss all of this as wishful thinking, or as nostalgia, or as foolishness. Yet our faith is rooted in reality—in the reality of the story of Israel, and in the reality of the experience of the disciples in the first century. The choice is ours: abandon all hope, or hold fast to it.

I choose to wait and wonder not in despair, for the evidence of the gospel is that in our barren times, in times of violence and of virus, of gloom and of fear, joy will come in the morning. That is our story. That is our faith. Let us wait and wonder in the conviction that death and darkness will give way to life and light. It happened before, long ago. And in that history lies our hope.

3

Anything but Ordinary Time

WHITE SOUL WORK

The Very Rev. Randolph Marshall Hollerith
Third Sunday after Pentecost, June 21, 2020

Four years ago, when I first arrived in the Diocese of Washington, I took part in a monthly orientation program with other clergy who were new to the diocese that year. The program was called Genesis, and it was designed to bring us together in order to build relationships, to spend good quality time with Bishop Mariann, and to better understand this new diocese that we now called home. To be honest, as I look back on it, I don't remember a lot about what we did during those meetings besides having the opportunity to get to know some new colleagues. But there was one session that sticks with me and remains fresh in my mind. It was the day we were invited to read and discuss a short story entitled, "Space Traders."

"Space Traders" is the kind of sci-fi story you might see on *The Twilight Zone*. It was originally written by Derrick Bell and then turned into a brief script by the diocese's very own Dr. Enid LaGesse. In short, the story centers around a group of very technologically advanced aliens who come to earth and promise to give the people of the United States enough wealth to end all our financial problems, special technology to fix all our environmental problems, and a brand-new power source that would end all our energy problems. The only catch is that in return for these gifts, America has to agree to put all African Americans aboard the alien ships and allow them to be taken away to the alien planet. Most of the story focuses on the public conversations and arguments that would take place if such an offer were made, and the story ends with a national referendum voted on and approved by the American people to trade African Americans for alien technologies. Crazy, right?

The day we discussed this story, we were a diverse group of highly educated and seasoned clergy. We were Black and White, male and female, LGBTQ and non-LGBTQ, old and young. At first, I thought the story was absolutely absurd, and I wondered why we were wasting our time talking about such things. When we were asked if we thought anything like this could ever really happen, the people of the United States trading African American lives for advanced technology, most of the White folks in the room thought it was ridiculous and could never happen. But what brought me up short was that most of the African Americans in the room thought it was not far-fetched at all and that under similar circumstances America would indeed make this trade.

I was floored. At first, I wondered why these colleagues, that I so respected, were being so dramatic, surely this was just a stupid science fiction story. But then I began to see that they were not being dramatic. Rather, with sadness in their eyes, they were being honest. And I realized that in spite of all my years of education and experience as an ordained priest, I still had blind spots to a reality that was painfully obvious to them—that racism is alive and well in America and still a very real threat. I was blind because I am White, and the story is only absurd to me because I do not have to deal with racism every single day of my life and they do. From their experience, this wild science fiction story was, at its core, talking about something very real. In that moment, I understood that despite everything I thought about myself, I was still blind, and I still had some very real work that I needed to do.

My friends, I know there are some of you out there who are right at this moment considering tuning me out or turning me off because you really do not want to hear me talk about this subject. With all the tragic news and all the protests in recent weeks, you are tired of hearing about racism, worn out from having to confront the pain that accompanies this topic, and you just want to talk about something else. But my friends, if we call ourselves Christians, if we take our faith seriously, especially if we are White, then the one thing we cannot do is turn away from this subject or try to hide from the pain. Because, we have brothers and sisters of color who need us. They need us to open our eyes and our ears, they need us listen to what they have to tell us. They need us to do the work that only we can do to realize the privilege our white skin affords us and then to eliminate that privilege. When we turn away, when we avoid the difficult issues, when we think that racism is not our problem, then we only reinforce our White privilege and nothing changes. The truth is, we can't afford to turn away, too much has taken place. This is our moment to do something meaningful to break the cycle of history, so we don't repeat yet again the same racist tragedies that we have seen throughout history, tragedies that are once again laid bare before us here in 2020 as they were in 1968, 1991, or 2014.

In our lessons for this morning, St. Paul says that in the waters of baptism we are buried with Christ (Romans 6:1b–11). Our old selves are crucified with him so that we might die to one way of being in the world and be reborn to a new way of being in the world—the way of Love. Moreover, Jesus tells us that we need not fear anything that can destroy the body, rather we need only concern ourselves with that which can destroy our souls. Friends, racism is destroying our souls and the soul of this nation. And those of us who are White have a special responsibility to make sure that this old self, this old way of being, that has existed since the beginning of America, that says White is right—this old self has to die or we can never really be reborn to something new—to the way of love.

The fact is, to deal with the root causes of racism, we have to deal with White supremacy and White privilege. It is not work that can be avoided or left to our brothers and sisters of color to somehow fix through protests or speeches. It will take much more than that to root it out, especially in its most subtle forms. It is our work, and in order to do it we are going to have to be willing to allow our old selves, our old ways of thinking to be crucified. We are going to have to be willing to uncover and bring into the light the assumptions, the behaviors, and the mindsets that many of us who are White are not even aware of. It is going to hurt, but we know from watching Jesus on the cross that there is no new life without struggle and pain. We don't have to have all the answers, but if we are willing to take up our cross and follow Jesus at this particular moment in our nation's history, then we must engage in what I call White soul work.

What is that? What is White soul work? Simply put, it is the process of having our eyes opened so that we can clearly see and help to dismantle the racist system that lies at the heart of our culture, a system that we often do not see precisely because we are White. Let's face it, most of us are good people, we would never consciously hurt, marginalize, or discriminate against someone else because of the color of their skin. As a result, some folks get defensive and resentful when they hear that they have to deal with their own White privilege. As Layla Saad writes in her book, *Me and White Supremacy* (and I paraphrase): *Our desire to be seen as good, by ourselves and others, prevents us from honestly looking at the ways we unknowingly participate in and are part of a racist culture. Our desire to be seen as good actually prevents us from doing good, because if we cannot see our-selves as part of the problem, then we cannot be part of the solution.*[1]

My friends, the real work needed to end racism has to start with the individual, it has to start with me, in me, through my hard work to come to terms with systemic racism that I may not see, to confront my participation in a racist system that I may not realize exists. That is White soul work. As Jim Golden writes,

> It is no accident that we learned about Helen Keller but not W.E.B. DuBois. We learned about the Watts and L.A. riots but not Tulsa or Wilmington. We learned about black ghet-tos but not Black Wall Street. We learned about "black crime," but white criminals were never lumped together and discussed in terms of their race. We learned about "states' rights" as the cause of the Civil War, but not that slavery was mentioned eighty times in the articles of secession. Privilege is having his-tory written so that you don't have to acknowledge uncomfort-able facts. Racism is perpetuated by people who refuse to learn or acknowledge this reality.[2]

Will you join me in this work? We all have work to do. Will you refrain from turning away, from changing the subject? I have no doubt that the Holy Spirit is at work amongst us right now in new and power-ful ways. She is stirring amongst the protestors, moving amongst people of goodwill, calling all of us, nudging us to live into the still unfulfilled American dream that all people are created equal.

Never forget that in our baptisms each of us was given the gift of the Holy Spirit. She is there to guide us and strengthen us to be better

---

1. Layla F. Saad, *Me and White Supremacy: Combat Racism, Change the World, and Become a Good Ancestor* (Naperville, IL: Sourcebooks, Kindle Edition, 2020), 43.

2. Jim Golden, "A New Curriculum for the History of Black People." *https://www.change. org/p/elizabeth-warren-how-the-history-of-black-people-is-taught-a-new-curriculum.* Altered in delivery.

than we are, and better than we thought we could be. She is there work-ing to build the beloved community, and as Dr. King reminds us, "It is this type of spirit and this type of love that can transform opposers into friends. It is this type of understanding goodwill that will transform the deep gloom of the old age into the exuberant gladness of the new age. It is this love which will bring about miracles in the hearts of men."[3] May it be so. May it be so. Good Lord, may it be so. Amen.

3. Martin Luther King Jr., "Facing the Challenge of a New Age," speech, Montgomery Improve-ment Association, Montgomery, Alabama, December 3, 1956. *https://kinginstitute.stanford.edu/king-papers/documents/facing-challenge-new-age-address-delivered-first-annual-institute-nonviolence.*

HOPE IN THE MIDST OF REALITY

The Rev. Canon Jan Naylor Cope
Seventh Sunday after Pentecost, July 19, 2020

Gracious God, help us always to seek the truth, come whence it may, cost what it will. Amen.

This morning, I invite you to join me in exploring hope in the midst of reality. Now, in the gospel you just heard, you might have noticed the language toward the end—of the fiery furnace, the weeping and gnashing of teeth, and Jesus saying, "Let anyone with ears listen!" (Matt. 11:15). You might logically ask where exactly do you see hope in that message? That would be a fair question, but stay with me because I do see hope in that gospel lesson. I see hope even in our current reality. If we look for hope, we will find it. Even more importantly, we have an opportunity if we come together and work together to bring hope to others.

That thirteenth chapter of Matthew (13:24–30, 36–43), from which our gospel lesson came, marks a turning point in Jesus's mode of teaching. Earlier in the gospel, we hear the Sermon on the Mount where Jesus is very clear and precise about his teaching. He calls us to turn the other cheek, go the extra mile, love our enemies, and pray for those who persecute us. Then, in this thirteenth chapter, he turns to parables and the disciples ask him, "Why are you teaching and telling us parables?" Apparently, Jesus's teaching was too clear and too hard because people were starting to turn away from him. He said, those who see don't perceive; those who hear don't listen and they don't understand. He repeatedly says, "Let anyone with ears listen!" That's for you and me, as well.

Parables were designed to engage the imagination and to challenge the conventional wisdom. Amy-Jill Levine says that parables are difficult because they "challenge us to look into the hidden aspects of our own values, our own lives. They bring to the surface unasked questions and they reveal the answers to the questions that we have always known but have refused to acknowledge."[4] The parable that you heard in the gospel lesson today is about the wheat and the weeds. The good news and hope in that lesson that I take away is that Jesus makes clear that at the end of the age, it's not up to us to judge the wheat from the weeds.

---

4. Amy-Jill Levine, *Short Stories by Jesus: The Enigmatic Parables of a Controversial Rabbi* (New York: HarperOne, Chalice Press, 2002), 3.

That's God's job—the same God we know to be steadfast, faithful, grace-filled, full of mercy, and abounding in steadfast love. I don't know about you, but I'd much prefer judgment coming from God than—no offense—from you or from me. That's the good news and the hope in that gospel lesson. Jesus then goes on to say that it is not our responsibility to seek to weed someone else's garden.

Jesus says earlier in the Sermon on the Mount that we need to take care of the log in our own eye before addressing the speck in someone else's. We are called to deeply reflect and wrestle with our own spiritual garden, the mix of wheat and weed. As we look across the landscape in our country and across the globe, we know that there are weeds that are infecting, poisoning, and killing the good in our country and across the globe. Over the course of the last four months, we've heard some powerful sermons coming from this Cathedral that have challenged us and also inspired us.

On Pentecost, our presiding bishop Michael Curry talked about the two pandemics: of course, the pandemic of COVID, where so many lives have been lost, but in that process it has also laid bare the underbelly of social injustice and inequities. We cannot fail to see the disproportionate number of infections and deaths that have come to persons of color. We can't unsee that, and we must not ever unsee that. Bishop Curry also spoke to the pandemic of the sin of our spiritual homes—the sin of racism, which has also been laid bare in these times. He preached a few short days after the shocking and brutal murder of George Floyd that sent shockwaves and people to the streets all across the country and across the globe. In that moment and in this movement, I see hope because people everywhere are saying, "No more." We cannot unsee what we have seen. We must not ever unsee what we have seen.

Bishop Curry offered words of hope, as he always does when he preaches. He reminded us that we are not victims of fate, that we are people of faith. As such, we follow Jesus, who taught us that love will make a way, even when there doesn't seem to be a way. We have work to do, you and me.

Our Bishop Mariann Edgar Budde referred to this time as a crucible moment in *Kairos* time, that all of us are called to come together and to continue this struggle, to continue this work, even when the cameras are gone. We will. We must. This Cathedral is committed to the two pandemics that we have seen and we continue to see with the coronavirus and the sin of racism.

Our Dean Randy Hollerith preached from this pulpit that those of us who are White have "White soul work" to do. It no longer works, it's no longer enough, for people of goodwill to stand silent, to not stand up, to not act, to not be heard. John Lewis taught us that when we see something that is not right, not fair, not just, we have a moral obligation to do something about it.

One of the signs of hope that I see in this reality is that the Black Lives Matter movement is continuing to this day. According to a *Washington Post* reporter, about 140 times each and every day, people are taking to the streets, joining in the struggle for justice and reconciliation. That's our call and our work, too.

In all of this, my own "White soul work"—I felt led to share with you some of my own work. Not because I'm some great exemplar, but because perhaps in my example, you might see something of yourselves. I felt led to do it. I'm reminded of my friend and colleague our Canon Theologian Kelly Brown Douglas preaching on Mother's Day, five years ago, after the brutal murder of Freddie Gray. She asked the question, "What are we teaching our children?" and she turned it to the imperative "What must we teach our children?"

So, I knew for me, the next chapter of my work needed to be to go back to my childhood. What did I learn at home? What did I learn from my community? What was the combination of the wheat and the weeds in my own life? I began that journey talking to my older brother Kenneth—four years older than I—who is generous and loving and wise and, most importantly, has the best memory of anyone I know, period. I asked him to reflect with me—what were we taught? He confirmed for me that our parents taught us that every person is worthy of our respect and our dignity, no exceptions; and that racial slurs and any sort of discrimination would not have been tolerated in our home. Were my parents perfect? No, none of us are, but they did their best to plant good seeds in us.

My mother taught me something else. I confess to you that I learned that lesson a little too well. She taught us that it wasn't polite to ask people personal questions, like how much something cost. I'm afraid that over time, I inculcated that to the point where I just didn't ask many questions. There were times when I should have asked a lot more than I have. And in a prayer of confession, I have learned that it's not so much the things that I've done, it's the things that I have left undone; the things that I have not said; the places I have not showed up. To try and get a better understanding of what I learned in my community, I had to go back there, too.

This is my reality. I grew up in a little town in South Texas named Refugio, which at its peak population had about five thousand people. There was a main drag that ran through the center of town named Alamo, of course. On one side of Alamo, that's where most of the White people lived. On the other side of Alamo, that's where the Black and the Brown people lived. There were three schools, three school entities that existed when I was growing up. There was the Refugio Independent School District that went from first grade through twelve. There was the parochial school, Our Lady of Refuge, that went from first grade to eighth grade. And then there was the Black school, Barefield, that was literally across the railroad tracks.

Now, you might ask why, when *Brown vs. the Board of Education* passed before I was even born, it wasn't until I was in the fifth or sixth grade that Black students came to my school. I remember some about that, but I couldn't trust my memory. So, I screwed up my courage and made the decision to reach out to one of my Black classmates I knew best, Mayola Shaw. I decided I would ask her to share her memories with me. Thanks to Google, I got her number. I called. I wasn't sure after forty years that she'd even remember me or that she'd be willing to talk to me. To my great relief and delight, she called me back. And I said, "Mayola, I seem to remember that in the fifth or sixth grade, you and Beverly Kay were in my classes." She said, "That's right, but that's not the full story."

She went on to tell me that we were fully integrated by about the sixth grade. All the students—and there weren't that many—came over from Barefield. She reminded me that there were tracks in our school system: the college bound, the maybe college bound, and the non-college bound. All the students from Barefield were put in the non-college-bound track. I guess they might have done some testing and it was only then that Mayola and Beverly joined my class. My White bubble had somewhat skipped over the full reality of that experience.

As part of my "White soul work," I'd also pulled out all of my high school yearbooks and looked at them with a different lens. My memory was that by high school things were really pretty well integrated and that turned out to be the case. But there was one thing I hadn't remembered and didn't notice: that in my high school, there was only one Black teacher—one—Mr. Marshall. I asked Mayola, "Did you notice or did you remember there was only one Black teacher in our school?" She laughed. Of course, she knew that! Of course, she remembered that vividly! She told me that for some reason, Black teachers had a hard time getting hired in our little town. They were hired in surrounding towns, but not ours.

Fast forward to 2020 and a sign of hope even in that reality. The mayor of my little hometown today is an alum of the Barefield School. Today, what remains of the Barefield School has been turned into a learning center so people will know the history of segregation in our little town. I'm also pleased to report that in my little town in early June, hundreds of White, Brown, and Black people took to the streets. In my little hometown, Black Lives Matter. Friends, wheat, and weeds exist.

It is our work to do. James Baldwin said, "If I love you, I have to make you conscious of the things you don't see."[5] It is time for us to wake up, listen up, join together in this urgent work—this Holy work we have to do. It is our turn. It is our time. It is our opportunity to make what's only been a dream, a reality. In the words of Jesus, "Let anyone with ears listen!" Let's go, friends! We have work to do! Amen.

---

5. Quoted in Debby Irving, *Waking Up White, and Finding Myself in the Story of Race* (Plano, TX: Elephant Room Press, 2014), 6.

LIFE-CHANGING FAITH

THE REV. CANON LEONARD L. HAMLIN SR.
Eleventh Sunday after Pentecost, August 16, 2020

I am often reminded of hearing many say that it's good to be here. In these days, it is good to be anywhere, but it is certainly good to be here. Over the past, perhaps months, I hear my father often saying as we would sit in certain moments together, "I don't know how individuals can make it without faith." I didn't realize then how much that made an impression upon my life, only to be wrestled with later on. But while I am grateful for this moment—recognizing the company of being with our dean as well as our vicar, whose presence and fellowship is greatly appreciated, as well as the worship team, who had pressed their way this morning—so that we might be able to connect one with another.

I am thankful to connect with those who are watching this morning, not in this space, but perhaps wherever you are—in your homes, perhaps in your workplaces and workspaces, those who have made use of the internet and the worldwide web. It is true that we have all learned to appreciate opportunities to connect.

Our connections today do not always resemble the familiar moments of yesterday, and our opportunities that we have now should be appreciated just as much as they were yesterday. And perhaps for some, who took them for granted, appreciated even more. We have all learned to appreciate not only six feet, but an opportunity to be in the same area. Many of us have quickly developed a different appreciation for FaceTime, for Zoom, for Skype, for Webex and other platforms that bring us, even digitally, face to face. I find myself in one moment complaining about being overtaxed by Zoom, but then grateful to see someone's face.

While I'm grateful for this moment, I'm always humbled by the responsibility that accompanies any preacher in a space like this. For while any preacher seeks to make a connection with the here—I may not see you directly—but through the power of the spirit, I know you're there. I was looking forward to meeting you on this day. So, wherever you are in your homes; wherever you are moving about, even watching, perhaps some that may see this later in the week; it is good to make a connection. I am humbled and joyful in knowing that you are there in your homes. Because you're not here, the space where you are has been transformed, even for just a moment, into a sanctuary right there.

Like many of you, I come this morning, and come to this moment, having been confronted, and at times feeling as if I've been assaulted, by the constant reporting and opinions on the realities which we face and in which we live. The continuing pandemics of racism and COVID, and all the tangible elements that have been brought to light even further, keep showing up at the door, keep showing up on the screen, keep showing up on the text, keep showing up in every place that I might turn.

I say that these pandemics have brought to light the tangible aspects and other aspects. And I say brought further into the light as opposed to some characterizing many elements as if they are being discovered for the first time. In trying to respond, not only have I been wrestling with the chapters of my own experience and listening to the narratives of others, but I have picked up publication after publication, read article after article, listened to program after program, specials that have been aired during different aspects of the week and time slots, all in an attempt to steady my spirit, while firmly planting my feet. I was even reminded this week of the opening words of Langston Hughes's notable poem "Mother to Son" that opens with the words, "Well, son, I tell you, life ain't been no crystal stair. It had tacks in it and splinters and boards torn up."[6]

I could go on in expressing that emotion and feeling that I was identifying with. But in the midst of my reflection, I was challenged to lift and to focus in on this fifteenth chapter of Matthew. It is a passage that in recent years has gained more scrutiny and examination, as close attention is being paid to the interaction between Jesus and a perceived outsider. It is an encounter that brings a seismic shift for us as we read the gospel; a seismic shift for us who walk in the faith; a seismic shift in all of us who follow the ministry of Jesus. If you are listening and paying close attention, you hear in this passage a shaking of the ground, a disturbing of what has always been, a transformation and a door swinging open to those who perhaps have been left out and casted out.

As we've been looking closely in here, Jesus encounters a woman who may be described by some as a member of the community that

---

6. Langston Hughes, "Mother to Son," *The Collected Poems of Langston Hughes* (New York: Vintage, 1995).

has been disavowed, disallowed, and disinherited. We know through another gospel writer that she was a Greek born in Syrian Phoenicia. She lived in the north country. We do not know her name, but her witness became part of the record and recorded in sacred texts that have transformed generations ever since. Her witness helped others to be able to do what they thought was impossible. Her witness and her faith allow things to be seen, not as they have always been seen, but to be seen in ways that they have never been seen before.

Jesus journeys to this region, as we look at this passage, and while there he comes face to face with this Canaanite woman. This encounter should speak to all of us as something happens when our limited concepts and the shaping of our humanity are invited to wrestle with the limitless and ever-present reality of divinity. The meeting appears to be confrontational at the onset, as she is crying out to Jesus to have mercy on her, as her daughter is suffering intensely. Jesus does not answer right away. And then even the disciples are in her way as they come to Jesus and urge—and the disciples had enough nerve to urge Jesus—and to cry out to him themselves, saying, "Send her away, for she keeps [crying] after us" (Matt. 15:23).

I always have to pause and note that we look at the elevated egos of the disciples as she is calling out to Jesus, but they interpret her calling as her calling out to us. Sometimes we're in the way thinking that we've got all the answers. When really, if we can just get closer to the one who has what we really need, our lives would be changed; our communities would be changed. But as they're trying to send her away—it was in this moment, as if they speak to the disciples' impatience, displeasure, and irritation—Jesus turns and addresses this Canaanite woman, this woman of mixed nationality. He addresses this woman who is a perceived, perhaps by the disciples, outsider.

I'm sure as she stood there—in the midst of Jesus's turning and beginning to address her—I'm sure she could feel the eyes upon her. In a world where she was, at this moment, seen as the outsider, she could feel in her time a spirit that still is present today for some. And a voice that is still being echoed out of some that would declare, "Go back to where you belong. That you don't fit in right now. You're not part of the in crowd." But she was at home in the moment. She stood firm in that moment. She was able to steel her back and lift up her head, and she was able to respond, in that moment. No matter what was being said around her, she knew that she had something within her. She was at home in the moment right where she needed to be.

Perhaps if we look at this moment closely, we better understand even James Baldwin, as he stated in one of his publications, "Perhaps home is not a place, but simply an irrevocable condition."[7] While this can be seen in the actuality of our natural existence—those who have a roof over their head, those who have an address by which they can be secure—we all would want to be in a place where we could have an irrevocable condition in our spirit that says, "I belong."

A condition that is not dependent on what people say about me, but a condition that I know through the power of the Holy Spirit. I know who I've been created to be. What a difference faith can make in our life. What a difference faith can make when we're addressing hard times and difficult situations. What a difference faith can make when we're seeing faith, not just in our life, but how it touches the lives of those who are around us and with us.

This Canaanite woman listened as Jesus replies to her cry for mercy by stating, "I was sent only to the lost sheep . . . of Israel" (Matt. 15:24). I could go on, but she does not let that faze her and cries again, "Lord, help me" (Matt. 15:25). Jesus responds in a manner that is the topic of discussion in the analysis by numerous theological and cultural commentators. Jesus responds by saying, "It is not right to take the children's bread and [toss] it to the dogs" (Matt. 15:26). The Canaanite woman, however—and what I would have you to hear and see is that this woman—is unfazed and unmuted by this challenge. As a matter of fact, the challenge even gave her more to hold on to; the challenge gave her something by which pushed her. Her faith was even fed by the difficulties that were present. And the challenges that came to her, she simply responds back, "You're right, master." In *The Message* translation, it says, "But beggar dogs do get scraps from the master's table" (Matt. 15:27).

She did not hear or shy away, but her faith made her rise up. Her faith made her speak up. Her faith made her stand up. It is at this point that the seismic shift that I was referring to is taking place. It is at this moment that the ground begins to change. It is at this moment that those of us who have been following Jesus's ministry feel the door swing open and a breeze coming in. It becomes apparent that here Jesus

---

7. James Baldwin, *Giovanni's Room* (1956), (London: Penguin, 1991), 92.

recognizes her faith. It is in this moment that we can see the power of faith and the difference faith can make, not just in the personal experience of our own lives, but in our family's lives, our community. But her faith moved her to challenge the accepted cultural norms. Sometimes we're moving because we're saying that's the way it's always been, but our faith says it doesn't have to be this way.

Our faith says that we can do better. Our faith says that there's a seat at the table for everyone. Our faith is able to do and to put us in places and to do what we've never thought was possible. Her faith opens the door for others to be identified as belonging to the beloved community. This woman's faith was strengthened and not limited by her own self-interest.

Because many of us, we all live to a certain degree and are motivated by self-interest. But if we paid close attention to her, her faith moved her because of her concern for another—her concern for her daughter, her concern for someone else other than herself. I remind us this morning, and even challenged myself to remember, that faith is more of a verb than it is a noun. We are called to possess a faith that is strengthened by our concern and our actions on behalf of one another, especially for those that have been relegated to being part of the disavowed, the disallowed, and, dare I say, disinherited. Jesus acknowledges, celebrates, and is even moved by her faith.

And the text says right then her daughter became well. I remind you by looking at what needs to change in our own lives, what needs to change in our community, what needs to change in our world, what a difference faith can make. What a difference faith in Jesus makes. I don't know what she heard about him, but she heard something that made her seek him out. I don't know what others told her about him, but they told her something that made her draw closer to him. I don't know what she might've heard about what he said, but she rested on his words and knew that he had what she needed. I remind you today that faith will move you and give you the strength to be like this woman. John Lewis reminds us on this day and his words still ring true. We need someone who is going to stand up, speak up, and speak out for people who need help, for people who need and who have been discriminated against, for people who are in need.[8] I remind you today that

---

8. Paraphrase from John Lewis and Michael D'Orso, *Walking with the Wind: A Memoir of the Movement* (New York: Simon & Schuster, 2015).

Henry Ward Beecher put it this way, "We should all have ambition. All ambitions are lawful, except those that climb upward on the miseries or credulities of mankind."[9]

We as a people of faith, as men and women and, dare I say, as a country and as a world, have the ability through faith to be instruments of ushering in and strengthening what is often termed "beloved community." I come out of a tradition and a heritage where on this morning, my mind's eye is remembering those people of faith that I grew up with. Those people of faith that Sunday after Sunday I stood in the midst of. Those people of faith, service after service, special moment after special moment, would gather, and after have been being beaten down all week, pressed down all week, pushed back all week, when they gathered with their faith, something would happen, and their lives and their spirit would be stirred. Faith would help them to lift their heads. Faith would help them to straighten their backs. Faith helped them to not just talk, but to move into action. It was by faith that Sunday after Sunday, special moment after special moment, we'd gather, and I could hear them lifting their voices saying, "We've come this far by faith, leaning on the Lord, trusting in his holy word. He's never failed us yet."[10] I can hear in that moment the melodious, and the sounds ringing out that said, "Oh, I can't turn around. We've come this far by faith."[11]

At this moment in your homes, in your sacred spaces and places, we've come too far to turn around because we've come this far by faith, and faith will lead us on. Amen.

---

9. Accredited to both Harriet Beecher Stowe and Joseph Conrad, Conrad credited here from Michael C. Thomsett and Linda Rose Thomsett, *A Speaker's Treasury of Quotations: Maxims, Witticisms and Quips for Speeches and Presentations* (Jefferson, NC: McFarland & Company, 2015), 9.

10. Albert A. Goodson, "We've Come This Far by Faith" (Brentwood, TN: Manna Music, 1965).

11. Ibid.

WHO DO YOU SAY I AM?
OUR ANSWER MATTERS

THE REV. CANON ROSEMARIE LOGAN DUNCAN
Twelfth Sunday after Pentecost, August 23, 2020

As a young child, I was told and taught a lot about Jesus from scripture, stories of his birth, his ministry. Born to and raised in faith at St. George's Episcopal Church here in Washington, the church of my maternal grandparents, parents, and a godparent, I heard a lot about Jesus from my family of faith, and I could tell you with relative certainty with a child's heart what I thought I knew. I sang that "Jesus loves me, yes, I know for the bible tells me so" with a child's understanding of this love with enthusiasm and joy. This was the foundation that would prepare me for my own journey of understanding of Jesus's identity and the development of my ever-deepening personal relationship with this Jesus, Son of Man—the Messiah.

Our gospel today (Matt. 16:13–20) triggered that memory as I realized that Jesus was helping the disciples in their own process of formation as his followers. We, like them, are confronted this day with two very specific questions from Jesus. The first: Who do people say that the Son of Man is? And the second: But who do you say that I am?

Today's gospel has fittingly been acknowledged as a pivotal point in Matthew's narrative of Jesus's Galilean ministry. The events to this point have repeatedly pressed the topic of faith and discipleship in the many stories of Jesus's preaching, teaching, and healing. Even foreigners and women, as in last Sunday's gospel, have expressed great faith in their acknowledging of this "Lord" as the agent of God's mercy (Matt. 15:21–28). Now it is time for Jesus's disciples who have followed him in his ministry to come clean and acknowledge the identity of this one who has called them and led them in this mission to the world.

Jesus and his disciples have been out on the road, making their way to Caesarea Philippi, a bustling city in the Galilee. It was a center for the worship of Syrian gods, Greek gods, and Caesar himself, and home to the elaborate marble temple of Herod the Great, father of the then ruling Herod Antipas.

We do not know why Jesus chose this place, but it is where he decides to ask the most crucial questions of his ministry. The disciples have heard people's comments and opinions, so now Jesus asks them what they've been hearing. Jesus takes this time with his disciples to do some public opinion research. What are people saying about me? Who do people say that the Son of Man is?

I have read this passage many times, but I was really struck this time around by the disciple's response to Jesus's first question. The disciples answer by naming people who are dead. The disciples have heard that some people suggest John the Baptist—a contemporary of Jesus recently beheaded by Herod. Others, the prophet Elijah, thought to return before the end times. Still others, Jeremiah, another one of Israel's prophets who had his own tensions with the authorities and suffered greatly for it. It is as though the people could not imagine the new thing happening before their eyes—life-changing, life-giving, kingdom of God stuff.

Jesus neither affirms nor denies any of what the disciples share. He simply listens, allowing his friends to offer up everything they think they know, based on other people's preferences, ideas, and opinions. As if to say: this is a good place to begin. This is where all explorations of faith begin, in naming what we've heard, examining what we've inherited, and reciting back the certainties others have handed to us, like my own childhood experiences. But at some point, the question of who Jesus is, must become personal. So, Jesus then asks the more challenging question, "But who do you say that I am?"

Now Matthew does not give us any detail about this scene, but I imagine the disciples falling into an awkward silence, avoiding eye contact with their teacher, thinking, "We weren't expecting that question." There is no escape, and this is no time for evasion. Then Simon, son of Jonah, answers with a declaration of faith that Jesus is, in fact, much more than anything the others said. Peter confessed that Jesus is the Messiah, the only begotten of God the Father.

Who would have expected this from Peter, the one who just two chapters earlier failed in his attempt to walk across the water to Jesus because his faith faltered, would be the one whose faith allows him to give the answer. It all becomes clear to him. Jesus, you are not simply a prophet. You aren't the reincarnation of John the Baptist, or Elijah, or Jeremiah.

Like Peter, we come to that moment, that shift when we move from simply knowing about Jesus to knowing him. It is about our transformed hearts. Peter's answer forms the foundation for the powerful movement that we are the inheritors and beneficiaries of. But the answer is just the beginning.

Jesus proceeds to bless him for it, "Blessed are you, Simon Son of Jonah! For flesh and blood has not revealed this to you, but my Father in heaven. And I tell you, you are Peter, and on this rock I will build my church" (Matt. 16:17–18). Now both Mark and Luke tell versions of this event, but Matthew is the only one with this blessing of Peter—the only one to even mention the church or to give instruction about how the disciples are to organize themselves after Jesus is gone. So, for Matthew, this question of Jesus isn't just for Peter. This is a question for the church, a question for us: Who do you say I am?

Church as the community of disciples and the kingdom of God are intimately bound in Matthew's conception of Jesus's mission, which from this point on in the gospel is linked to Jesus's passion, death, and resurrection. The church is what continues Jesus's mission to the world—centered on ministry with the poor, the hurting, the sick, the forgotten, and the rejected.

With this context, Paul's words to the Romans are instructive and take on particular meaning and urgency for our own time:

> I appeal to you therefore, brothers and sisters, by the mercies of God, to present your bodies as a living sacrifice, holy and acceptable to God, which is your spiritual worship. Do not be conformed to this world, but be transformed by the renewing of your minds, so that you may discern what is the will of God—what is good and acceptable and perfect. (Rom. 12:1–2)

Martin Luther King's sermon in the *Strength to Love* captures this text with two powerful words: transformed nonconformity. By conforming, not to the world but to God, our actions speak much louder than any words possibly could. King notes how the pressures for cultural conformity, to "condition our minds and feet to move to the rhythmic drumbeat of the status quo," are immense.[12] But the church—that's you and me folks—needs to discover ways to live very much in the world but not of the world. King, writes, "The hope of a secure and livable world lies with disciplined nonconformists, who are dedicated to justice,

---

12. Martin Luther King Jr., *Strength to Love* (Boston: Beacon Press, 1963), 11.

peace, and brotherhood. . . . In any cause that concerns the progress of mankind, put your faith in the nonconformist!"[13]

We should never abandon the world, nor should we embrace it as it is, but work to bring the kingdom of God to it. Grounded in love we witness and testify to God's life, love, and presence in our lives and the world. You see, who we say Jesus is matters. It matters for every moment of our individual and collective lives as the family of God.

With so much going on in our world, we may find ourselves wondering, who do we say Jesus is as we confront institutional and structural racism and discrimination? Who do we say Jesus is as COVID-19 continues to spread in our nation? Who do we say Jesus is as we face deep divisions in our country? Who do we say Jesus is when we are faced with decisions that have no easy answers? Who we say Jesus is has everything to do with who we are, how we live, and who we will be.

It reveals how we live and what we stand up for. It guides our decisions and determines the actions we take and the words we speak. My sisters, brothers, and siblings, God is still living and moving and working in the world. And as those who proclaim Jesus as Messiah, we have the power to be the voices of forgiveness, and mercy and love—of justice and of compassion, of healing and of wholeness.

The question that Jesus asked the disciples is a question that continues to be asked this day, to each one of us. Jesus is looking us all in the eye, patiently waiting for our reply. "Who do you say that I am?" But this day, I can say that Jesus, who loves me and teaches me to love—my savior, my friend, and the center of my joy is waiting for your response. Amen.

---

13. Ibid., 16–17.

MORE THAN A FEELING

THE RT. REV. MARIANN EDGAR BUDDE
Thirteenth Sunday after Pentecost, August 30, 2020

Let love be genuine. . . . Do not be overcome by evil, but overcome evil
with good. (Rom. 12:9, 21)

I'd like to begin with a question. When and how did you first learn that
love is more than a feeling?

The word itself holds layers of meaning. We use the word "love"
to describe our preferences for ice cream or music; feelings we have for
those closest to us, ranging from grandparents to lovers; our actions,
and the impact of our actions on others.

A hard way to learn that love is more than a feeling is when someone who professes to love you treats you in ways that are not loving. It
happens to all of us at some point because those who love us are not
perfect, nor are we perfect in our love for them. In most loving relationships, the gap between our words and deeds is the terrain for growth in
love. It's where we strengthen love's muscles of forgiveness, acceptance,
and our desire to be better people than we sometimes are. Learning to
love well is a lifelong process of trial and error and trial again. We also
learn that what doesn't feel like love at first might be the most loving
thing we can do for another. Think of a parent saying no to a toddler
who wants to play with fire.

Sometimes, however, those who say that they love us seem to have
no appreciation for, or concern about, the disconnect between their feelings of love and what we receive from them. It's as if their love is an
internal experience for them alone that doesn't need to translate into
loving words or deeds. I had that experience as a child, and I carry with
me a memory of the day, somewhere around the age of twelve, when I
said to myself, "That is not love. If I ever have a kid, I'm never going to
do that."

I also remember what it felt like years later to recognize that people
have different capacities for love; that some, frankly, aren't very good
at it and aren't interested in getting better. That helped me to forgive
those who had hurt me through their poor skills at love, and to seek the
best possible relationship with them while at the same time wanting to
be someone who acts in ways that others actually experience as loving.

I often fail in love, as those close to me will tell you. But I'm willing to learn and to grow.

Let me now say what some of you may already be thinking, given what's happening now in our country. There is a parallel between our definitions of love and of racism. As with love, most of us who are White begin with an understanding of racism that's rooted in our feelings. We don't like being told we're racist, because we don't harbor racist feelings, at least none that we're conscious of or want to admit. We certainly would never say or do the things that blatant racists do, those who unapologetically believe that people with lighter skin are superior to those whose skin is black or brown. If your definition of racism remains on the level of feelings, okay, but as with love, your impact for good will be limited.

A more accurate definition of racism includes not only how we feel and how we treat an individual person of a different race, but also how willing we are to accept and complacently benefit from a society organized in such ways that people of color suffer more on every scale of wellbeing. We want to say that all lives matter because they do. But as a country, we don't act as if Black and Brown lives matter as much as White lives. We don't. The disparities are everywhere—in health care, education, housing, policing, and in our churches. As Ibram X. Kendi writes, "One either allows racial inequities to persevere, as a racist, or confronts racial inequities, as an antiracist. . . . The claim of 'not racist' neutrality is a mask for racism."[14] As with love, what matters is less how we feel inside, and what we actually commit our lives to changing in a racist society.

Circling back now to how we grow in love: one way that we grow is when we realize that we're willing to act in ways that others experience as loving even when it costs us, when, as Jesus said, we have to make sacrifices and take on suffering. That's when it dawns on us that sacrificial love is a choice. How we feel in a given moment is irrelevant.

The truth is, no loving relationship can survive if we aren't willing to make sacrifices, to persist in love, persevere in choosing to love, even when loving feelings are absent. Fortunately, feelings of love wax and wane and then return in a deeper way. Our capacity to love deepens

14. Ibram X. Kendi, *How to Be an Antiracist* (London: One World Publications, Penguin Random House, 2019), 9.

and grows so that we have more love to offer, which is something we'll miss if we walk away too soon. I don't mean to imply that we never walk away, for sometimes our capacity to love isn't large enough to hold what love requires or out of self-love we end an unloving relationship. But those are tragedies of a different kind.

In these days of transition from summer to fall, I've been taking stock of my life over the last six months. It's a humbling exercise at any time, but especially as so much has changed and so much has been lost, when we've all had to adapt to new realities and face hard truths. Because there are people who look to me for guidance and hope, I've been asking myself what they have learned from my example. What am I teaching, through how I live my life, about what it looks like to love in challenging times?

Suffice it to say that there's been plenty to grieve and confess, and much for which to give thanks. Some things I'm proud of; others I'm not. Widening the lens to consider all that's happening in our country, it's clear that everything depends now upon our capacity to love, to choose love. There's a lot at stake whenever we refuse to love or cannot love when love is needed because we've never practiced those muscles.

As I turn my gaze toward the future, I find myself called back to the core practice and postures of a Jesus-focused life. It's not that I wasn't praying in the last six months—in some ways I've never prayed harder in my life. But the rhythms of my life and the practices that sustain me suffered in all the upheaval. Perhaps that's been true for you. It's understandable, and perhaps it was necessary. I don't know about you, but I'm ready for a reset and rededication.

In the Episcopal Church, our presiding bishop Michael Curry has called us all to practices that help us strengthen our love muscles, to receive Jesus's love for us and then to live in such a way that others experience His love through us. Those practices are called, appropriately, the Way of Love. There is nothing new or earth-shattering about them. They simply express the kind of intentionality necessary for growth. For in love, as in any other realms in life, we don't drift toward our highest aspirations according to how we feel on a given day. There is sacrifice involved, discipline and practice.

The harsh truth is that if we don't grow in our capacity to love, we become part of the problems we see all around us, and not the solution. The good news is that with effort, we can grow.

Let love be genuine, St. Paul writes as the opening line for one of
the most compelling descriptions of what love in action looks like. If
you have a Bible, you might look up the passage in Romans, chapter
12, write it down for yourself, and post it in a place where you can see it
every day. It wasn't Paul's first attempt to describe such love. He wrote
a similar passage in the letter we know as 1 Corinthians, one that no
doubt you have heard many times at weddings:

> If I speak in the tongues of mortals and of angels but do not
> have love, I am a noisy gong or a clanging cymbal. . . . Love
> is patient; love is kind; love is not envious or boastful or arro-
> gant or rude. It does not insist on its own way; it is not irritable
> or resentful; it does not rejoice in wrongdoing, but rejoices in
> the truth. It bears all things, believes all things, hopes all things,
> endures all things. Love never ends. (1 Cor. 13:1–8)

The passage from Romans is similar yet strikes different themes:

> Let love be genuine;
> hate what is evil, hold fast to what is good;
> love one another with mutual affection. . . .
> Rejoice in hope, be patient in suffering, persevere in prayer.
> Contribute to the needs of the saints; extend hospitality
>   to strangers.
> Bless those who persecute you; bless and do not curse them.
> Rejoice with those who rejoice, weep with those who weep.
> . . . do not claim to be wiser than you are.
> Do not repay anyone evil for evil, but take thought for what is
>   noble in the sight of all. . . .
> Do not be overcome by evil, but overcome evil with good.
>
> (Rom. 12:9–21)

These are compelling words to live by for anyone, for the call to
love in action is universal. But for those of us who claim to be Christians, they aren't optional. They are our mandate. The only commandment Jesus gave us is to love one another as He loves us. Only
one, but it takes a lifetime of practice to fulfill. No one drifts into this
kind of love—we must want it, and work for it, be willing to fail at it,
and try again.

So here is my invitation and my challenge to you as the season turns from summer to fall: Take stock. As they say in twelve-step spirituality, make a moral inventory of your capacity to love right now.

- Where are you loving well? Be sure to celebrate that.
- Where have you fallen short?
- How do those whom you profess to love experience your love? Do you know?
- How far does your circle of love extend?

After taking stock, ask yourself this:

How might I grow in my capacity to receive love and offer love?

If you're Christian, you might want to add Jesus into your question:

How might I increase my awareness of Jesus in my life and be a channel of his love for others in deeper ways?

If you're inclined to accept this invitation, one more thing: best not do this alone. It's not that you can't, but it's harder. We all benefit from being part of a community in which to practice love. If in COVID time you've fallen away from your community of faith, why not recommit to it now or find another that helps you grow? In that community, dare to go deep with someone, or a group of someones, in spiritual practice.

A word to the church leaders, particularly in the Diocese of Washington: Our most important work isn't getting back into our buildings, as great as that will be. Our most important task is to create as many opportunities as we can for our people to grow in love.

In closing, let me ask again with one notch greater specificity:

What one step might you take this day, this week, this fall to grow in love?

For your sake and that of everyone around you, I urge you to take that step. Take it so that you may know more of God's love for you. Take it so that others may know that love through it. Take it so that together we might help overcome the evil of this world with the goodness that flows from love.

KINGDOM ECONOMICS ARE
NOT WALL STREET ECONOMICS

The Rev. Canon Jan Naylor Cope
Sixteenth Sunday after Pentecost, September 20, 2020

If I were to invite you to name your favorite parable, what would it be? And if you, like me, have a lot of favorites—what are your two or three favorite parables? Even though I can't see it, in my mind's eye I can sort of picture our YouTube live chat quickly getting populated by parables—that's a great thing. Even though I can't see them, I can imagine some of the answers: the Good Samaritan, or the Prodigal Son, maybe the Mustard Seed, or the Sower. I can also imagine some that maybe aren't at the top of your list. Take, for example, the parable the last time I preached—the one about the wheat and the weeds. You remember it—the closing image is that of the eternal fire and the furnace and the weeping and gnashing of teeth. Perhaps today's parable, the Laborers in the Vineyard, may not have been at the top of your list, but that's okay. I would posit the view [that] the message in the parable today is as relevant in Jesus's teaching to his disciples two thousand years ago as it is to you and me today. I'm going to invite you to join me in delving more deeply into what Jesus was saying and continues to say.

We know that parables were one of Jesus's favorite forms of teaching. For the next three Sundays, there are going to be parables. So, what might we look at when considering these stories?

As we look at today's parable, I'm indebted to the scholarship of Jewish New Testament scholar Amy-Jill Levine, whose wonderful book *Short Stories by Jesus* helps to open these things up for all of us. Levine makes the point that we might be better off thinking less about what they mean and more about what they do: ". . . remind, provoke, refine, disturb" to cause us to look at things in a slightly different way.[15] She also says the parables, "if we take them seriously not as answers but as invitations, can continue to inform our lives even as our lives continue to open up the parables to new readings."[16] I would submit to new understandings.

---

15. Amy-Jill Levine, *Short Stories by Jesus: The Enigmatic Parables of a Controversial Rabbi* (New York: HarperOne, 2014), 4.

16. Ibid., 297.

So, let's look at today's parable. One of the first clues for us in understanding the parable is the way it begins. Jesus says "the kingdom of Heaven is like . . ." (Matt. 20:1), so we know from the very beginning Jesus is not articulating the world as it currently existed, but more about the world as God intended it to be. We know, looking at that parable, that it turns our notions of what's right and what's fair upside down. I mean, let's face it. Anyone overseeing an MBA program would not lift up that parable as a model case study on how to implement a cost-basis analysis. That's not what it's about. Kingdom economics are different than Wall Street economics.

Moving on in the story (Matt. 20:1–16), the landowner hires the first round of laborers, who were day laborers. They were dependent on work each day to have the resources to feed and sustain their families. A denarius was a typical day's wage for that work, which for laborers in the field would have begun at six in the morning and concluded at six in the evening. A denarius was not generous, but enough for them to take care of their families. The landowner continues to go out to hire more laborers, and he says that he will pay them whatever is right. The Greek translation is closer to whatever is just, whatever is proper. And the Hebrew root underneath that, *tz-d-k*, is about justice and righteousness and charity. That begins to give us a view of what's going on in the story.

Then at five o'clock, he goes, once again. Now, you can only imagine if the laborers have been waiting for work all day, in order to feed their families, what they must have been going through in the last hour of the working day, and not being hired. When the text reads "standing idly," it basically means literally without work. The fact that they're still waiting means they're still hoping. They're still hoping that someone might hire them and they're willing to accept whatever that person would be willing to pay, because something is better than nothing.

You see, the kingdom of Heaven is about God's economics, not Wall Street's. I don't know about you, in terms of the larger lesson for our time in 2020, but so far 2020 is not looking much like the kingdom of Heaven to me. This weekend, we mark the grim milestone of two hundred thousand lives lost to COVID. Two hundred thousand. We know that in the peak of this pandemic, the unemployment rate has never been higher since the Great Depression. We know that millions of people have lost their jobs and lost their ability to provide for themselves and for their families.

It's been a particularly hard week in our country, as the hurricanes have assaulted the south and the wildfires have run rampant in the west. If that's not bad enough, on Friday as the sun was setting and Rosh Hashana was dawning, Justice Ruth Bader Ginsburg died. Much like the landowner who evidenced *tz-d-k*—that teaching in the Torah of justice and righteousness—Justice Ginsburg lived her life learning that teaching. Throughout her life, she was dedicated to giving voice to so many who for so long had no voice. Particularly as a woman, and on behalf of a very grateful nation, I say, thank you. Exceedingly well done, good and faithful servant.

In this year, 2020, many other things have been laid bare. Two weeks ago in the *New York Times* Sunday magazine, the title was "America on Hunger's Edge."[17] The cover photo was what first caught my attention and what continues to haunt me. The cover photo is of a four-year-old named Sonia Rodriguez who was sitting cross-legged and barefoot on the floor, cradling a loaf of bread. In the photojournalism article that unfolds in the magazine, we see the work of a photojournalist who, over the course of three months, traveled across the country, beginning in New York and ending in San Diego, taking photos of what's going on in our country. The article states that nearly one in eight adults says that in this time they don't have enough food to feed their families. Part of what it lays bare is what's been hidden in plain sight—that millions of Americans struggle to put food on the table.

Sonia Rodriquez's mother is disabled. She receives $900 a month in disability benefits. For her mother and for Sonia and her two brothers, she doesn't always make it to the end of the month. The photo captures a loaf of bread and some other provisions that the Salvation Army provided. The story tells us that Sonia and her brothers said to their mother how excited they were, because at least that night. they would not go to sleep hungry with no food in their tummies. Where do we look for hope and our call in the midst of that?

Where is God's economics coming to bear in these times that we're in? The truth is, as I look across the country and the notes that we receive from so many of you, I see the hope and I see the answers.

---

17. Brenda Ann Kenneally, "America at Hunger's Edge," *The New York Times Magazine*, September 2, 2020. *https://www.nytimes.com/interactive/2020/09/02/magazine/food-insecurity-hunger-us.html*.

Today's parable is all about loving God and loving our neighbor. Part of that is sharing what we've been given. We've seen how so many of you are helping to stock food banks across this country. How so many places of worship, including this Cathedral, have had food drives, helping to meet the needs of our neighbor. You inspire me. The message this morning is, we can't stop. There's more for us to do. Deuteronomy 15:11 says that there will never cease to be those in need and that God commands us to open our hands to the poor and needy in our land.

We've had challenging times before and we've done it; we've gotten through it by loving God and loving our neighbor and doing it together. My prayer for you and for me this time is that when generations after us look back, they will see how we met the moment—loving God, loving our neighbor. Together, we can do this, and we must. Amen.

THE GRAPES OF WRATH

THE REV. CANON DANA COLLEY CORSELLO
Eighteenth Sunday after Pentecost, October 4, 2020

From our psalm this morning, the fourteenth verse: *Turn again, O God of Hosts; look down from heaven, and see; have regard for this vine, the stock that your right hand planted* (Ps. 80:14–15).

If the Cathedral had a billboard outside on Wisconsin Avenue advertising the title of my sermon, I doubt "The Grapes of Wrath" would make passersby want to come inside and listen. And for you, who receive our email blasts about upcoming Sunday preachers, I'm certain you couldn't press "delete" fast enough. Perhaps if I were offering a lecture on John Steinbeck's great American novel of the same name—but certainly not on the parable of the Wicked Tenants.

On its face the parable (Matt. 21:33–46) is a horror story. At least two people are beaten, two stoned, and three murdered, including the vineyard owner's heir.

And it is assumed that the landowner will seek a bloodbath of revenge. This is ugly stuff. According to Matthew's gospel, Jesus was in a "mood" when he told it.

You see, the day before, Jesus entered Jerusalem for the final time. Hosannas rained down on him as he paraded through the streets on a donkey. But the mood soured as soon as Jesus headed to the temple to confront the money changers. The next morning the opponents accost him. Who did he think he was? On whose authority was he teaching, healing, forgiving, judging, cursing? But instead of backing down, Jesus called out their greed and inhumanity, telling them that tax collectors and prostitutes would enter the kingdom of God before they would.

Of course, the parable of the wicked tenants is a thinly veiled allegory of the rejection and crucifixion of Jesus, and it is shot through with judgment and wrath. Israel is Yahweh's vineyard. The Prophet Isaiah had warned that there would be consequences when Yahweh went to harvest the fruits of his labor, only to have the vineyards of Jerusalem and Judah yield sour, wild grapes (Isa. 5:4b). Scripture often uses the trampling of grapes as a metaphor for judgment and destruction. Listen to the violent language Isaiah uses to describe God's anger in chapter 63:

I have trodden the wine press alone,
and from the peoples no one was with me;
I trod them in my anger and trampled them in my wrath;
their juice spattered on my garments, and stained all my robes.
For the day of vengeance was in my heart,
and the year for my redeeming work had come. (Isa. 63:3–4)

The goriness of grapes is most famously evoked in the book of Revelation, where an angel "swung his sickle over the earth and gathered the vintage of the earth, and he threw it into the great wine press of the wrath of God. And the wine press was trodden outside the city, and blood flowed from the wine press, as high as a horse's bridle, for a distance of about two hundred miles" (Rev. 14:19–20).

A lake of blood as deep as a horse's bridle and two hundred miles long? Wow!

This passage, with its apocalyptic reversal of oppression, inspired Julia Ward Howe's famous pro-Union, anti-slavery anthem of 1861, "Battle Hymn of the Republic":

Mine eyes have seen the glory of the coming of the Lord:
He is trampling out the vintage where the grapes of wrath
    are stored;
He hath loosed the fateful lightning of His terrible swift sword:
His truth is marching on.[18]

John Steinbeck used the lyrics of Howe's anthem to title his 1939 novel about the exploitation of Depression-era tenant farmers. It tells the story of the Joad family—poor folk from Oklahoma, trapped in the economic miseries of the Dust Bowl, who set their hopes on the promised land of California's breadbasket. Upon arriving, they find the state oversaturated with migrant laborers like themselves, low wages, and workers exploited by big corporate farmers to the point of starvation. In the book, the "grapes of wrath" refers to the purposeful destruction of food to keep prices high: "[A]nd in the eyes of the hungry there is a growing wrath. In the souls of the people the grapes of wrath are filling and growing heavy, growing heavy for the vintage."[19]

---

18. Julia Ward Howe. "Battle Hymn of the Republic," *The Atlantic* 9, no. 52 (February 1862), public domain.

19. John Steinbeck, *The Grapes of Wrath* (New York: Viking Press, 1939), 238.

My friends, what is it about avarice and power, what is the unmet need in us, that leads us to exploit and oppress another human being for profit? Are we hardwired this way? Was Paul right when he wrote in the first chapter of his letter to the Romans, "So they are without excuse; for though they knew God . . . they became futile in their thinking and their senseless minds were darkened. . . . they exchanged the truth about God for a lie" (Rom. 1:20–21, 25).

Now, amidst other national calamities, we are being forced to reckon with our country's original sin—the exploitation and enslavement of, and genocide against, Brown and Black bodies. There is no getting around it. My naming it does not mean I am rewriting our history, much less that I am unpatriotic. No, quite the opposite. It means that I love this nation. But for it to reflect the divine spark that lies within each and every American, it and the White Christian church, including my church, the Episcopal Church, has sins to acknowledge and atone for. "In the souls of the people the grapes of wrath are filling and growing heavy, growing heavy for the vintage."[20]

David P. Gushee, distinguished university professor of Christian ethics at Mercer University, explicates this in his book, *After Evangelicalism: The Path to a New Christianity*. He says our nation's fate was set in motion when the fifteenth-century conquerors from Spain, Portugal, and Britain began colonizing the world in the name of Christ. They rationalized heresies about the lower worth of people with darker skin; and they convinced themselves that God's laws against murder, adultery, theft did not apply to them. Gushee, who is White, writes, "*We* were white and Christian and European and better; *they* were "red" and "brown" and "black," and heathen and native and worse. While we were entitled to rule, they were slated to suffer, serve, and die."[21] This same narrative was used to justify anti-Semitism and the persecution and subjugation of Jews.

This grand delusion was the American soil in which white supremacy grew over the course of centuries. Despite the historical probability that the Aramaic-speaking Jesus was a dark-skinned Semite, White men inevitably envisioned a God made in *their* image. As a result, God and Jesus's Whiteness has been reflected in all mediums of

---

20. Ibid.

21. David P. Gushee, "White American Christianity Is Rooted in Colonial Empire-Building," September/October 2020. *https://sojo.net/magazine/septemberoctober-2020/white-american-christianity-rooted-colonial-empire-building*.

art through the centuries, especially stained glass and painting. Jesus, as the best and highest of human beings, has remained a White man in the White imagination.

White Christians contorted aspects of their faith practice and the bible to justify and accommodate themselves to the profitable institution of slavery. We've come a long way since, but there is still work and repentance to be done. We cannot preach that we are all made in the image of God and then muzzle ourselves when our civic leaders maneuver to secure White patriarchy, subjugate the Black and Brown vote, and obfuscate our nation's history. When we reject some of God's people, we are rejecting the God who made them—and sowing the sourest of grapes. No, the love God has for you and for me and the aforementioned politicians is so vast and so merciful that we, too, can be free from our self-inflicted bondage. We do not have to bear the brunt of our nation's original sin or be shamed by the color of our white skin or enslaved by the power that comes with it. Sin does not own us. God does. To acknowledge the privileges of white skin does not indict us a racist.

But it does mean we have the responsibility to advocate for the vulnerable—widows, orphans, immigrants, and the poor and anyone considered "other"—to ensure they can flourish just as we have flourished.

I have never understood why those who call themselves Christian cannot accept the fact that in God's sphere there is enough to go around.

From the terrible winepress of the vestiges of white supremacy and systemic racism comes a terrible wrath. It is up to us to disavow the hubris that makes us vulnerable to the violence and judgment we have too often brought down upon others. The mystical winepress of Christ delivers us and nourishes us with the sacrificial image that Jesus offered himself—as the true Vine—into God's winepress, to spare his branches, you and me, from God's wrath.

> Mine eyes have seen the glory of the coming of the Lord:
> He is trampling out the vintage where the grapes of wrath are
>   stored;
> He hath loosed the fateful lightning of His terrible swift sword:
> His truth is marching on.

Glory, glory, glory alleluia! Amen.

STEPPING UP TO THE PLATE

THE RT. REV. MARIANN EDGAR BUDDE
Nineteenth Sunday after Pentecost, October 11, 2020

Once more Jesus spoke to the people in parables, saying: "The kingdom of heaven may be compared to a king who gave a wedding banquet for his son. He sent his slaves to call those who had been invited to the wedding banquet, but they would not come. Again he sent other slaves, saying, 'Tell those who have been invited: Look, I have prepared my dinner, my oxen and my fat calves have been slaughtered, and everything is ready; come to the wedding banquet.' But they made light of it and went away, one to his farm, another to his business, while the rest seized his slaves, mistreated them, and killed them. The king was enraged. He sent his troops, destroyed those murderers, and burned their city. Then he said to his slaves, 'The wedding is ready, but those invited were not worthy. Go therefore into the main streets, and invite everyone you find to the wedding banquet.' Those slaves went out into the streets and gathered all whom they found, both good and bad; so the wedding hall was filled with guests."

But when the king came in to see the guests, he noticed a man there who was not wearing a wedding robe, and he said to him, 'Friend, how did you get in here without a wedding robe?' And he was speechless. Then the king said to the attendants, 'Bind him hand and foot, and throw him into the outer darkness, where there will be weeping and gnashing of teeth.' For many are called, but few are chosen." (Matt. 22:1-14)

In the last few months, I've been called upon by numerous people and organizations to do things for them. Some requests are relatively small and manageable; others require considerable commitments of time and energy. Receiving such requests has always been a part of my life, as it surely has been of yours. What feels different now is the level of intensity. There is an urgency and at times even a desperation in the asking. I understand why—this is a stressful time. A lot is being asked of everyone. How tired we are when the request comes may not be the most important data point.

The best way I can describe how it feels when these requests come is with an expression from the great American pastime: *stepping up to the plate.*

Baseball players step up to home plate when it's their turn at bat, unless the manager replaces them with someone else. How they feel about stepping up to the plate when it's their turn is irrelevant. Stepping up to the plate is what baseball players do.

It's a singular task. Yes, baseball is a team sport, but the team doesn't go to bat all at once. When you're up, for that excruciating and exhilarating moment, all eyes are on you. So, it's easy to understand how the phrase "stepping up to the plate" crossed over from baseball into other areas of life to describe those moments when someone acts alone in response to a crisis or an opportunity, when one person takes the initiative, accepts responsibility, and does what needs to be done.

As an aside, given that we are a bilingual diocese, I wondered how "stepping up to the plate" would translate into Spanish. It turns out that the exact translation *subir al plato* isn't an expression. The closest parallel I could find comes from the Castilian sport of bullfighting: *coger el toro por los cuernos*, which crosses over smoothly as an expression in English: to take the bull by the horns. There's another expression in Spanish that doesn't cross over into English well, but made me smile: *ponerle el cascabel al gato*, which literally means "to put a bell on a cat." Its idiomatic translation: to have the courage to do what others dare not do.

Stepping up to the plate. Taking the bull by the horns. Putting a bell on a cat.

Drawing from scripture and from life, I'm going to describe three ways we can experience this call to step up to the proverbial plate. My hope is that you'll hear something that validates your experience and gives you a sense of how important you are when the call comes. I know it's hard now. I know you're tired. But who you are and what you're being called upon to offer—small or large—matters more than you'll ever know.

We've just heard a mashing together of two of Jesus's most disturbing parables found in the last chapters of the Gospel of Matthew. Context is important here. Jesus is near the end of his life. He's in Jerusalem, with his back against the wall. In increasingly hostile debates, his adversaries are throwing at him everything they've got. He responds in the best way he knows how, by telling stories with exaggerated characters in extreme circumstances in order to convey a message for those with ears to hear.

The first parable is about a wedding banquet to which the invited guests couldn't be bothered to attend, so the king does away with them and orders the doors be opened for all to come. The second parable is about a man who shows up to a wedding banquet poorly dressed for the occasion. He, too, is thrown into outer darkness. Assuming the man had a garment but didn't make the effort to put it on, both have something to say about the dangers of half-hearted responses to the great opportunities of life.

So here we go—stepping up to the plate in three ways:

The first is with clarity and confidence. This is when we feel we're ready and well equipped for whatever task is before us. It can be small or big; something we're excited about or that we dread. Whatever the circumstance, we're confident we can do what's required. In some instances—surely the most important—we have the sense that we must do them.

Two particularly clear moments in Jesus's life come to mind here. The first is from the beginning of his public ministry, as recounted in the Gospel of Luke, chapter four. The text tells us that Jesus returns to his hometown of Nazareth from his forty days of trial and testing in the wildness "filled with the power of the Spirit." He goes to synagogue on the Sabbath, as was his custom, and took his turn to read from the scroll of the prophet Isaiah. This was the appointed text:

> "The Spirit of the Lord is upon me, because he has anointed me to bring good news to the poor. He has sent me to proclaim release to the captives and recovery of sight to the blind, to let the oppressed go free, to proclaim the year of the Lord's favor." (Luke 4:18)

Jesus rolls up the scroll and sits down. The room grows quiet and all eyes are on him. Then Jesus says: "This scripture has been fulfilled in your hearing" (Luke 4:21), by which he meant, "I am the one. I have come to do these things." He was clear. He was equipped. He stepped up to the plate.

Another moment of confident stepping up comes at the end of Jesus's life, as told in the Gospel of John, chapter eighteen, but with a decidedly different tone and outcome. Jesus has been arrested, and the religious authorities want him dead. As they don't have the power to crucify him, they want Pilate, the puppet leader for Rome, to do it for them. Pilate doesn't understand why Jesus's own people are so keen to kill him. Finally, he summons Jesus and asks, "Who are you? Are you the King of the Jews?" (cf. John 18:33). Jesus replies: "My kingdom is not of this world. . . . For this I was born, and for this I came into the world, to bear witness to the truth. Everyone who belongs to the truth listens to my voice" (cf. John 18:36–37). Jesus refuses to say anything more. He knew that his time had come and he was ready.

That kind of clarity is, in my experience, relatively rare, but when it comes, you know it. As one person said to me in a way that I've never forgotten, "I have been preparing my whole life for this moment."

Has there been or is there now a moment like that for you? Are you seeing that kind of clarity taking shape for someone else?

Five years ago, the bishops in the Episcopal Church elected Michael Curry as our presiding bishop. Prior to the election itself, when the final slate of four bishops had been announced, it was clear that Michael Curry knew that he was called to the position. You could tell by the way he handled himself, the generosity with which he engaged the other candidates, his ability to identify with a wide range of people, the clarity of his vision, and how he spoke directly, definitively, and non-defensively to address the concerns some were raising about his leadership. As bishops, we all knew how the vote would go, and yet we were all holding our breath. On the day of the election, as we made our way to the church where we would cast our votes, I happened to walk alongside Bishop Curry. I said to him, "For a time such as this, Michael," harkening back to the biblical heroine, Esther, at a definitive stepping up to the plate moment for her. He stopped, took my hand, and said, "Pray for me, sister. Pray that I never lose sight of Jesus." He knew, and he was ready.

That's one way we're called to step up to the plate. When it happens to you, step up with confidence. The world needs you.

But another, far more common way we're called to step up is on the opposite end of the experience spectrum: when we feel anything but ready, when we know that we don't have what is needed but feel called upon anyway.

The biblical examples of this experience are many, which is reassuring given how often we feel this way ourselves. A common response among the prophets, those in ancient Israel whom God called for particular tasks at a particular time, was to politely point out to God why they were the wrong person for the job. Moses insisted that he couldn't possibly tell the ruler of Egypt to release the Israelites from slavery because he stuttered. Jeremiah told God that no one would listen to him because he was only a boy. Isaiah first responded to the call with a sense of shame. "Woe is me!" he said, "for I am a man of unclean lips" (Isa. 6:5). In each case, God responded by saying, in effect, "I know who you are. I know your shortcomings. Step up anyway." There is a similar refrain among Jesus's disciples, most notably with Simon Peter, who told Jesus when he called, "Stay away from me. I am a sinful man" (cf. Luke 5:8). Jesus's response (and I'm paraphrasing a bit): "Tell me something I don't know. Now step out of your boat and up to the plate. I need you to help me fish for people."

There's a clear message throughout scripture that whenever God calls or life itself summons, most people feel both unworthy and unprepared. The good news is that God makes possible what we cannot, so that it may be clear, as St. Paul writes of his own experience, "that this extraordinary power comes from God and does not belong to us" (cf. 2 Cor. 4:7).

I live my entire life inside the miracle of the loaves and fish, the story of how Jesus takes an insufficient offering of food and with it feeds a multitude. Its universal, timeless message is that when we offer what we have, even when we know it's not enough, God can work miracles.

So let me speak directly to all who feel stretched beyond your limits, who are doing all that you can and more to hold life together and it's not enough: you are my heroes. You're stepping up to a plate that you didn't ask for; you are showing up where you are needed every day. I want you to know that God sees you. I see you. Part of the reason people like me are willingly taking on more and more is we see what you're doing. What's being asked of us pales in comparison to what's being asked of you. I pray that you are given all the strength you need to keep going, because what you are doing is holding up the world. I pray that you're given respite from time to time by others willing to step up so that you can get a break.

There is another side to the experience of inadequacy. Sometimes as a result of our ill-preparedness and incompetence, when we step up to the plate, we fail and God doesn't fill in the gap. The consequences of our failure are real. It hurts. But when we accept failure as a part of growth; when we persevere and learn from our failures, we get stronger, and the next time it's our turn, we're better prepared. Sometimes God seems to invite us to step up to the plate when we're not ready so that we might learn and grow.

A few years ago, I came across a short essay written by Ira Glass, the host and executive producer of the popular radio show and podcast, *This American Life*. Addressing an audience of young artists, he speaks directly to this process of getting better through failure:

> Nobody tells this to people who are beginners, and I really wish somebody had told this to me.
>
> All of us who do creative work, we get into it because we have good taste. But it's like there is this gap. For the first couple years that you're making stuff, what you're making isn't good. . . . what you're making is a disappointment to you. A lot of people never get past that phase. They quit.
>
> Everybody I know who does interesting, creative work went through years . . . where they could tell that what they were making wasn't as good as they wanted it to be. They knew it fell short. Everybody goes through that.
>
> And if you are just starting out or if you are still in this phase, you gotta know it's normal.
>
> The most important thing you can do is do a lot of work. . . . It is only going through a volume of work that you're going to catch up and close that gap so that work you make will be as good as your ambitions.[22]

Stepping up to the plate when you aren't ready is the price of beginning. It's what you have to do, time and again, when moving toward something important, becoming the person who is able to do or accomplish what is now beyond your ability. You show up, take your place in the lineup, and step up to the plate, swing and miss, and miss, and miss, until one day you make contact.

Where in your life might you be in the long arc of hard work, failure, and getting ready for a future call?

Now for the third, and for today, the last way we're called to step up to the plate. For this I harken back to a sermon preached here on September 27 by the Archbishop of Canterbury, Justin Welby. Archbishop Welby told the story of biblical patriarch Jacob, whom he portrayed in deservedly harsh terms: "a lonely victim of self-imposed family trauma"

---

22. Ira Glass, *What Every Successful Person Knows But Doesn't Say*. Text at *https://jamesclear. com/ira-glass-failure*.

and "a narcissistic con man." This is a man who has cheated both his father and his brother, yet God's grace and love were greater than his sins and failing.[23]

Here's the sentence that has stayed with me since I heard the Archbishop preach: "Jacob's complexity of action and motivation is met in God, not by simplifying or condensing, but by calling." God doesn't excuse, condone, or seem to be bothered by the long history of Jacob's sin. God picks him up out of his morass and sets him on a different path, giving him something worthy to do.[24]

I can't tell you how many times I've been rescued from the downward spiral of my thoughts, anxieties, or foolish actions by the call to step up to something else. The call doesn't take away or solve the ambiguities and contradictions of my life, but for a time I'm lifted out of them, free to think about something else, or better yet, to do something good for someone else. I think this is what St. Paul is getting at with the words we heard read this morning from the Letter to the Philippians: ". . . whatever is true, whatever is honorable, whatever is just, whatever is pure, whatever is pleasing, whatever is commendable, if there is any excellence and if there is anything worthy of praise, think about these things" (Phil. 4:8). When you're stuck in the ruts of your life, God will set your sights higher.

This past Labor Day weekend, feelings of sadness were washing over me. We had said goodbye to our adult children and sweet toddler grandson, not knowing when we'll be able to see them again. It was clear then that we would be in pandemic mode for the foreseeable future. I had a lot of work to do and didn't feel like doing any of it. It was as pure a depressive state as I've been in for a while, and I was perfectly content to sink further down.

Then I remembered that a neighbor was organizing what she called a Yard Give Away to help immigrant families. Feeling as poorly as I did, I almost blew it off, but then thought better of it. So I packed up our car with extra dishes, pots and pans, blankets, clothes, and some furniture we didn't need. The next day I drove to the site of the giveaway—a basketball court near an apartment complex where you

---

23. Washington National Cathedral, Holy Eucharist Service, September 27, 2020. *https:// www.youtube.com/watch?v=lyr6VcmYbJU&t=1s*.

24. Ibid.

could smell poverty in the air. A dozen people were organizing the donations into what looked like the first floor of a department store, while a line of people stood outside waiting for the gate to open. For about two hours, it felt like Christmas morning. I know that what I gave away helped some people, but being there, stepping up to a different plate, lifted me out of my crippling sadness into a space of gratitude. I was, and still am, the same person with the same struggles. But stepping up to something else allowed me, if only for a time, to break free and serve a higher good.

Let me close as I began, acknowledging that a lot is being asked of all of us right now, and of some more than others. We'd be made of stone if we didn't want to walk away from it all, to stop the world and get off, to step away from the hard things. Every word I've offered here is meant as encouragement. If you are in any way feeling called to step up, trust that there's more at play and more at stake than how you feel. What's more, there is a tremendous feeling of satisfaction that comes when we take our turn at the braver, necessary things, when we fulfill the deeper purposes of our lives, and when we feel ourselves accepted, even in our brokenness, and called to do something big for something good. Don't miss it.

If it's your turn, step up to the plate; take the bull by the horns; put a bell on that cat. At that moment, you may feel alone, but you're not. The communion of saints is behind you. The people who love you are with you. The Spirit of the Lord is upon you because God has anointed you, chosen you, for this.

WHAT SHALL I RENDER?

The Rev. Canon Leonard L. Hamlin Sr.
Twentieth Sunday after Pentecost, October 18, 2020

Certainly, as we gather on this morning, I must confess that I always look forward to Sunday. That might be expected from a member of the clergy or a preacher, but my anticipation for Sunday runs much deeper than simply the rituals of worship or the practices of our own religion.

On my way to this moment, I have had several occasions to reflect and also discuss with many the passing of time since we entered the challenges back in March and the moment of acknowledgment of the present pandemic. If we think for a moment and reflect upon the time that has gone by, we were thrusted into the center of these circumstances. Very quickly we were moved—and almost caught up—where we changed our habits overnight. Prior to this moment of acknowledgment, we had been hearing about the possibilities—and also the prospects of what could happen—but we tried to find comfort along the edges, hoping not to be drawn closer to the center. But the moment arrived, whether we wanted it to arrive or not. The moment arrived where we were moved from the fringes and had to grasp the realities that were confronting us—for better or for worse, for richer or for poorer, in sickness and in health. We were immediately wed to the moment.

This is why I look forward, though, to Sunday. If we think about that moment, our routines and our lives were interrupted and they were disrupted. I look forward to the encounter and the meeting that takes place on Sunday. It is a day that disrupts the routines that somehow have been trying to get a hold of me. A day that seeks to call us not to conform, but to transform. I look forward to Sunday because there's something about Sunday that is unlike any other day of the week. Because it allows the ground that I'm on, and the place where I stand, to shift from ordinary to extraordinary. It is a day that opens my thoughts to shift from impossibilities to possibilities. It is a day to take that which has been weighing me down and set it down. It is a day to try and shake off some of that, which I had no business carrying and let it go.

It is a day that allows for the examination and the re-examination of what I may have sought to avoid, but now I can embrace with faith, strength and gain the courage to face it head on. It is a day that moves all of us from the fringes of life into the very core of where we find our life. Somehow—although many of you who are connecting with us are not here—whether you're in your living rooms, your dining rooms, your bedrooms; all of a sudden those ordinary places have become extraordinary sanctuaries. Although we may not see your faces, we recognize your presence. Although you may feel that you have been isolated, I remind you, you are never separated.

When we look on this day, our separation is not isolation. Because here, when we look at today, our speaking is not about a God who just sees us, but more importantly, it is about a God who is with us. No matter where you are today, I remind you, we stand here lifting up and letting you know that God is with you in a moment like this. As much as I would like to lighten the moment found in the gospel (Matt. 22:15–22) this morning, I am compelled by its content and the calling of the spirit to move to the core of the text that is always present but sometimes not heard clearly. Because the gospel and the words of Jesus have a way of disrupting, disturbing, and upsetting our routines, there is a tension and a meeting in this text of two forces moving in opposite directions.

And if we're not careful, we can be caught up going in the wrong direction and not moving with the kind of flow and intent that we ought to have in times like these. One is moving with a focus and a plan shaped by their selfish desires, and the other by Jesus who has a focus that is shaped by the selfless service found in seeking God's will.

The religious authorities and certain political influences of the day planned and plotted in order that they might trip Jesus up, or trap Jesus by drawing him into the center of their debate and conflict. What they did not realize was that Jesus was not trying to move away from the center of life's critical questions, but he wanted to place himself dead center. Or let me rephrase that, place himself at life's center, in order that they would hear what they needed to hear, to get out of the routines and the focus that they had to take the temporary and somehow transform it into the eternal.

The text, for a moment, rests upon their questions that they thought would bring Jesus down, but their question only helped to lift him up. They try to preface their question with words of flattery. They try to get him to think that they thought highly of who he was, and so we hear their words when they say, "Teacher, we know that you are sincere, and teach the way of God in accordance with truth, and show deference to no one; for you do not regard people with partiality" (Matt. 22:16). Listen to how they paint the picture and try to get him to fall for this kind of facade. And then they immediately move to asking, almost with a demanding tone, "Tell us, then, what you think. Is it lawful to pay taxes to the emperor, or not?" (Matt. 22:17). Jesus steps right into the center and calls us to join him there as he answers their question after careful examination of the coin used for tax in that day. It was here, printed and casted with the emperor's image pressed upon its face, and Jesus looks at the coin, has them carefully examine it. And he tells them, "Give therefore to the emperor the things that are the emperor's, and to God the things that are God's" (Matt. 22:21).

It is not the answer that they expected. Perhaps it's not the answer that we would have expected. But Jesus gets to the heart of the matter while they, perhaps, try to trip him up while hoping he addresses the issue by skirting the issue. Jesus could have gotten caught up in whether or not one should pay their taxes, and in the honest responsibility on both sides to engage in fair and just practices for the benefit of all, and for the functioning of government for the care of all of those around us. Jesus could have spent time talking about civic duty and the accountability we should uphold in meeting the requirements set upon each of us as we examine and hear the need to assist the poor; the need to provide care for our sick; to deliver essential services not to those considered at the high rung or those considered special, but especially to those who have been marginalized, ostracized, racialized in order that their importance would never be minimized.

He gives the straightforward and simple answer but raises a key question. You may not see it printed on the page, but the question is right there. He says, "Give the emperor what belongs to him, but give to God what belongs to God." The question and focus is not what I give to hear the emperor. The real question today is, what do I give to God? The real wrestle is, "Have I come prepared on this day and every day of my life to give him my best?" On this day, have I really thought about who is first in my priority, who is at the center of my life, and who is at the center of all of my joy? They left God out when Jesus was trying to make sure God was brought in. They had closed the doors when Jesus was trying to open the doors. They had shut down their thinking, had drawn their conclusions. They had made up their minds about what they should do when God was calling them to do more than what they had already done.

It is at the center of all that is taking place in our lives that God is working and speaking. They were focused on someone's failure to pay taxes when no one was asking the question, "God, what would you have me to do for my brother and my sister? God, what would you have me to do for my son and my daughter? God, what would you have me to do for the sick and the shutout? God, what would you have me to do in the highways and byways, in the dark where all of those who are crying out, their voices need to be?"

I am reminded this morning of one of the most noted deans of preachers, Dr. Gardner Taylor, who often reminded many of us preachers that we have to be careful to not be intimidated by the crowd or the circumstances we encounter and be guilty of preaching what might be called a suburban gospel. A gospel that is comfortable camping out on the edge of the city. It does not deal with the real issues of life. It embraces simply manageable themes that are inoffensive and only offers prudential advice.[25]

Well, I'm grateful today to join with my colleagues. Today, I'm grateful for the leadership of our dean that is not letting us get comfortable here, on the fringe and the outskirts of the city, but to press to the core of what is happening today. That no matter where you are, that you know that there's somebody here praying for you. Somebody here lifting you up. Somebody here who is not comfortable to live life on the edge of the city, but to be at the center of where life's traffic is really taking. "What shall I render and what shall I give?"

All week I have been challenged by almost a deafening sound of politics, posturing, positioning, marketing, promoting, and advertising and attempts at influencing my life and your life that has at times sent my spirit drifting. But the gospel has a way of interrupting those patterns. It has a way of disrupting the chaos. It has a way of asking me the question, "What shall I give?" In another translation it says, "What shall I say render unto God?" (Ps. 116:12, KJV).

I can remember hearing in the days gone by choirs, who often lifted up that selection in that gospel hymn, "What shall I render to God for all of his blessings? What shall I render? And what shall I give?

---

25. Paraphrased, Gardner Taylor, "It Is Finished," L.K. Williams Ministers' Institutes sermon, Bishop College, Dallas, Texas, 1976.

All I can render is my body and my soul. That's all I can render. That's all I can give. God has everything. And everything belongs to him. God has everything and everything belongs to him."[26]

I remind you today. It is our giving, not our receiving, that transforms the world. I learned very early in my twenty-two years of pastoring that out of all of the statements, declarations, assertions, and sermons that were offered, declared, and given, there was one statement that caused more disruption, more disturbance, and more unsettling above all the others that I made. It was simply saying to an individual or to an assembly that I love you.

It caused more problems than saying there's a meeting on this night, that we were short with something else. To tell someone "I love you" causes them to wrestle with truth or falsehood. Saying "I love you" opens the door to vulnerability. Saying "I love you" causes an examination that some will never feel. Saying that I love you will make those who have never gotten up before rise up out of circumstances they never thought they would get out of.

Today we're not called to camp out on the fringes of life, but we dare to stand at the center and declare our love for God; our love of neighbor; our love of every man, woman, boy, and girl. The love that is needed from every parent, child, neighbor, and for even every stranger. I remind you today, if you want to turn the world upside down, call someone and tell them "I love you." Call someone and offer the best that God has given you.

On today, what shall I render? And on today, I'm reminded of standing with my mom, standing with my parents, standing with family. And we would stand and sing, "Come, thou fount of every blessing, tune my heart to sing that grace; streams of mercy never ceasing call for songs of loudest praise. Teach me some melodious sonnet, sung by flaming tongues above. Praise the Mount, oh, fix me on it, mount of thy redeeming love."[27]

Today, what shall I render? Love. Unceasing. Love with no limits. In your home, in your connections, whether it's digital or in person, tell someone that "God loves you. And so do I."

Amen.

---

26. Traditional.
27. Robert Robinson, "Come, thou Fount of Every Blessing" (1758).

I SOUGHT MY NEIGHBOR

THE VERY REV. RANDOLPH MARSHALL HOLLERITH
Twenty-first Sunday after Pentecost, October 25, 2020

It seems a little ironic to me in this season of presidential debates that we have in our gospel for this morning (Matt. 22:34–46) what some might consider a debate between Jesus and the opponents of his day. But truth be told, this wasn't a debate between Jesus and the Pharisees, it was another attempt on the part of the religious authorities to play "gotcha" with Jesus, an attempt to try and catch him saying something they could then use to discredit him. (Wow, I guess that does sound a lot like a presidential debate.) In any case, our lesson for this morning is a continuation of our lesson from last week. Last Sunday the Sadducees wanted to discredit Jesus by asking him whether it was lawful to pay taxes to Caesar. They were trying to trap him into a no-win situation because if he said it was lawful to pay the Roman tax, then he would alienate the crowds who loved him and hated paying taxes to the Roman invaders. If he said it wasn't lawful, then, well, Jesus could be arrested by the Roman authorities for sedition. As you may remember, Jesus brilliantly dodged both attempts to corner him by saying—give to Caesar what is Caesar's and to God what is God's.

This week, another group of religious authorities take their shot at Jesus hoping to discredit him. This time the Pharisees ask him which of God's commandments is the greatest, the most important. Now, you must understand that there were 613 commandments in the Jewish law, and the Pharisees were hoping that whatever commandment Jesus chose he would open himself up to criticism because of the 612 he didn't choose. Once again, Jesus brilliantly dances his way out of the corner they are trying to trap him in by giving them two commandments: the Shema from the book of Deuteronomy (cf. 6:5), "Love God with all your heart, and with all your soul, and with all your mind," and a second commandment from the book of Leviticus (19:18), "Love your neighbor as yourself." By doing this, rather than opening himself up to criticism, Jesus perfectly summarizes all 613 laws by joining together love of God with love of neighbor.

"I sought my soul, but my soul I could not see; I sought my God, but my God eluded me; I sought my neighbor, and I found all three."[28] My friends, in this time of struggle in which we live, this time of strife and division, in the midst of a tragic and deadly pandemic and on the cusp of the most hotly contested presidential election in memory, our gospel lesson for this morning is a reminder of our fundamental task as Christians—to love God and to love our neighbor. It is a call to reground ourselves in the essential work of our lives. What Jesus wants us to know this morning is that these two commandments are deeply intertwined. As Audrey West wrote in *The Christian Century*, "Do you want to know how to love God with your whole self? Practice loving your neighbor. Do you want to know how to love your neighbor? Practice loving God. Repeat. Then do it again."[29]

Yet, these two simple commandments are easier said than done. After all, who is my neighbor and what does it mean to love my neighbor and to love God? First, love in this context is not a feeling. We aren't being commanded to feel a certain way. It isn't about liking or being fond of someone. In this context, love is all about commitment. When I love God, I am committed to care about what God cares about in the world. That means, as Bishop Curry says, that I "refuse to accept and acquiesce to the way things are." Rather, I "pray and work for the way things could be."[30] When I love my neighbor, I am committed to their wellbeing just like I am committed to my own wellbeing. I am committed to their wellbeing whether I like them or not, in fact, most especially when I don't like them.

"I sought my soul, but my soul I could not see; I sought my God, but my God eluded me; I sought my neighbor, and I found all three."[31] What does it mean to love your neighbor, what does it look like? The best answer I know comes from St. Paul in his famous passage from Corinthians, the one we often read at weddings. Here St. Paul gives us a checklist for love in action: "Love is patient; love is kind; love is not envious or boastful or arrogant or rude. It does not insist on its own way; it is not irritable or resentful; it does not rejoice in wrongdoing,

---

28. William Blake. *https://www.famousquotes.com/quote/william-blake-quotes-1015205*.

29. Audrey West, "Living by the Word: October 25, 30A (Matthew 22:34-46)," *The Christian Century*, September 29, 2020. *https://www.christiancentury.org/article/living-word/october-25-30a-matthew-2234-46*.

30. Michael Curry, *Love Is the Way* (New York: Avery–Penguin Books, 2020), 118.

31. Attributed to William Blake, "Auguries of Innocence," public domain.

but rejoices in the truth. It bears all things, believes all things, hopes all things, endures all things" (1 Cor. 13:4–7). This is what love as commitment looks like. This means in order to love God we must strive to be kind, patient, generous, unassuming, humble, and polite to everyone we encounter. It means being willing to listen to our neighbor rather than lecturing them about what we think. It means striving to be pleasant and always speak the truth no matter what our neighbor says or does. It means doing all these things for the people we like the least as well as the people we like the most. How different would our nation look if we lived this way even ten percent of the time? How much better off would we be if we learned to lead with love?

Did you see the article in *The Wall Street Journal* this past Wednesday about the Mitchell and the Gates families who live next door to each other in suburban Pittsburgh? These two families of five are not only neighbors (literally), but they are good friends. The Mitchells are lifelong Democrats with a Biden/Harris sign proudly planted in their front yard. The Gateses are staunch Republicans with a Trump/Pence sign proudly displayed in theirs. These two families disagree politically on just about everything, but their friendship is bigger than their politics, which means they don't define each other by their politics or reduce each other to their different political opinions. Tragically, both families were so disturbed by the amount of anger, vitriol, and hatred they were witnessing between people of different political ideologies that they felt it necessary to put a second sign in each of their yards. That sign, right next to their Biden or Trump sign, said, "We Love them," with a large yellow arrow pointing to their neighbor. As Bart Gates said in the article, "Our fundamental job as parents is to be a good role model for our children. We don't see them as Democrats. They are the Mitchells. We know they are good people who live next door."[32] For these two couples, this was their small way to love their neighbor, their small way to witness to the fact that people can strongly disagree and still honor and respect each other. I say this is tragic because when did we forget this basic fact? How did we get to the place where the only thing we feel for our political opponents is contempt? Friends, if we consider ourselves Christians, then this cannot be the way we live in the world.

---

32. Clare Ansberry, "How Neighbors Split on Politics Stay Close," *The Wall Street Journal*, October 21, 2020.

"I sought my soul, but my soul I could not see; I sought my God, but my God eluded me; I sought my neighbor, and I found all three." My friends, ask yourself what I can do in my own small way to love God and to love my neighbor? In Greek, the word "neighbor" literally means "near me." In this sense, our job is to strive to love, in whatever way we can, each person we encounter, each person who comes "near me." During these days of pandemic, that can be as simple as wearing a mask to protect each person who comes "near me." But whatever the case, we should never underestimate the power of these small acts of love that we put out into the world. As Bishop Curry writes in his new book, *Love Is the Way*:

> My job is to plant seeds of love, and to keep on planting, even— or especially—when bad weather comes. It's folly to think I can know the grand plan, how my small action fits into the larger whole. All I can do is check myself, again and again: Do my actions look like love? If they are truly loving, then they are part of the grand movement of love in the world, which is the movement of God in the world. . . . It is impossible to know, in the moment, how a small act of goodness will reverberate through time. [This] notion is empowering and it is frightening— because it means that we're all capable of changing the world, and responsible for finding those opportunities to protect, feed, grow, and guide love. We can all plant seeds, though only some of us may be so lucky as to sit in their shade.[33]

Indeed, my friends, we can all plant seeds, seeds of love, one encounter at a time. This is the work that God is calling us to do, no, commanding us to do. It is the work our world needs the most and the only thing that will pull us out of the hole we have dug for ourselves. For as St. Paul reminds us—without love, I gain nothing; without love, I am nothing. Amen.

---

33. Curry, *Love Is the Way*, 199.

THE SOLID ROCK

THE MOST REV. MICHAEL B. CURRY
All Saints Day, November 1, 2020

Before I begin, I want to say a word of thanks to Bishop Mariann Budde and Dean Randy Hollerith and the team and the staff of this Cathedral and diocese, to thank them for this invitation to preach this morning on this All Saints Day. Five years ago, I was installed as presiding bishop of our church. I count that a great blessing in my life, and I thank God for it. They were kind enough to say, "Why don't you come on back on your anniversary?" So, thank you to them. Thank you to the Cathedral. Thank you to the wonderful Cathedral Congregation online and thank you to the people of the Episcopal Church.

Allow me, if you will, to offer some reflections on a text that comes at the end of the Sermon on the Mount. We just heard the beatitudes from the Sermon on the Mount and these words of Jesus and that sermon from Matthew, chapter seven. Jesus said, referring to the Sermon on the Mount, "Everyone then who hears these words of mine and acts on them will be like a wise man who built his house on rock. The rain fell, the floods came, and the winds blew and beat on that house, but it did not fall, because it had been founded on rock" (Matt. 7:24–25).

My grandma used to love the hymn based on this text that says, "My hope is built on nothing less than Jesus's blood and righteousness. I dare not trust the sweetest frame, but wholly lean on Jesus's name. On Christ, the solid rock I stand, all other ground is sinking sand."[34]

In the Sermon on the Mount, which begins with the beatitudes—blessed are the poor and the poor in spirit, and blessed are the merciful, the compassionate—there are teachings of Jesus that Matthew has ingeniously brought together and put in one place. They have been called the Sermon on the Mount because the setting where Jesus spoke those words was on a mountaintop. Blessed are the poor. Blessed are the poor in spirit. Blessed are the merciful, the compassionate. Blessed are those who hunger and thirst that God's righteous justice might prevail in all the world. Blessed are the peacemakers. Blessed are you when you are persecuted for righteousness' sake—when you are persecuted just because

---

34. Edward Mote, "The Immutable Basis for a Sinner's Hope," 1834, public domain.

you tried to stand for love and compassion and decency. Blessed are you when you're persecuted like that, for so the prophets who came before you were persecuted. When you do this, when you're compassionate peacemakers, justice seekers, when you do unto others as you would have them do unto you, when you love, love, love—even your enemies—when you do that, you are the light of the world, the salt of the earth.

Charles Marsh, who teaches at the University of Virginia, wrote a book on the spirituality of the civil rights movement. He says of Jesus and his teachings, "Jesus founded the most revolutionary movement in human history. It was a movement built on the unconditional love of God for the world and the mandate to a community who followed him to live that love in the world."[35]

Those first followers took Jesus at his word. They dared to live his way of love, and his way of love changed them and they in turn changed the society around them.

Jesus says of these teachings of his, "Everyone who hears them will be like someone who built their house on solid rock."

The storms came, the winds came, the rain came, the thunder roared, the lightning flashed, and the earth even quaked. But that house did not fall. It will not fall. Built on the teachings of Jesus, it cannot fall because it's built on a rock. "On Christ, the solid rock I stand. All other ground is sinking sand."

Some years ago when I was the bishop of North Carolina, the good people of the diocese were kind enough to grant me a sabbatical leave for three months, after I had been there six or seven years, to rest and to do some study and reflection. I made a decision that I wanted to study the Sermon on the Mount, Matthew, chapters five, six, and seven. I also decided that I wanted to take violin lessons, and I did. Somebody asked, "Do you play the violin?" I said, "No, that's an overstatement. I took violin lessons." That's about as much as I can say of my art history. But I took violin lessons, and I did do some rest. I did study the Sermon on the Mount.

While I was at it—I hadn't planned to do this ahead of time—I got curious and I started reading up on the arguments of Christians in the nineteenth century over the issue of chattel slavery in America. There were those who made arguments in favor of the maintenance of

---

35. Charles Marsh, *The Beloved Community: How Faith Shapes Social Justice, From the Civil Rights Movement to Today* (New York: Basic Books, 2006), 81.

slavery as being justified biblically. There were those, the abolitionists, who argued against the institution of slavery as contrary to the word and the will of God on biblical basis.

So, I started reading some of the arguments on both sides and I noticed an interesting pattern: those who argued for the maintenance of human slavery of one person enslaving another person, one child of God enslaving another, of one human being created in the image and likeness of God, as Genesis 1 says . . . I began to see a pattern. Those who argued for the continuation and maintenance of human slavery never used Jesus and his teachings. They never touched where Jesus said, "You shall love the Lord, your God, and your neighbor as yourself." They never touched Jesus when he said, "Do unto others, as you would have them do unto you." They avoided the teachings of Jesus like the plague. Where Jesus said, "As you did it to the least of these who are members of my family, you have done it unto me." They avoided the Jesus who said, "Love your enemies. Bless those who curse. Pray for those who despitefully use you." They avoided the Jesus of the parable of the Good Samaritan. They avoided Jesus like the plague, because if bigotry is your game, Jesus is not the name.

But those who argued for an end to slavery, they ran to Jesus. They quoted him; they cited him; they referred to him because the way of Jesus is the way of love. The way of love is the way of life that liberates us all. The old slaves understood this well, when they sang, "If you cannot preach like Peter, and you cannot pray like Paul, you just tell the love of Jesus, how he died to save us all."[36] Not some of us; he died to save us all. And I realized something: when we, who are Christians, build our lives as Christians on anything other than the teachings of Jesus, whose way is love, we are building our house of faith on shifting sand. But when built on Jesus and his way of love, that house is built on solid rock. It will not be easy, but it is built on solid rock. Rock that can stand the test of time. Rock that not even the very quaking of the earth can destabilize.

I believe with all my heart that the way of love that Jesus has taught us is the way to heal our nation, the way to bring about true justice, the way to set us all free—all of us. The choice is ours: chaos or community. I believe that Jesus and his way of love has shown

---

36. "There Is a Balm in Gilead," African-American spiritual, public domain.

us the way to community—beyond the chaos to community that reflects something akin to the beloved community. Something akin to what Jesus called the kingdom of God. Something akin to the reign of God's love. Something akin to what John in the Revelation saw as a new heaven and a new earth. Something akin to that heaven in Revelation, chapter seven, when John looked up and saw in heaven, and he said, "Behold, I saw a host that no man could number, a folk from every stripe, every type I saw, every race, every nationality, every political party. I saw all types of humanity. All God's children."[37] Oh, heaven's a lot bigger than we thought it was because grace is greater than we could ever imagine.

I'm a Christian. I'm a follower of Jesus because I believe that Jesus has shown us the way, the way to become the beloved community of God. That is the way for us, America, with all of our divisions, with all of the injustices, that way of love is the way of life.

On the great seal of the United States, created and devised by the founders, you may remember that it's the one that on the front has the eagle and above the eagle, there are these banners and inscribed on the banners, the Latin words *E pluribus Unum,* "from many one." *E pluribus Unum.* That Latin phrase comes from the writings of Cicero in ancient Rome in the days of the Roman Republic. It was Cicero who wrote and said, "When every person loves the other the same way he loves himself, then one from many, *E pluribus Unum,* becomes possible."[38]

On the great seal of the United States is the hope and the vision that many diverse people, all of God's children, might come together and become one nation under God, indivisible with liberty and justice for all—that this American experiment might actually be a reflection of God's dream of a beloved community whereas the old slaves used to say, "there's plenty, good room, plenty, good room, plenty good room for all God's children." And that the key to becoming *E pluribus Unum* is love. When I love you as much as I love myself, when we love each other, *E pluribus Unum* America becomes possible. I'm a follower of Jesus because I believe he was right.

---

37. Revelation 7:9, paraphrase.

38. Cicero, *De Amicitia (On Friendship),* trans. and with introduction and notes by Andrew P. Peabody, Loeb Classical Library (Boston: Little, Brown, and Co., 1887), book 1, section 56, p. 154, public domain.

Originally, I was going to preach this sermon from the great Canterbury pulpit at the National Cathedral. When the Bishop and Dean invited me to come, it was pre-COVID. My plan was to be in Washington and preach for the morning service. Then COVID-19 hit and then the pandemic. I held off making a final decision, still hoping that maybe there was some way I could get to Washington. Finally, I realized that it just wasn't wise to do so. I must tell you that I was disappointed because I was looking forward to it. I was disappointed, but I figured, okay, I can borrow a church somewhere in Raleigh. You know, I used to be bishop there. I'm sure somebody would let me borrow a pulpit.

Then it dawned on me, wait a minute, this is the Sunday, the Feast of All Saints, just before an election in America, in a critical moment in our life and history. Go over to St. Augustine's University, one of our historically Black colleges, founded by the Episcopal Church. Go over to St. Augustine's and preach from that pulpit. The Reverend Hershey Mallette Stephens and all the staff here and all the folk here were kind enough to make this possible. Before coming here, I remembered this chapel. I remembered that this very building in which I stand is composed of rocks and stones quarried from this very land. That this very pulpit where I'm preaching from is made of rock and stone quarried from this very land. This college, this university was founded through America's worst nightmare, in the midst and after the Civil War itself.

The bishop of this diocese, Thomas Atkinson, and many other people after the decimation of the war, realized that even in the midst of despair, you must carve out a stone of hope. They carved out a stone of hope to start a school, to educate newly freed and emancipated slaves. This very school started by Episcopalians in North Carolina and the Freedmen's Bureau of North Carolina in days as James Weldon Johnson said, "When hope unborn had died,"[39] they carved out, chiseled out stones of hope.

They started this school to educate newly freed slaves and their descendants. This very chapel was built by the hands of former slaves, where they could worship the God and Father of us all. This very school has educated generations of people. Teachers and scholars, and once upon a time, most of the nurses who were public health nurses in the Carolinas and in Southern Virginia, were educated right here at St.

---

39. James Weldon Johnson, "Lift Every Voice and Sing." *https://poets.org/poem/lift-every-voice-and-sing.*

Agnes Hospital and School. This school produced most of the Black Episcopal clergy in the Episcopal Church. At one time, it sent teachers out into the world to educate. This school has made a difference. It has carved out hope, chiseling it from stones of despair.

I realized that this very sacred place may be a wonderful reminder to all of us that even in the darkest midnight, as long as there is a God, there is hope. Even when there is crucifixion, as long as there's a God, there's a resurrection. The old preachers used to say, as long as there is God, Easter is always coming.

I'm a follower of Jesus because I believe his teachings, his spirit, his example. He is the solid rock on which we can stand. He was right. He's right today.

"My hope is built on nothing less than Jesus's blood and righteousness. I dare not trust the sweetest frame, but wholly lean on Jesus's name. On Christ, the solid rock I stand, all other ground is sinking sand."

God love you. God bless you. And may God hold us all in those almighty hands of love.

WHAT IT MEANS TO PRAY
FOR HEALING, UNITY, AND HOPE

THE RT. REV. MARIANN EDGAR BUDDE
Election Day, November 4, 2020

[Bishop Mariann preached this homily at the Service of Healing, Unity, and Hope at Washington National Cathedral on November 4, 2020.]

"You are the salt of the earth; but if salt has lost its taste, how can its saltiness be restored? It is no longer good for anything, but is thrown out and trampled under foot. You are the light of the world. A city built on a hill cannot be hidden. No one after lighting a lamp puts it under the bushel basket, but on the lampstand, and it gives light to all in the house. In the same way, let your light shine before others, so that they may see your good works and give glory to your Father in heaven. (Matt. 5:13-16)

In his most recent book, *Love Is the Way: Holding onto Hope in Troubling Times*, Presiding Bishop Michael Curry has a chapter that you're drawn to read by the title alone: "What Desmond Tutu and Dolly Parton Have in Common." The short answer is their dreams. He quotes Dolly Parton telling of the dreams that helped her rise from crushing poverty in Appalachia. Desmond Tutu dedicated most of his life to holding onto the dream that one day his native South Africa would be free from the evil of apartheid.[40]

Lest you think the chapter then falls into platitudes about dreams, Bishop Curry pivots to events in his own life, and in particular, what happened in the years 1967–68 when he was a teenager. In 1967 his mother died. 1968 was the year his two heroes—Martin Luther King Jr. and Robert Kennedy—died. What held him together in those years was the example of his father and of the Black Church, and this sense from those around him that you just keep going in the face of struggle. You don't give up. Most importantly, for all in his world, Jesus wasn't somewhere up in the sky. Jesus was right there, in the struggle with them.

Curry's point throughout this chapter comes in the form of a gentle exhortation: if you're going to live by your dreams, be prepared to go deep, and to live deeply, and to face the despair of disappointment when you bump up against the crucible steel of life. But when you do, he writes,

---

40. Curry, *Love Is the Way*, 70–94.

trust that hope will see you through. Curry then cites the "Ten Commandments of Non-Violence" that was part of the essential teaching and training for those involved with King in the civil rights movement.[41]

Here are the first nine:

- Meditate daily on the teachings and life of Jesus.
- Remember always that the non-violent movement seeks justice and reconciliation—not victory.
- Walk and talk in the manner of love, for God is love.
- Pray daily to be used by God in order that all might be free.
- Sacrifice personal wishes in order that all might be free.
- Observe with both friend and foe the ordinary rules of courtesy.
- Seek to perform regular service for others and for the world.
- Refrain from the violence of fist, tongue, or heart.
- Strive to be in good spiritual and bodily health.

We are in this for the long haul, and if we're going to live and walk in the love of Jesus, we need to have clarity about what that means.

We gather today in prayer for healing, for unity, and for hope.

This I know, from personal experience, about the healing process: If your body sustains a deep wound, and a scab or thin layer of skin forms on the surface, it can look as if healing is taking place. But if the connective tissue underneath the skin doesn't come together in its own process, that part of the wound can get infected and grow worse. Though the deeper wound is hidden for a time underneath the scab or skin, it's not healing at all. So, as we pray for healing in our nation, we do well to remember that there is little to be gained and, in fact, much harm to be done, if we tend too quickly to the surface of things while ignoring the wounds underneath.

May we pray for deep healing.

This is what I know about unity: that it often comes at the expense of those whose inclusion is too costly for the dominant group. This is as true on the playground and in family relationships as it is in the wider society. Then that exclusion is often forgotten by those who have settled for what the prophet Isaiah called "peace when there is no peace" (cf. Isa. 57:21).

---

41. "Ten Commandments of Non-Violence," quoted in Curry, *Love Is the Way*, 92–94.

We don't have to look far for examples from our history: after the Civil War and the political whiplash of a white supremacist becoming president after the assassination of President Lincoln, followed by a president committed to reconstruction of the South and real liberties for those formerly enslaved, followed by other presidents who looked away while White leaders in the South committed to dismantling all the gains Blacks had made. As that dismantling was taking place there was a constant drumbeat for national unity between North and South. Monuments all over the country were erected, and stained-glass windows, like the one that was once in this Cathedral, were commissioned and installed, all in the service of unity among Whites. We know who was excluded from that unity, excluded from the ideals of democracy and liberty and justice for all. Some of the most shameful events of our history—many of which were suppressed from our collective memory—come from that time.

As we pray for unity, may we remember that the kind of unity worthy of the kingdom of God and represented in the mosaic of this nation is not one that will come by exclusion, but with the hard work of reconciling.

This I know about hope: it isn't something we need to manufacture. It is God's gift. Hope often rises from despair. It can stir our hearts even when we have reason to give up. I wish I could tell you how this happens; I only know that it does. Hope resists platitudes or wishful thinking. It allows for grief and all its manifestations. It never chastises us for being exhausted and worried. It doesn't ask us to pretend that everything is going to be okay when we don't know if that's true, at least in the short term.

But what hope does—and thank God for hope—is help us rise again, not from our strength, but from the strength that comes to us from the deepest wells of the human spirit, where God's divine spirit meets us.

There is a cost to this hope, and we must choose it, because it refuses to deny the reality of suffering. You may have heard a refrain from St. Paul on the importance of suffering. He writes that we need to embrace suffering, for suffering is what produces endurance, and endurance produces character, and character produces hope—and this hope does not disappoint because God's love has been poured into our hearts through the Holy Spirit that has been given to us (Rom. 5:1–5). The source of our hope is the amazing love of God.

In this time of waiting for the results of this election to be revealed, let me simply say that not only do we believe, as theological bedrock, that every person is a beloved child of God, we also believe that every citizen has a right to cast a vote. Those votes need to be counted, and so we must wait. And it's not helpful—it's a bit embarrassing, and frankly outrageous—for our president to cast doubt on the normal practices of democracy and the heroic efforts of so many during this pandemic to exercise their right to vote. We will wait for the results and take it from there. Whatever the outcome, the practice, the discipline, the call to love is the same. We pray for deep peace. We pray for unity that excludes no one. And we set our sights on hope.

I love the biblical passage about letting our light shine. But I wish it said let Jesus's light shine. I'm not as confident about mine, but I can let His light shine. And I'm letting him be the salt, not me. I'm placing my hope that God will prevail in the end.

And in the meantime?

Last night my husband Paul and I went down to Black Lives Matter Plaza. There were dozens of young people there. Some were singing; some were shouting; some held up signs. There was a lot of drumming. It was chaotic and peaceful. The police were respectfully keeping distant watch. An equal number of journalists and news reporters were there with their cameras and lights, ready to tell the world what was about to transpire.

But there wasn't much happening that was newsworthy. We walked around a bit more. Then I met a group of people who are part of a group known as the "Nonviolent Peaceforce." The Nonviolent Peaceforce places people trained in nonviolence into some of the most politically charged and volatile situations around the world, to be instruments of peace. There is a DC Peaceforce and they were there last night, and they were praying, walking around, talking to people. I spoke to the leader. He said, "We are all people of faith, and we feel called to the work of peacemaking." It is work to which all followers of Jesus are called.

We begin by meditating on the teachings of Jesus. Then we are to walk and talk in the manner of love, for God is love. We are to pray daily to be used by God in order that all might be free; sacrifice personal wishes in order that all might be free; observe with both friend and foe the ordinary rules of courtesy; seek to perform regular service for others and for the world. We can refrain from the violence of fist, tongue, or heart. And strive to be in good spiritual and bodily health.

If we do those things, then surely the light of Jesus will shine through us as we dare to hope and to dream and to work for true healing and unity. May it be so. Amen.

HOLDING ON TO HOPE

THE MOST REV. MICHAEL B. CURRY
November 4, 2020

> When Jesus saw the crowds, he went up the mountain; and
> after he sat down, his disciples came to him. Then he began to
> speak and taught them. . . . (Matt. 5:1–2)

The Beatitudes, just read in a variety of voices from around our country, are part of a compendium of some of the teachings of Jesus that tradition has called the Sermon on the Mount. They are so named because the setting for these teachings of Jesus is on a mountaintop. That is not an incidental detail.

In 1939 the late Zora Neale Hurston published a novel that retold the biblical story of Moses and the Hebrew freedom movement recorded in the book of Exodus. She told it in the idiom of African slaves in America, but she wrote it as an ingenious critique of lynching and the immorality of Jim Crow segregation here at home, and a critique of the rising tide of fascism, authoritarianism, hatred, and bigotry around the world that would lead to the Second World War. She titled the book, *Moses, Man of the Mountain.*

"When Jesus saw the crowds, he went up the mountain and taught them."[42]

The mountain is not an incidental background detail. When Jesus saw the crowds, he went up the mountain and began to teach them. Matthew was deliberately and intentionally invoking the memory of Moses around what Jesus was doing in the Sermon on the Mount.

It was on a mountain called Sinai that God confronted Moses and challenged him to live beyond mere self-interest and to give his life in the service of God's cause of human freedom. "Go down, Moses, way down in Egypt land, and tell ole Pharaoh, let my people go."

Years later when the Israelites had won freedom, it was on that same mountain that Moses received the Ten Commandments: God's law and principles for living with freedom.

---

42. Zora Neale Hurston, *Moses, Man of the Mountain* (New York: HarperCollins; reprint ed., 2010).

And at the end of his life, it was on another mountain, Mt. Nebo, that God allowed Moses to, as the slaves use to say, look over yonder to behold a promised land.

Centuries after Moses, in Memphis, Tennessee, a follower of Jesus named Martin, on the night before he was martyred for freedom's cause, spoke of hope in the biblical language of the mountain. "I've been to the mountaintop, and I've seen the promised land."[43] No, the mountain is not an incidental detail.

The mountaintop: That is where prophets and poets look over yonder, to behold not what is, but what ought to be. To behold the promised land of God; a new heaven, a new earth, the kingdom of God, the reign of God's love breaking in, the beckoning of the beloved community, a reconfiguration of the landscape of reality from the nightmare it often is into the promised land of God's dream for the human family and all creation.

"When Jesus saw the crowds, he went up the mountain and taught them."

What did he reveal from that mountaintop? He told them about the way to the promised land.

> Blessed are you when you're poor and broken-hearted. Here's the way.
> Blessed are you when you're compassionate and merciful. This is the way.
> Blessed are you when you're humble and meek. This is the way.
> Blessed are you peacemakers who will not cease from striving until human beings learn to lay down their swords and shields down by the riverside to study war no more.
> This is the way to the promised land.
>
> Blessed are you when you hunger and thirst that God's righteous justice might prevail in every society, in every age, for all time.
> This is the way.
>
> Do unto others, as you would have them do unto you.
> Love God, your neighbor, yourself.
> Love when they spit, shout and call you everything but a child of God.
> Love!

---

43. Martin Luther King Jr., "I've Been to the Mountaintop," April 3, 1968.

This is the way, the way to the promised land.
When you live something like this, when you look something
    like this,
when *we* love like this, then we are on our way to the promised
    land.

You may be thinking, this sounds wonderful in church, but will it
work in the world? Can such lofty ideals about hope, beloved community, and the reign of God be translated into human reality and society?
Some years ago, I was in the public library working on a sermon. I took
a break and walked around the stacks looking at books. In the religion
section I came upon a little book with an old black binding, published
by St. Martin's Press, titled, *The Great Sayings of Jesus.*

The forward to the book was written by Richard Holloway, who
once served as the primus or presiding bishop of the Scottish Episcopal
Church. He said that in the gospels generally and, "In the Sermon on
the Mount, in particular, we get from Jesus something of God's dream
for a transformed creation. But the epilogue [the rest of the gospel
story] reminds us that the dream is costly, that dreams are cruelly dis-
posed of by the world as we know it. Yet the dream lives on, nothing can
kill it for long; and Jesus goes on breaking out of the tombs into which
we have consigned him."[44]

"The dream lives on." Do not underestimate the power of a
dream, a moral principle, eternal verities, virtues, and values that lift us
up and move us forward. For true and noble ideals and the dream of a
promised land have their source in the God who the Bible says is love.
And God, as my grandmother's generation used to say, God is still on
the throne!

Our ideals, values, principles, and dreams of beloved community
matter. They matter because they drive us beyond service of self alone,
to commitment to the greater good of us all. They matter because they
give us an actual picture of God's reign of love, and a reason to struggle
and make it real. They matter to our lives as people of faith. They matter to our life in civil society. They matter to our life as a nation and as a
world. Our values matter!

---

44. John William Drane, ed., *The Great Sayings of Jesus: Proverbs, Parables, and Prayers*
(New York: St. Martin's Press, 1999).

They matter in some simple and yet significant ways. A number of years ago, Robert Fulghum wrote a wonderful book titled, *All I Really Need to Know I Learned in Kindergarten.*[45]

Here is a list of the things—the values—he learned:

- Share everything.
- Play fair.
- Don't hit people.
- Clean up your own mess.
- Don't take things that aren't yours.
- Say you're sorry when you hurt somebody.
- Wash your hands before you eat.
- Flush.
- When you go out into the world, watch out for traffic, hold hands, and stick together.

Imagine a world in which these basic values *don't* matter.

Share everything? Imagine a world in which the value of sharing is replaced by greed and selfishness.

Play fair? No, cheat, lie, steal. That would make for an interesting World Series, NBA Championship, Super Bowl, election, democracy.

Wash your hands before you eat. No, let's spread the germs.

Flush? I rest my case.

"When you go out into the world, watch out for traffic, hold hands, and stick together."

No, it's everyone for themselves.

Our values matter! A world, a society, a life devoid of values and ideals that ennoble, that lift up and liberate, is a world descending into the abyss, a world that is a dystopian vision of hell on earth.

Mahatma Gandhi knew something about the power of ideals, dreams, and values, and is reputed to have said:

Your beliefs become your thoughts,
Your thoughts become your words,
Your words become your actions,
Your actions become your habits,

---

45. Robert Fulghum, *All I Really Need to Know I Learned in Kindergarten* (Evanston, IL: Press of Ward Schori, 1988).

Your habits become your values,
Your values become your destiny.

Our values matter!

The values and dreams we hold as a nation, our shared American values, they matter even more. We hold this prayer service in the midst of a national election, in the context of profound divisions that left unhealed could prove injurious to the fabric of democracy itself. The right to vote and to participate in the democratic process is a value of the highest order.

To be sure, no form of governance attains perfection. The preamble to the Constitution wisely reminds us that each generation must continue the evolving work of forming "a more perfect union."[46] No, our democracy is not perfect, but it offers the best hope yet devised for government that fosters human freedom, equal justice under the law, the dignity and the equality of every human being made, as the Bible says, in the image of God.

Reinhold Niebuhr said it well, "Man's capacity for justice makes democracy possible; but man's inclination to injustice makes democracy necessary."[47]

Despite our flaws and failings, we have some shared values. One of them is the preservation and perfection of representative democracy itself, "that government of the people, by the people and for the people shall not perish from the earth."[48]

We don't think of it this way very often, but love for each other is a value on which our democracy depends. On the Great Seal of the United States, above the bald eagle, are banners on which the Latin words, *E pluribus Unum* are written. Those words, *E pluribus Unum*, literally mean, "one out of many." One nation from many diverse people.

But do you know where those words come from? They come from the writings of Cicero who lived during the time of the Roman Republic. Cicero said, "When each person loves the other as much as himself,

---

46. The Preamble, Constitution of the United States. *https://constitution.congress.gov/constitution/preamble/*.

47. Reinhold Niebuhr, *Children of Light and Children of Darkness* (1944) foreword. *https://www.oxfordreference.com/view/10.1093/acref/9780191843730.001.0001/q-oro-ed5-00007882*.

48. Abraham Lincoln, Gettysburg Address, November 19, 1863.

it makes one out of many."[49] Cicero, who gave us those words, said that love for each other is the way to make *E pluribus Unum* real. Jesus of Nazareth taught us that. Moses taught us that. America, listen to Cicero, Jesus, Moses. Love is the way to make *E pluribus Unum* real. Love is the way to be America for real.

We have some shared values.

Thomas Jefferson gave voice to these shared values in the Declaration of Independence.

> We hold these truths to be self-evident, that all men are created equal, that they are endowed by their Creator with certain unalienable Rights, that among these are Life, Liberty and the pursuit of Happiness.[50]

We have shared national values. Abraham Lincoln gave voice to them when he said in the Gettysburg Address:

> Fourscore and seven years ago our fathers brought forth on this continent, a new nation, conceived in Liberty, and dedicated to the proposition that all men are created equal.[51]

We have shared national values. Every one of us was taught these words as a child in school.

> I pledge allegiance to the flag
> of the United States of America
> And to the republic for which it stands
> One nation, Under God, Indivisible
> With liberty, And justice, For all.[52]

We sing our shared values.

> America. America.
> God shed his grace on thee.

---

49. Cicero, *De Amicitia (On Friendship)*, trans. and with introduction and notes by Andrew P. Peabody, Loeb Classical Library (Boston: Little, Brown, and Co., 1887), public domain, *https://sourcebooks.fordham.edu/ancient/cicero-friendship.asp*.

50. Declaration of Independence, July 4, 1776. *https://www.archives.gov/founding-docs/declaration-transcript*.

51. Lincoln, Gettysburg Address.

52. Francis Bellamy, Pledge of Allegiance, first published for Columbus Day, on September 8, 1892, in the Boston magazine *The Youth's Companion*.

And crown thy good with brotherhood.
From sea to shining sea.[53]

At a church picnic, many years ago when I was a parish priest, I happened to be sitting at a picnic table with parishioners, several of whom were veterans of World War II and Korea. One of the men sitting there, then well into his eighties, was one of the Tuskegee Airman, the first Black air unit to fight.

He started talking about Eleanor Roosevelt, and he spoke of her with great reverence and respect. He went on to explain why. In the beginning the Tuskegee airmen were being trained to fly, yet they were prohibited from flying and fighting for their country because of the color of their skin.

At the time there was a great debate in Congress and the country as to whether or not a Black person had the lung capacity to handle altitude. And, if they had the brain capacity to handle the intellectual rigors of flying. Scientists were brought in to argue the case on both sides. Nothing changed. The Tuskegee Airmen kept training.

The tide turned when Eleanor Roosevelt, First Lady of the United States, went to Tuskegee and brought the press with her. While the cameras flashed, she got in a plane piloted by a Tuskegee airman and flew for forty-five minutes over the Alabama countryside. The picture of her in the plane with the Black airmen went viral. And it changed the debate.

What led Eleanor Roosevelt to stand with them? In a spiritual biography of Eleanor Roosevelt, Harold Ivan Smith said she "wanted her critics to join her in working toward a new America that lived out the Declaration of Independence and the Beatitudes of Jesus."[54] She was holding on to deep American ideals, the values of this country. And lifting up the values of God.

What led the Tuskegee Airmen to fly, fight, and even die for their country? Between 1943 and 1945 those airmen flew over fifteen thousand sorties. Recognitions included ninety-six Distinguished Flying Crosses, a Silver Star, fourteen Bronze Stars, seven hundred forty-four Air Medals, and eight Purple Hearts. In 2007 President George W. Bush awarded three hundred Tuskegee Airmen the Congressional Gold Medal.

---

53. Katherine Lee Bates, "America the Beautiful 1893, public domain.

54. Harold Ivan Smith, *Eleanor: A Spiritual Biography: The Faith of the 20th Century's Most Influential Woman* (New York: Westminster John Knox Press, 2017).

I was raised by folk like those guys sitting at that picnic table. In her living room, my grandma proudly displayed the pictures of her two sons who fought in World War II, serving in segregated units within the Army Air Corps. My wife has her grandfather's discharge papers; he fought in a Black unit in World War I. This I know: They loved America even when America didn't love us. They believed in America because—even when America falls short—the values and ideals of America, the dream of America, stands tall and true and will one day see us through.

So, whatever your politics, however you have or will cast your vote, however this election unfolds, wherever the course of racial reckoning and pandemic take us, whether we are in the valley or the mountain-top, hold on to the hope of America. Hold on to hope grounded in our shared values and ideals. Hold on to God's dream. Hold on and struggle and walk and pray for our nation, in the words of James Weldon Johnson:

> God of our weary years,
> God of our silent tears,
> Thou who has brought us thus far on the way;
> Thou who has by Thy might
> Led us into the light,
> Keep us forever in the path, we pray.
> Lest our feet stray from the places, our God, where we met
>   Thee,
> Lest, our hearts drunk with the wine of the world, we forget
>   Thee;
> Shadowed beneath Thy hand,
> May we forever stand,
> True to our God,
> True to our native land.[55]

---

55. James Weldon Johnson, "Lift Every Voice and Sing." Copyright © 1917, 1921, 1935 James Weldon Johnson, renewed 1963 by Grace Nail Johnson. Used by permission of Viking Penguin, a division of Penguin Books USA Inc.

GOSPEL VALUES

The Very Rev. Randolph Marshall Hollerith
Twenty-third Sunday after Pentecost, November 8, 2020

Do you remember these words from years past?

> These are difficult times for our country, and I pledge to him tonight to do all in my power to help him lead us through the many challenges we face. I urge all Americans who supported me to join me in not just congratulating him, but offering our next president our goodwill and earnest effort to find ways to come together, to find the necessary compromises, to bridge our differences and help restore our prosperity.[56] (John McCain on losing the election to Barack Obama)

> Almost a century and a half ago, Senator Stephen Douglas told Abraham Lincoln, who had just defeated him for the presidency: "Partisan feeling must yield to patriotism. I'm with you, Mr. President, and God bless you." Well, in that same spirit, I say to President-Elect Bush that what remains of partisan rancor must now be put aside, and may God bless his stewardship of this country.[57] (Al Gore on losing the election to George W. Bush)

> Our constitutional democracy enshrines the peaceful transfer of power and we don't just respect that, we cherish it.[58] (Hillary Clinton on losing the election to Donald Trump)

> I have said repeatedly in this campaign that the president was my opponent and not my enemy. And I wish him well. And I pledge my support in whatever advances the cause of a better America because that's what the race was about in the first

---

56. "Transcript: McCain's Concession Speech," *The New York Times*, November 5, 2008. *https://www.nytimes.com/2008/11/04/us/politics/04text-mccain.html?smid=url-share.*

57. "Text of Gore's Concession Speech," *The New York Times*, December 13, 2000. *https://www.nytimes.com/2000/12/13/politics/text-of-goreacutes-concession-speech.html?smid=url-share.*

58. "How to Lose an Election: A Brief History of the Presidential Concession Speech," *All Things Considered*, National Public Radio, November 2, 2020. *https://www.npr.org/2020/11/02/929085584/how-to-lose-an-election-a-brief-history-of-the-presidential-concession-speech.*

place, a better America as we go into the next century.[59] (Bob Dole on losing the election to Bill Clinton)

And finally, this extraordinary letter left by George H. W. Bush in the oval office for Bill Clinton:

Dear Bill, When I walked into this office just now I felt the same sense of wonder and respect that I felt four years ago. I know you will feel that, too. I wish you great happiness here. I never felt the loneliness some Presidents have described. There will be very tough times, made even more difficult by criticism you may not think is fair. I'm not a very good one to give advice; but just don't let the critics discourage you or push you off course. You will be our President when you read this note. I wish you well. I wish your family well. Your success now is our country's success. I am rooting hard for you. Good luck—George[60]

I know there are many of you out there this morning who are overjoyed by the results of our current election, and I know there are many others who are sad and disappointed. In recent days, I have been doing a lot of thinking about elections past. Truth be told, I was pleased with the outcome of some of them and disheartened by the outcome of others, but in almost every case I was proud of our democratic process and the way that in the end each candidate honored the values of our democracy. Hard fought, sometimes vicious campaigns, ended with a winner and a loser, joy and sadness, triumph, and defeat—yet, as evidenced by the words above, a common love for the sacredness of our democracy took precedence over everything else. In each case, these politicians realized that there were values at stake that were larger than their own political desires and aspirations, values that in the end superseded their ambitions.

Our parable this morning about the ten bridesmaids is a story about being ready, about being prepared. As a precursor to the message

---

59. "Remarks by Dole in Conceding Defeat by Clinton," *The New York Times*, November 6, 1996. *https://www.nytimes.com/1996/11/06/us/remarks-by-dole-in-conceding-defeat-by-clinton.html?smid=url-share.*

60. Gillian Brockell, "'Dear Bill': The Classy Letters Left in the Oval Office from One President to Another," *The Washington Post*, January 20, 2021.

of Advent, we are reminded today to keep our proverbial lamps trimmed and full because Christ the bridegroom is coming, and we must remain alert and ready to receive him. From the point of view of our current situation, our gospel for this morning speaks to me about the need we continually have to keep our metaphorical lamps full, not of oil, but of the values that we need in order to shine the light of Christ's love in the world and push back the darkness of despair. It speaks to me of the need to protect those values and stand up for those values, because without them there is only darkness. Values that point to the essence of our faith and our democracy—love, justice, freedom, equality, dignity, hope, forgiveness, self-sacrifice, and service. The very same values that I think undergirded each of the statements made above by those losing candidates. As George Washington said in his farewell address in 1796:

> Of all the dispositions and habits which lead to political pros-
> perity, religion and morality are indispensable supports. In vain
> would that man claim the tribute of patriotism who should
> labor to subvert these great pillars of human happiness, these
> firmest props of the duties of men and citizens. The mere pol-
> itician, equally with the pious man, ought to respect and to
> cherish them.[61]

My friends, the truth of the matter is the message of the gospel has deeply political implications. In all times and in all places, the teachings of Jesus have far-reaching consequences for how we govern ourselves, for how we treat one another; the gospel has much to say about what we should value in all human interactions. From my point of view, to say there is nothing political in what Jesus taught is to not understand the gospel. But the gospel is not partisan. It is not the property of one polit-ical party or another. In fact, as Washington pointed out, the way of love taught and lived by Jesus Christ offers much needed critique to each and every political party. As a result, in the months to come, we who consider ourselves followers of Jesus, must work to lift up the values of the gospel that stand above party, to lift up the values that critique our politics, values that stand above any and all political platforms. It is

---

61. Transcript of President George Washington's Farewell Address (1796). *https://www. ourdocuments.gov/doc.php?flash=false&doc=15&page=transcript.*

those values that claim my heart and soul, and it is those values that our country needs now more than ever.

In an article written earlier this week, Mitch Albom, who wrote *Tuesdays with Morrie,* said, "The truth is, our future won't be determined by who we choose to lead us this week. It will be determined by how we act after we do."[62] He's right, isn't he? The election is over, but we remain an extremely divided nation. While I celebrate that we have our first female vice president, a woman of color, whose election smashes yet another barrier to full inclusion, Albom is right, having a new president and vice president won't mean as much if we are not willing as a people to look beyond our political affiliations and work for the common good of all Americans. We have to put the healing of the nation above our political loyalties—always remembering, as Bishop Mariann reminded us in her sermon earlier this week, that this doesn't mean plastering over the unfinished work we need to do, this does not mean promoting healing over justice, this means continuing to pursue justice so that our healing as a nation can be real and lasting.

My friends, we have so much work to do, and while we are supposed to disagree in our democracy, while we are supposed to argue our competing ideas, we are not supposed to hate one another, that is not the way, hate is not the way. We have to uplift the values of honor and decency, the value of recognizing that we are all in this together. We have to cling to the truth that honesty matters, integrity matters. As Bishop Curry said in an interview this week on *The Today Show,* "I want to suggest that we can find common ground when we make a decision that I care about you as much as I care about myself, and when we do that, we can disagree without being disagreeable. We can find common ground, and we can heal this country."[63]

In our parable for this morning, five of the ten bridesmaids were wise and kept their lamps trimmed and full of oil. We must be wise and do the same thing. Between now and the return of our Lord, it's up to us to keep our lamps trimmed and full, full of what St. Paul describes as the fruits of the Spirit—love, joy, peace, patience, kindness, generosity, faithfulness,

---

62. Mitch Albom, "Election Will Be Meaningless If We Don't Change Our Ways," *The Detroit Free Press,* November 1, 2020.

63. "Bishop Curry Offers Advice for Divided Americans to 'Heal This Country,'" *The Today Show,* November 5, 2020. *https://www.today.com/news/bishop-curry-shares-advice-during-election-today-show-t197641.*

gentleness, and self-control. Each of us, in our own way, from wherever we are in life, has to shine the light of Christ's love and forgiveness across our strained and divided nation, promoting the values of our democracy that surpass political parties, recognizing that I cannot be truly free and safe as an American until I am willing to make sure that you are truly free and safe as well. We have a long way to go, and we have a lot of work left to do, but this democracy of ours is a gift from God and it deserves our very best efforts to preserve and protect it. Amen.

FINDING HOPE IN GOD OUR HOME

THE REV. CANON ROSEMARIE LOGAN DUNCAN
Twenty-fourth Sunday after Pentecost, November 15, 2020

Lord, you have been our refuge from one generation to another.
Before the mountains were brought forth, or the land and the
earth were born, from age to age you are God. (Ps. 90:1–2)[64]

These opening verses of Psalm 90 relay the greatness and steadfastness of God—and right now words of this assurance are a comfort to the heart. What you may not know about Psalm 90 is that it is the only psalm attributed to Moses, suggesting that it the oldest in the psalter. And just to give a bit of context, Moses and people of Israel were out in the wilderness. It would be forty long years before they reached the Promised Land. Almost all of those who were part of the Exodus would die along the way, including Moses's sister, Miriam, and his brother, Aaron.

So Moses begins with this sense of home, "Lord, you have been our refuge from one generation to another." The New International Version, translates it this way, "Lord, you have been our dwelling place throughout all generations," but the New Living Translation makes it more direct, "Lord, through all the generations you have been our home."

So, home—it's not a place at all, but a person. To be with God is to be at home, wherever you are. It makes sense that Moses is associated with this text. Moses knew homelessness—he was raised as a foster child. He grew up to become a fugitive from Egyptian law, then he crossed the border to live in the land of Midian as an alien with a past. He lives the rest of his life as a migrant, camping in tents, pulling up stakes and moving from one spot to the next with the people of Israel. He never even makes it to the Promised Land that he's been leading them to—he never makes it to that physical destination, but he is at home in the Lord.

And if we think about it, Moses represents many who are the most vulnerable of our day, for human experience is constant throughout history.

---

64. Unless otherwise noted, the quotations from Psalm 90 contained in this sermon are from *The Book of Common Prayer* (New York: The Church Hymnal Corporation, 2007), 717–719.

Now, Psalm 90 may sound familiar to many of you because it is often read at funerals. And it's no wonder, given the content. The language of Psalm 90 is that of someone who is acutely aware of mortality, "You sweep us away like a dream; we fade away suddenly like grass. In the morning it is green and flourishes; in the evening it is dried up and withered" (Ps. 90:5–6).

The psalmist has grown tired and introspective. Looking back over his life gives him a keen sense of limitation and failure. That, of course, also comes with age. Our memories aren't always heartwarming. They're often filled with regret. In my sixty years, my regrets are much more about the things I haven't done over the things I have. Whatever your regrets—fill in the blank—being human means having regrets because we live in time. The psalmist stands with an open heart before God in confession, fully aware of his failures and the dead ends of his life. And I know that talking about sin and confession is uncomfortable for many, but confession isn't about beating yourself up. It is about honesty. It's about owning up to the truth about ourselves that God already knows anyway. We prayed that in earnest as we started our worship, "Almighty God, to you all hearts are open, all desires known, and from you no secrets are hid."

Psalm 90 isn't so much a personal prayer but a corporate one, and I think that's too important not to point out. The pronouns in Psalm 90 are all plural. They are all about us—our iniquity, our sin. Ancient Israel knew that there was a place for corporate confession. They knew that evil could be systemic. And they also knew their own sin against God.

It is not easy for us as Americans to name and claim our societal evils—the sins of our collective history or our present reality. Racism and White privilege, violence, poverty are deeply rooted in the culture in which we live and breathe, and we are corporately responsible to confess and address these realities of our common life. This is a psalm of corporate confession, but it doesn't just end there. For after confession comes a request: "So teach us to number our days that we may apply our hearts to wisdom" (Ps. 90:12).

With this request, the psalm turns toward hope. And what is this wisdom? It is being able to discern how our lives are interconnected with God and with one another. And to truly engage each other requires both trust and risk. This is particularly true in the time we are living.

Sometimes I look around at our deeply troubled world, our divisions and our distrust in our nation, our lack of faith and discouragement, and I'm inclined to think my feeble efforts at resolving things aren't going to matter much in the whole scheme of things.

And that is why the message of Jesus's parable of the talents (Matt. 25:14–30) remains relevant today. Now, it could be easy just to get stuck thinking that the parable is all about money, but this parable is really an invitation to a full-hearted response to God's lavish gifts of faith and purpose. And that purpose is building the kingdom of God. Our choice is how we will use God's gifts so generously bestowed. Will we multiply or bury, embrace, or reject? And the question is for us as individuals as well as a community.

We are living in an uniquely challenging period in history. We are in the middle of the worst global pandemic of our lifetimes, with COVID cases surging across our nation and the world and more than 245,000 deaths in this country. The unexpected consequence of this health crisis, however, has been to reveal the deep wounds of our society that have been denied, suppressed, and too often ignored.

Over the past months we have experienced an awakening to the institutional and societal structures that keep us separated, and they are many and they are deep—racial, political, socioeconomic, and cultural, just to start. And as the memories of thousands of people taking to the streets in protest this summer fades as we move to the next news cycle, we must remember Breonna Taylor, George Floyd, Ahmaud Arbery, and continue to say their names because Black Lives Matter. There is still more work to be done to mend the very fabric of our nation that feels so torn. We need what Bishop Curry calls a "great relationship revival"[65] that demands we see one another as beloved children of God. But we can't accomplish this without love, without trust, without vulnerability, without risk.

It has been said, "What God does first and best and most often is to trust people with their moment in history."[66] God is trusting us now with our moment in history. It is ours to do something with. As people of faith, if we truly want to see the kingdom in our day, it is

---

65. Curry, *Love Is the Way*, 207.

66. Quoted in Edward White, *Saying Goodbye: A Time of Growth for Congregations* (Herndon, VA: Alban Institute, 1990), 92.

going to come by our full use of what God has placed in our care. We have today's parable to inspire us to choose another way—a new way of living together, to stare fear in the face and stand on the side of Christ; to be bold enough to take a stand in the face of what tries to render us helpless and hopeless. We have not been entrusted with the gospel of Jesus Christ to treat it as personal treasure to place on a shelf for our own comfort. No. Now is not the time to deny the power of the gospel. Pretending we don't have that power—by avoiding our responsibility to use that power to help the most vulnerable, to fight for justice, and to build God's kingdom—is not an option. Dear friends, may we not be afraid. In the midst of these uncertain times, God who is our refuge, our home, God who is faithful from one generation to another will empower us for the days before us. Amen.

THE STORY WE WRITE

THE REV. CANON KELLY BROWN DOUGLAS
Last Sunday after Pentecost, November 22, 2020

Good morning, Cathedral family worldwide. I remember one day, when my son was in elementary school, he came home very excited about a new subject they were introduced to that day: history. He then eagerly went on to tell me some of the things that he had learned. At the end of exhausting the day's history lesson, he stopped and said, "So, Mommy, I really still don't understand. What is history?" I remember telling him that history was about the story that people write with their lives in their time. With that answer, he got this big smile on his face and he said, "Oh, cool! So, I can make history with my life!" To which I smiled and said, "Yes, yes, you sure can."

Cathedral community, today is the feast day of Christ the King. This day marks for us the end of the long season of Pentecost, the end of our liturgical year, as it is the last Sunday before Advent. But this day is also about much more than that. For inasmuch as we proclaim that Christ is King of Kings and Lord of Lords, as we did in this morning's collect, then this is the day we recognize that through Christ, the story of heaven comes down to earth. To proclaim that Christ is King is to affirm the story of God's kingdom, that the future that God promises us all will be breaking into our history. And for those of us who claim to be followers of the Jesus that is Christ, this is the story, that on this day, we are invited into—the story we are invited to write with our very lives. Simply put, as people of faith, we are invited to partner with God in bringing our world, in this our time, just a little bit closer to God's promised, just future. We are invited to make history with God, with our very lives.

And so, the question is, what kind of story is it? What is the story that we are invited to write with our lives that breaks into our history through Christ the King? I like to think of it as a story defined by the P's of God's promise. And so, it is a story that begins with the *powerless*.

Whatever you did or didn't do unto the least of these, you did or didn't do unto me, Jesus tells us. Our gospel reading this morning makes clear to us that the promise of God that breaks into our history through Christ the King is one of uncompromising identification and solidarity with the hungry, the thirsty, the poor, the stranger, the imprisoned—that is, with those who are on the underside of justice, essentially those who have no power in this world. And so it is that the story we are invited to write with our lives is one that must begin with the powerless in our time. It is with the powerless that God's kingdom, that God's promised future is inaugurated in this our history.

Cathedral community, here is the thing: inasmuch as God's just future means a restoration of and respect for the sacred dignity of all of God's people—and it does—then it must begin, to borrow from the words of Missouri's newly elected Congresswoman Cori Bush, with whom she describes as "the counted outs, the forgotten abouts, the marginalized and the push asides."[67] Those, she says, "who have the least, who have suffered the worst."[68]

Let us make no mistake about it. It is only when they who are the least of these, when they who have experienced the harsh realities of injustice—it is only when they are free to live into the fullness of their created humanity and potential, that God's justice can be realized.

Her name was Pamela Rush. Catherine Flowers tells us in a recent *New York Times* article[69] that Pamela was the 42-year-old mother of two children, living with them in a single-wide trailer in Lowndes County, Alabama. The trailer had gaps in the walls where possums and wild animals could squeeze in, Flowers writes. She continues that it was musty, poorly ventilated, and poorly lit. Pamela's daughter's bedroom had mold everywhere, leaving her daughter with asthma. Outside of the trailer, a pipe spewed raw sewage on the ground. Pamela could not afford to move. She said she and her children were trapped, trapped in the death-dealing inhumanity of poverty. Soon COVID-19 would ravage Lowndes County and in July, Pamela would succumb to it, leaving behind her two children.

The story that Christ the King invites us to write with our lives is one that begins with the children of the Pamelas in our world. It is when they have enough to eat, when they have clean water to drink, a

---

67. Cori Bush (@CoriBush), Twitter post, November 3, 2020. *https://twitter.com/CoriBush/status/1323841396378402816?s=20.*

68. Cori Bush, "This Is Our Moment . . . I Love You: Cori Bush's Electrifying Acceptance Speech," *The Guardian*, November 5, 2020. *https://www.theguardian.com/us-news/2020/nov/05/cori-bush-congresswoman-st-louis-missouri-speech.*

69. Catherine Flowers, "Mold, Possums, and Pools of Sewage: No One Should Have to Live Like This," *The New York Times*, November 14, 2020. *https://www.nytimes.com/2020/11/14/opinion/sunday/coronavirus-poverty-us.html.*

safe bedroom to sleep in, clothes to wear, means to care for their health; when they are free to grow into whomever God has put them on this earth to be, it is then that we will know that we are writing a story that at least bends toward the justice and mercy that is God's promised future for all of God's people. And so what kind of story is it that Christ the King invites us to write with our lives? It is a story that begins with the powerless, and it is one that is *personal*. "When did you see me?" they asked Jesus. And Jesus answered, "Truly I tell you, just as you did it to one of the least of these who are members of my family, you did it to me" (Matt. 25:40).

As God's kingdom breaks into our history through Christ, it breaks in as a personal story. For it was the case that Jesus saw himself in the face of the weak and the vulnerable, of those on the underside of justice. It was personal for him. And as it was for Jesus, it is to be for us. The way to God's promises begins with us seeing the other in ourselves, and ourselves in the other. It is in this way that the story we are invited to write with our lives is indeed personal.

Here is the thing: behind the statistics of poverty, police brutality, and the daily counts of COVID are real people—they are persons like you and like me—they are somebody's fathers, somebody's mothers, daughters, sons, and children. And so it is that the story we were invited to write with our lives begins not with what seems like the out of reach, improbable, and impersonal task of changing systems and structures (though change them we must); but this story begins with the probable, which is recognizing and affirming the value, the worth, the dignity, the personhood of those who are just like us but find themselves trapped in the violent cycles of systemic and structural injury and injustice.

Zay Jones, a wide receiver for the Los Angeles Raiders, said that one day he was in a store shopping with his cousin, and an elderly White woman approached them and said, "I'm from Minneapolis and I just want you to know that you matter." Jones said, "I could see it was very sincere and heartfelt." And so, he asked for permission to hug her, even amid the coronavirus pandemic. He said, "I just felt like that was the right thing to do," Jones recalled. And in an instant, he said, "She just kind of fell into my arms. And she just started crying."[70]

---

70. Gina Vivenetto, "NFL Player Shares Kind Words Elderly White Woman Told Him at Store," *The Today Show*, originally on Twitter (Zay Jones, zay@zayjones11, May 30, 2020). *https://www.today.com/news/raiders-player-zay-jones-shares-kind-words-stranger-told-him-t182931*.

Doing justice is within our reach. It is about affirming the person-hood of one another. That is the personal story that Christ the King invites us to write with our lives.

And as it is personal, it is also *partial*. That is, it is partial to the values that are God's. And here is the thing, those values don't change—they are not subject to the mercurial and changing personalities of partisan politics of our times. No, they are steadfast, as they reflect the steadfastness of a God who is love. And so, during these times that are ours, when bigotry overwhelms goodness and privilege masquerades as justice and greatness overrides graciousness, we are to show forth the generosity, the righteousness, the compassion that is the promise of God's love. These are the values that we are to be partial to at all times. Simply put, when all around us "goes low," we are to "reach high," reach-ing for the values that are God's heaven.

Shawn Dromgoole is a 29-year-old Black man who has lived in the same Nashville neighborhood his entire life. He said that he watched as his neighborhood became gentrified and fewer and fewer people who looked like him remained in the neighborhood. And so, with each pass-ing year, he said he felt more and more unwelcome and more and more afraid. After watching what happened to Ahmaud Arbery, he said, "I was afraid to leave my porch. I was afraid to walk by myself in my childhood neighborhood because I was afraid that I wouldn't live to see another day. . . . When I shared my fear on social media, my neighbor said, 'We will walk with you.'"[71]

". . . whatever is true, whatever is honorable, whatever is right, whatever is of good repute, if there is any excellence and anything wor-thy of praise," Paul says, "we must dwell on them" (cf. Phil. 4:8). And so, the neighbors defied the values that fostered fear. And they walked. That is what it means to write with our lives a story that is partial to the ways and values of God's promised future.

And if we do this, then the story we write must ultimately be one defined by *prayer*. Of all of the images that run through my mind when I think of Jesus, the one that always stands out to me the most is that of Jesus going off to a lonely place to pray. The Jesus that is Christ the

---

71. Sydney Page, "A Black Man Was Afraid to Walk in His Gentrified Com-munity. So 75 Neighbors Walked with Him," *The Washington Post*, June 3, 2020. *https://www.washingtonpost.com/lifestyle/2020/06/03/black-man-was-afraid-walk-his-gentrified-community-so-75-neighbors-walked-with-him/.*

King invites us to write a story with our lives that is marked by prayer. To pray is to recognize that it is not all up to us, but there is a power that is beyond us that will indeed complete the work of justice, even as it sustains us in doing that work in our time. For, it is through prayer that we can actually reach beyond ourselves to the mystery that is God's transforming power. It is prayer that connects us to God's very promise. Indeed, that we pray signifies our faith in the God who promises us a more just future. It is for this reason that the late Congressman John Lewis would say, "Without prayer, without faith in God almighty, the civil rights movement would have been like a bird without wings."[72]

And so it was, on the Sunday after a week of protests, following George Floyd's murder, the Alfred Street Baptist Church, in Alexandria, Virginia, sponsored a day of prayer on the National Mall where thousands gathered. As one man explained, "After all that is going on, coming here to pray makes me feel that change is going to come, because God is with us."[73]

There is no getting around it. Prayer is at the heart of the story that Jesus who is Christ the King invites us to write with our lives.

And so, there you have it. What is the story of God's promised future that on this day, Christ the King invites us to write with our lives? It is a story that reflects the P's of that promise—it is a story that begins with the powerless, a story that is personal, partial, and defined by prayer.

Cathedral family, my great-grandmother, whom I knew, was born into slavery. She died when I was about six or seven years old. Given the world into which my great-grandmother was born, and even the one in which she died, I know that she could never, ever have fathomed a Black president or a Black, South Asian female vice president. This is the story that my son now has inherited. It reflects a history that my great-grandmother, his great-great-grandmother, didn't get to experience. Yet, it is her story of hope that he and his children and his children's children can continue to write with their lives. It is a story of a future where all of God's children can truly achieve their dreams and

72. Kim Lawton, "John Lewis Extended Interview," *Religion & Ethics Newsweekly*, January 16, 2004. *https://www.pbs.org/wnet/religionandethics/2004/01/16/january-16-2004-john-lewis-extended-interview/2897/*.

73. Alfred Street Baptist Church in Alexandria, Virginia, June 2020.

live into the fullness of their created potential. This is a story that bends toward the justice that is the promise of God.

"Oh, cool!" my son said. "I can make history." Cathedral family, we can make history. We can make it through the stories that we write with our lives—left for us to decide is the kind of stories we want to write, and thus, the side of history we want to be on.

On this day, we are invited to be on the side of history that is Christ the King's, the side of history that is God's just future coming to earth, and thus to write the story that begins with the powerless, that is personal, that is partial and is defined by prayer. We are invited to write that story of promise. May it be so.

4

Time to Be of a New Mind: Healers

THE GIFT OF YOUR ROSE

The Rt. Rev. Mariann Edgar Budde
Second Sunday of Advent, December 6, 2020

Comfort, O comfort my people, says your God. Speak tenderly to Jerusalem, and cry to her that she has served her term, that her penalty is paid, that she has received from the Lord's hand double for all her sins. (Isa. 40:1)

The beginning of the good news of Jesus Christ, the Son of God. As it is written in the prophet Isaiah, "See, I am sending my messenger ahead of you, who will prepare your way; the voice crying out in the wilderness: Prepare the way of the Lord, make his paths straight. . . ." (Mark 1:1-8)

Be still, my soul. The Lord is on thy side.
Bear patiently the cross of grief or pain.
Leave to thy God to order and provide.
In every change, He faithful will remain.
Be still, my soul. Thy best, thy heavenly friend
through thorny ways leads to a joyful end.[1]

Good morning. I'd like to begin with an excerpt from a story that always comes to my mind in December. It's not a Christmas story, but it speaks to me of the miracle and mystery of what we celebrate at Christmas. This comes from the story of a prince—a little prince.

> The Little Prince lay down and wept at the sight of five hundred roses in a garden. You see, on the planet he ruled, he had a single rose who had told him that she was unique. Yet here were five hundred roses, just like her, in one garden. "She

---

1. Katherine von Schlegel, "Be Still My Soul," trans. Jane Borthwick, *The United Methodist Hymnal*, #534.

would be very much annoyed if she knew," he said to himself. "She would cough most dreadfully and pretend that she was dying, to avoid being laughed at. And I should be obliged to pretend that I was nursing her back to life. . . . "I thought that I was rich," he thought sadly, "with a flower unique in all the universe." If she were but an ordinary rose, who, then, was he?

Then the Little Prince met a fox who taught him an important lesson about love. "To me," the fox said, "you are nothing more than a little boy who is just like a thousand other little boys. I have no need of you. And you have no need of me. I am just a fox, like a hundred thousand other foxes. But if you tame me, then we shall need each other. To me, you will be unique in all the world, and I will be the same for you."

The Little Prince returned to the garden of five hundred roses and realized that for all their beauty, he felt nothing for them. But he loved his rose far away on his tiny planet—the rose he watered and sheltered and cared for. "It is the time you have wasted for your rose that makes her so important," the fox told the Little Prince. "You are responsible for your rose."[2]

Like the one rose, the entirety of the Christian faith rests on an astonishing spiritual proposition: When God chose to redeem the world, God did not send an army, or a committee, or a plan. God sent one person. Jesus lived in a particular place and time. He was born of Mary. Through his one life we see the human face of God. We who call ourselves Christians are those who feel so drawn to that one life that we seek to live our lives in light of his. The gospel of our lives—our good news—is our story of how his life makes a difference in ours.

According to the gospel of Mark, the earliest written account of Jesus's life, his story begins not in the manger, but with a voice that cries out, "In the wilderness, 'prepare the way of the Lord, make his paths straight'" (Mark 1:3).

The season of Advent is one of preparation. But what are we preparing for exactly? For Christians, this is simply another way of asking how we are to live. It's a haunting question in a world that needs so

---

2. Antoine de Saint-Exupéry, *The Little Prince* (New York: Harcourt Brace Jovanovich, 1943; 1971), 77–87.

much. For those who feel Jesus's claim on our lives, what or who is our rose? For what and for whom are we responsible?

Our first responsibility must always be for the one life with which we have been uniquely entrusted. No one else can live our lives for us, nor can we live another person's life. While we dare never minimize the impact of inequity and trauma, nor the randomness of fortune and disaster, we can and must choose our response to life. We decide how we will live, and to what degree we will allow the love of God in. We are responsible for our rose.

Our second responsibility is within our particular sphere of relationships—family, friends, and community. It's no small task to love well those closest to us, and to own our part in the universal imperfection of relationships. It's a daily discipline to seek the best in one another and forgive the worst. Every day we choose how we will show up with and for each other, to do our part, and more when life demands it. We are responsible for our rose.

A third responsibility is for our work, our contribution to the greater good. Through work, we take our energies and gifts and offer them up and out, beyond us. The realm of work is complicated and it changes over time. Sometimes our work is related to what we do for a living, but not always, for our work is always more than our job. Sometimes work plays a big part of our identity, but other times it's simply doing what needs to be done. Sometimes we're recognized for our work, but often not. Sometimes our work puts us right in the center of things, but most of the time we're in a supporting role for someone else. Case in point: John the Baptist, the patron saint of Advent. His entire life was a prologue for Jesus's ministry.

Work helps us find our place and connect to something bigger. The former Czech president and poet Vaclav Havel said it this way: "By perceiving ourselves as part of the river, we take responsibility for the river as a whole."[3] We are responsible for our rose.

Even in normal times, whatever that means, life rarely affords the luxury of apportioning equal allotments of energy to each of these three realms of responsibility. More typical is for one area to take priority for a time, be it self, relationships, or work.

When the focus needs to be on ourselves, in a time of intense development, maturing, or rest, it can feel selfish and self-indulgent. Yet

---

3. Vaclav Havel, *Letters to Olga* (New York: Henry Holt, 1982), 301.

more than one wise mentor has said to a restless soul, "Self-sacrifice isn't worth much if you don't have much of a self to begin with." It's a lesson I've learned and relearned many times. I am responsible for my rose. And you are responsible for yours.

In a similar way, when life requires us to drop everything for the sake of one we love, there is no option but to go. Once when a family member needed emergency surgery, I brought with me into the surgical waiting room all of my work for the coming weekend. I had a sermon to write, a wedding to prepare for, and meetings to plan. The extent of this health crisis had not fully registered, and I was trying to fit it in with my other responsibilities. I may have been in shock. It took the reality check of a friend, who gently but firmly told me that I wasn't going into work that weekend. When someone in our immediate circle needs us, we belong there. We are responsible for our rose.

Yet there are also times when our work requires that kind of singular focus and energy, for creativity's sake, or to accomplish whatever it is that we feel called to. When work demands it, the other realms of self and relationships can suffer. It's a dangerous way to live indefinitely, but sometimes it feels necessary for a greater good. A few years ago, *The New York Times* ran a story about a group of scientists at the National Institutes of Health who realized that they were nearing a breakthrough in a treatment for a rare form of leukemia. Driven by the hope of this new treatment, they worked around the clock for weeks, missing their children's soccer games and piano recitals so that someone else might live to see their own children play.

The same determined focus is evident now, as those who have the skill and capacity to create and distribute a vaccine are working at great sacrifice so that we might see a better day. It's happening in our schools and hospitals and nursing homes and households: sacrificing yourselves for others' sake. If you are among those tending to your work so that others might live, thank you.

In ways we still can't fully measure, the events of 2020 have affected everything within our circles of responsibility—our own lives, our relationships, and what constitutes our work. It's as if we're all in a cosmic game of 52-card pickup, and we're all scrambling on the floor to pick up the pieces of our lives.

As we consider how Jesus would have us live now, could we dare to believe that He first invites us to be still just long enough to acknowledge that impact and what's required of us considering all that's happened and is happening?

It's a rubber-meets-the-road kind of spiritual question: If Jesus is indeed God's way of redeeming the world, if Jesus is God's way of healing us, where do we need him most right now? Where do you need him? Where do I?

Our answers will differ according to our circumstances and the particular claims on our lives. His promise, however, is the same: Jesus comes and makes his home with us, wherever we are. He is the light that darkness cannot overcome. He is the love that shows up where love is most needed. That's something to hold onto amid all that we've lost. Presiding Bishop Curry said in a recent interview, "The truth of Christmas may be more profoundly true for us this year because everything else has been stripped away. We are not helpless. We are not alone. There's a God that cares enough to come into this world."[4]

Be still, my soul. The Lord is on thy side . . . through every change, he faithful will remain.[5]

One way for us to live, then, is to embrace the particularity of our lives in this moment and focus on singular, specific expressions of love. So often we worry that we're not doing enough. If that's your worry, as it is mine, might we all agree, right now, to let that worry go, and choose instead, as Mother Teresa advised, to do small things with great love?

I first read the story of the Little Prince when I was a new parent, adjusting to the enormous shifting of energy and life priorities that parenting required. I was both comforted and challenged by the image of the rose—comforted in that I knew with unmistakable clarity where my responsibility lay, and challenged because I realized that if I didn't rise to this, if I couldn't love this one child, then all my efforts to love and to give in other realms would mean nothing. Now that child is a young man with a babe, with a rose, of his own.

---

4. Sarah Pulliam Bailey, "Closed for Christmas, Washington National Cathedral Is More Popular Than Ever," *The Washington Post*, November 27, 2020. *https://www.washingtonpost.com/religion/closed-for-christmas-washington-national-cathedral-is-more-popular-than-ever/2020/11/27/ab71990a-2f50-11eb-96c2-aac3f162215d_story.html.*

5. Katharina Amalia Dorothea von Schlegel, "Be Still My Soul" 1752, trans. Jane B. Harthwick (1855), public domain.

It turns out that intentional expressions of love expand our capacity to love. The love we offer, no matter how small, has a way of multiplying as it goes forth from us. When we choose to love the lives we have been given, we have more love to share. When we tend to our relationships, we build a foundation of compassion and health that reaches generations. When we do work with love, we share in God's redeeming of the world.

I think of the Little Prince every year as Christmas approaches, because of the one rose. *Lo, how a rose ere blooming*—we'll sing this season—*It came a flower bright, amid the cold of winter, when half spent was the night.*

There is striking singularity about the Christian faith, focused as it is on one person, one babe born long ago. Yet it is the power and presence of that one life, living in us, that holds the promise of all that is good and just and true, all that we long for for ourselves and hope for our children's children. In the face of all that this world cries out for, it may not feel like enough, but it is God's way, in and through us. For Christians, Jesus is our rose. And we are his. Amen.

TEARS OF LOVE

THE RT. REV. MARIANN EDGAR BUDDE
Christmas Eve, December 24, 2020

The people who walked in darkness have seen a great light. (Isa. 9:2)

I'm both sad and happy to celebrate with you this way—sad that we can't be physically together, either here or in your own churches, and happy that while we're all in our particular spaces, we are gathered in this common space. We are united in our humanity, our hope for a better day, our love for those who have a particular claim on our hearts, and our prayers tonight for peace and goodwill in all the earth.

Many of our loved ones aren't with us; some we won't see again on this side of heaven. Others are physically distant, which hurts all the more at Christmas. Still others may be physically close but emotionally distant, which is a sorrow all its own. Some of you, I know, are alone tonight, although we're here to assure you that you're not alone. Tonight is the celebration of *Emmanuel*—God-with-us. We are with one another through a great mystery, and I'm not talking about technology, as wonderful as it is. We are bound together by the love of God revealed to us in Jesus's birth.

I have a candle next to me to honor you and all those we hold in our hearts, and to remind us, as scripture teaches, that the light of Christ shines in the darkness and the darkness did not and cannot overcome it.

The country music singer Alan Jackson wrote a Christmas song that tells the story of Jesus's birth pretty much according to the biblical accounts. It begins with those who made their way to the Christ child following a star. Then it tells of the animals in the manger, imagining them being still, as animals often are when they sense that something important is happening.

The heart of the song is its refrain, which hones in on the angels present that night. But there's no mention of them telling the shepherds not to be afraid, or of the heavenly chorus praising God. In this song, the angels cry. That's the entire refrain: *"And the angels cried."*[6] As soon as I heard it, I knew that it was true.

---

6. Alan Jackson, vocalist, "Honky Tonk Christmas" by Alan Jackson, 1993.

We've cried so many tears this year. Tears of grief and rage. Tears of disappointment, frustration, and fear. Tears of loneliness and longing. Tears in awe of those who are sacrificing so much for our sake. Tears of gratitude for hope on the horizon. And as an older friend used to say whenever we met and she would cry, "Tears of joy, Mariann. Tears of joy." They weren't really tears of joy, but I loved the fact that she remembered joy as she cried.

Of course the angels cried. And if you've ever held a newborn in your arms, you know why. They cried for love. They cried knowing that it was for love God had sent His Son. They cried because they knew the child's destiny was to grow into a man who would love as God loves and suffer as only love can suffer. They cried knowing that they could do nothing to protect this beautiful child from the cost of a love that would lead from the manger to the cross. The angels cried.

There are particular moments when we're given eyes to see as God sees and hearts to love as God loves. One such moment is at the birth of a child. We look into the eyes of a miracle. We hold the miracle in our arms, and in that moment, our love is pure and complete. And like the angels, we cry.

Another such moment is at the end of life. God bless the intensive care doctors, nurses, and chaplains who are now sometimes the only ones present when a person dies of COVID-19. A chaplain in California describes how he holds a phone or an iPad up so that loved ones can say goodbye. "It's so clear every time that the one dying is so loved. But the amount of crying I've done this year . . . it's hard."[7] In death we're given eyes to see as God sees and hearts to love as God loves. And like the angels, we cry.

The former Archbishop of Canterbury Rowan Williams once said that if you want to know what God is really like—in other words, how the creative power at the heart of our universe really works—look no further than the manger and the cross. "God acts by giving away all strength and success as we understand them. The universe lives by a love that refuses to bully us or force us, the love of the manger and the cross."[8]

---

7. Jack Jenkins, "For Chaplains, Being Vaccinated First Brings a Mix of Emotions," *Religion News Service*, December 23, 2020.

8. Rowan Williams, Christmas sermon, Canterbury Cathedral, December 25, 2004. Text at *www.thinkinganglicans.org.uk*.

There is something worrying about this, Williams concedes. We'd like our God to be more powerful than a baby or a man sentenced to die. We Christians are forever trying, with the best of intentions, to make God bigger, espousing certainties easily disputed in face of the facts. The truth is we don't know what to do with a God who gives all power away; with healing that comes through suffering; with love that meets us in our vulnerabilities and stays there with us, rather than providing the escape from it that we so desperately want.

But that's how it is with God.

If you want to find God in your life, look no further than the manger and the cross, which is to say, where life is beginning and ending in you. Look in the places where you know the least and fear the most. Look in the eyes of those you love more than love itself, and in the eyes of those whom you struggle to love. Look in the mirror; listen to the sound of your own voice; consider the beating of your own heart. Then cast your gaze across the globe and ponder the same love manifest in places we hear of marked by great sorrow and suffering. And like the angels, don't be afraid to let your heart break. Let your tears flow at the sorrow and the joy of it all, the wonder of life and the mystery of love. For Christ comes to your place of tears.

There's another song in my head tonight. It's not a Christmas song, but it is about tears. The acapella group Sweet Honey in the Rock sings about a Black woman who washes floors to send her kids to college, who always makes sure that there's food on the table, and who stays up late listening to her children's hurt and rage. Everyone turns to her.

> *The father, the children, the brothers turn to her. And everybody White turns to her.*

But where does she turn? Sweet Honey sings:

> *There oughta be a woman can break down, sit down, break down, sit down.*[9]

Hold that image of a strong Black woman breaking down, crying her eyes out, alone. Then when the tears are done, watch her as she takes a breath, gets up, and carries on. While I am in no way comparing myself to that amazing woman, I am ashamed to say that I have cried

---

9. Sweet Honey in the Rock, vocalists, "Good News," "There Oughta Be a Woman," by Bernice Johnson Reagon, 1982.

like that this year—tears like a river, alone. But here's the thing: when there were no more tears to cry and I got up, I was okay. I knew that I wasn't alone. Emmanuel, God-with-us, was with me, in the tears and the rising.

What I'm saying to you is that if you feel a good cry coming on, tonight or any night, it's more than okay. It makes all the sense in the world. If not, that's okay, too. Perhaps you're the one to witness another person's tears tonight, or to hold a space for joy. Maybe your Christmas task this year is to shield joy.

But if or when the tears come, let them come. When they subside and you wonder what to do next, take a breath and allow yourself to feel God with you and for you. You'll know what to do next. You'll rise.

Remember this: the world isn't saved by any of us trying harder, but neither are we bystanders in this world. You and I are invited into an amazing mystery; first, to experience something of God's love in a way that actually matters, and then to embody—to incarnate—that love for someone else. Jesus comes to us when we make a home for him, and through us, his light and love shines on.

Will you pray with me?

O God, we are your manger tonight, each one of us. Help us to grow large enough inside to hold you and to hold the mystery of love, the sorrow of a broken heart, the miracle of our beating hearts. We are here with our tears of sadness, tears of joy, and tears of love. Amen.

WORD MADE FLESH

The Rev. Patrick L. Keyser
First Sunday after Christmas, December 27, 2020

"And the Word became flesh and lived among us." (John 1:14)

A very Merry Christmas to you all. Every year I delight in the fact that the church's celebration of Christmas is founded on the idea that the joy and celebration of the wonderful news of the coming of a Savior who is Christ the Lord cannot be contained in just one day and should thus continue for twelve days. This year, though, that joy of Christmas is tinged with a great deal of grief and sadness for so many of us. I have felt this mix of joy and sadness very acutely myself in recent days as I have been looking back on this year in its closing days. There has been tremendous, incalculable loss—loss of life, livelihood, jobs, relationships, hopes, dreams. And then came Christmas, a day that for many, though by no means all of us, is associated with joy, celebration, and spending time with loved ones. This year Christmas came with loss, as well. Traditions and rituals were significantly disrupted—churches were mostly empty, gathering with loved ones was difficult if not impossible. Many felt the sting of grief, missing the presence of those who have died this past year. Many others felt the weight of anxiety, unsure how much longer they could pay to put food on the table and keep a roof over their head. It was a difficult and heavy day, a day of absence. In her sermon on Christmas Eve, Bishop Mariann invited us to weep when we felt the need to weep—to join the angels who cried at the birth of the Christ child. This invitation was a blessed reminder for all of us at the end of a year in which the loss has been so great and there has been so much that breaks the heart.

The toll of this year has indeed been great, but amidst it all we have also caught glimpses of the resiliency of the human spirit. As I reflected on the past year, I looked especially for the moments of grace and the unexpected blessings in the face of such horror—both in my own life and in the stories of others. There are, of course, countless stories from day-to-day life that go unreported—of neighbors coming together to care for each, to deliver food, medicine, and other essentials to those in need, of friends reaching to those who are isolated and alone. There are, too, particular moments known to us from the past nine months that came to my mind. In the very early days of this pandemic when their country had become one of the places hardest hit by the virus and death ravaged their land, Italians in lockdown took to their balconies to sing together songs of hope and encouragement in scenes that charmed the world. A few months later millions of people across this country, from the biggest cities to the smallest towns, took to the streets in the wake of the killing of George Floyd to protest racism and ongoing police brutality in what seems to be the largest movement in the history of this country.

There are, too, numerous moments from the life of this Cathedral congregation—of gathering this fall to baptize and welcome new members to the family of God, of the weekly coffee hours that we have shared with so many of you across these months, of the new community of worshippers across this country and across the world that has emerged since March. All are moments of grace in difficult times. All moments when the light shines through the darkness, we might say. I see, too, that all are rooted in a desire, a longing, for connection in a time when we have been so physically separated from each other. It is one of the cruelest features of this pandemic time that the very thing that humans look to to navigate difficult times—the sort of human connection that comes through physical proximity and human touch— that is precisely what must be avoided in order to prevent the spread of this terrible virus. We are creatures of flesh and blood, created to be in community, and our inability to experience this basic need is, I think, at the root of so much of the grief and sorrow we are feeling.

It is in that very place where the message of Christmas meets us this year, offering us good news once again, good news that has a lot to say about flesh and blood. Christmas Eve brings us the beloved narrative from Luke's gospel, with shepherds, angels, and the precious newborn child resting in the manger. Luke tells a story situated in a very particular time and place—he even lists the names of the emperor and the governor of the region at the time of the Christ child's birth. John's gospel, on the other hand, approaches the story from a different angle, taking a cosmic perspective in its prologue we heard this morning. John's prologue is like a good piece of poetry—something that is best experienced by just letting it wash over you and sink into your being. Echoing the opening words of Genesis, John takes us to the beginning, something we cannot completely wrap our minds around and something our words cannot fully describe. In the beginning was the Word. This term, in the

Greek *logos*, was long used in philosophy and then adopted into religious discourse, most notably here in John 1. The Word was there in the beginning—the Word with God, the Word that is God. The Word was there at creation, and through him all things came into being.

This talk of *logos*, of the Word, might seem very abstract. I ask you to stick with me, because though that may seem to be the case, the central truth that John's prologue reveals to us is anything but that. For this passage reaches its climax in the proclamation that "the Word became flesh and lived among us." It is an extraordinary, even scandalous claim. Omnipotent, almighty God, who was in the beginning, who created all things, this God took on human flesh, our fragile humanity, and lived among us. No other major world religion makes this astonishing claim—that God became human. It was no easy task for early Christians to wrap their heads around it either. How could it be that a child born of Mary was also fully God? How could it be that though no one has ever seen God, this Jesus, who is close to the Father's heart, makes God known to us? A great deal of contemplation, discussion, and even conflict emerged from the reflections on what in theological terms is called the incarnation, from the Latin meaning "to make into flesh." This expression has a very visceral quality to it. The Latin, in fact, can either be translated as flesh or meat—think of connections with words like "carnivore" or "carne" in some Romance languages. Incarnation is, then, the language of meat, of flesh, of our humanity. One more brief etymological note will offer further insight to this absolutely crucial verse from John 1. The word translated as "lived" really means "to tent" or "to tabernacle." "Lived" certainly conveys the meaning in a more accessible way in modern English, but we should understand this word to have a real depth of meaning to it, of coming and dwelling, of making a home among us.

What becomes so very clear, then, is that the incarnation, our belief that in Jesus the Word indeed became flesh and lived among us, is a testament to God's longing to be close to us. It is God's way of showing that there are no limits to what God will do to seek us out and find us. There are absolutely no limits to the love God shows us. The loving creator of all that is chose to take on humanity, to share our human life so that we might in turn share with Christ in the divine life. Jesus comes to us in solidarity, sharing our humanity, our struggles, sorrows, joys, and yearnings. The loneliness that may seem so consuming, the grief and sorrow that pierces your heart, the tears that will not stop—Jesus comes right alongside us and says, "I too have known that loneliness, that grief, that sorrow. I too have wept. You are not alone." This is "Immanuel." This is "God with us."

The incarnation shows us with total clarity that creation, our humanity, and our bodies are fundamentally good and indeed a primary way in which we encounter God. God enters into the world; heaven comes down to earth. Jesus shows that creation itself can bear the holiness of God. The incarnation guides our understanding of the power and importance of sacrament, that in the simple things of this earth—bread, wine, water, oil, human touch—with these simple things we can come face to face with the presence and power of God. Our hearts long for these sacramental encounters because our hearts long for God. As people of the incarnation, we desire incarnate, fleshy encounters with God and one another.

That of course reveals a great paradox and a great challenge of this time we are living through—how can we be people of the incarnation in a time when we are physically isolated from one another, when so much of our lives is mediated virtually? What does the incarnation have to say to us in a time when tangible, fleshy human encounters are so severely limited? We must first acknowledge the difficulty that is so real and so strongly felt. We long to be together again, we long for sacrament, for sharing together again in the sacred meal of bread and wine. Our inability to do that grieves so many hearts. There is difficulty, no doubt, but the good news of this day, the good news of Christmas, is that no matter the circumstances, no matter the struggles or pains of this life, God is with us. There is no limit to what God will do to seek us out and find us. Jesus, the Christ, became flesh and lived among us. We encounter that divine presence through the centuries-old rituals of the church, but we trust too that God is revealed to us in countless other ways as well—in the wonder of creation, in compassionate care and service shown to others, in worship and prayer in your home this very day. Nothing, not even the horrors of this pandemic, can stop God's presence and love from breaking into our world and coming to us. That is the joy and promise of Christmas. It is the good news of which the angels sang, which the shepherds first heard long ago, which propelled the wise men on their journey. It is good news to us too, here and now in this year of such pain and sorrow. God comes and makes a home among us and says, "I am with you—I have come to make all things new." Amen.

JESUS AND MARY'S RELATIONSHIP STATUS: IT'S COMPLICATED

The Rev. Canon Dana Colley Corsello
Second Sunday after Christmas, January 3, 2021

Good morning, Merry Christmas, and Happy New Year! What a treat to wish you the hat trick of all greetings. I have often wondered if this passage from Luke's gospel (Luke 2:41–52) triggered the mandatory head count of every tour since the first century. If you've ever chaperoned children on a field trip or taken adults on a mission trip, you know exactly what I mean. Perhaps Jesus being left behind in Jerusalem, and his parents not discovering his absence until they walked at least twenty-five miles toward home, is the reason why every head is accounted for before the bus pulls away.

To our modern sensibilities this event would be a dereliction of parental duties, and child protective services would be summoned. In first-century Palestine though, the caravan traveling back to Nazareth would have been made up of family and friends—a community of trust in which this village looked after one another's children.

I know this scenario very well. My two sons were literally born into the church family of St. James's in Richmond, Virginia. Once my husband wrestled them into the building on Sundays, we hardly saw them or knew where they were. Usually, a young girl had one of them on her hip and was "mothering them" for the morning. Our pediatrician, another member of the parish, warned me, "You're thinking that everyone is watching your boys, but in fact, everyone thinks that too, so no one is really watching them." She was correct. One Sunday, my baby Casper escaped from the undercroft where we were enjoying coffee hour, crawled up the stairs to the narthex, out the door onto the portico, and was headed down the steps to the sidewalk and the busy street below. We had no idea. It wasn't until our sexton, James, came and found me and said, "Does this belong to you?" Let's just say that our hearts stopped when we learned where James had rescued him. This passage has always hits a little too close to home.

And let's just say that I, like most parents, would want to wring Jesus's neck for being so oblivious and hanging back in the temple when he knew exactly where he was supposed to be—in the caravan headed home. I am sure many of you have known that feeling when your child vanishes at the grocery store or an amusement park. One of sheer panic—then great, rushing relief—even a dissipating anger that accompanies your reunion. The text says Mary and Joseph experienced great "anxiety" over their search for Jesus—the Greek translates this as *pain*.

More, though, than just an interesting story about the missing years of Jesus's childhood, this text from Luke shares with us a tinge of the heartache Mary and Joseph must have felt when they realize their adolescent child is pulling away and individuating. It is obvious; this is the moment they become "parents" and God becomes both abba and amma father and mother. As far as we know, this is Jesus's first real awareness of his parentage, and it intuitively comes to him in his Father's house. I can't help but relate to Mary and her constant undertow bewilderment. Keep in mind, she does not "treasure all these things in her heart" (cf. Luke 2:19) until they return safely to Nazareth and Jesus agrees to be obedient.

Knowing how Jesus's life on earth unfolds, the word that keeps coming to me about Mary's journey with Jesus is "beleaguered."

Throughout December, I hosted a series of evening reflections based on traditional Advent texts. These reflections were given by a scholar/preacher, a chaplain, a monk, and a spiritual writer. Debie Thomas, who writes for the webzine, *Journey with Jesus*, offered a beautiful, powerful reflection on the Annunciation and several of its key lines from the first chapter of Luke, one being verse 31, "And now, you will conceive in your womb and bear a son."

But she focused only on three words, "You will bear." Debie reminded us that Mary bore a great deal more than an infant. It was Simeon, after his blessing of the infant Jesus in the temple, who warned Mary about destiny's child, "and a sword will pierce your own soul too" (Luke 2:35).

Debie began and I quote, "Mary bore the scandal of an unplanned pregnancy in a culture that shunned or stoned women in her condition. Mary bore the initial suspicion and disappointment of her fiancé Joseph; she bore the pain of labor and delivery of her firstborn child in threadbare circumstances, far from her home and kin. She bore the terror of all refugees who flee their homes and homelands to save their children; she bore the complicated guilt and relief of the survivor whose own baby lived while countless others in Herod's realm died in his place; she bore the horror of all parents whose children go missing and, when she finally found her twelve-year-old boy discussing theology in the temple, she bore the bewilderment of having a child who was already surpassing her; and a young man she could neither contain nor comprehend."[10]

One of the last trials in this exhaustive list of Mary's anguish was this: "Mary, like so many mothers and fathers across history, stood under a lynching tree and bore the unspeakable pain of watching her son die. . . . Alongside that horror, she bore the public humiliation of having a supposed criminal for a son."[11] End quote. Grief is apparently the price of love. And I must add, the deep wells of courage, patience, and tenacity required to parent are not unique to mothers.

Knowing all of this, I have always been troubled and confounded by the curt, distant tone in which Jesus speaks or talks *about* Mary. He addresses her as "woman" in John; he doesn't speak to her at all in Mark's gospel, only *about* her; in Luke, Jesus says the shocking: "Whoever comes to me and does not hate father and mother . . . cannot be my disciple" (14:26); and in Matthew when Mary and his brothers want to speak to him, he denies them as his kin. A knife to the heart. A sword to her soul.

For those of us mere mortals, Jesus's indifference is hard to take. How can he be so callus? He wept over Lazarus, John was his beloved disciple, and Mary Magdalene—she held a piece of his heart, too. But he couldn't express a smidge of public affection for the woman who birthed him? Thank goodness he had the wherewithal to ensure Mary's wellbeing after his death when he presented her to John and said, "Here is your mother" (John 19:27).

In my humble estimation, the relationship between Mary and Jesus is defined by his divinity rather than his humanity. It's not that he rejected her, instead when it came to her, he erected guardrails between the two. I think it had to be this way or Jesus would not have made his way to the cross—his mission could not be hampered by the human guilt of devastating his human mother. He placed these guardrails around his heart just before he turned thirteen because

---

10. Debie Thomas, "Advent Reflections," Washington National Cathedral Webinar, December 23, 2020, *www.cathedral.org*.

11. Ibid.

according to Jewish tradition, that's when boys become men. It was the only way. And as you know, we often hurt those we love the most, knowing that even during the Calvary moments of our own lives, they won't abandon us.

Friends, know that we can take comfort in the visions of Dame Julian of Norwich, the fourteenth-century English mystic. It was on her deathbed that Julian experienced visions of Christ becoming animate, flesh and blood, speaking to her from the crucifix that stood on her bedside table. During her eleventh Revelation she describes Jesus peering down from the cross to his right where Mary would have been standing on Calvary. Julian sees a ghostly Mary "exalted and noble and glorious and pleasing to him above all creatures"[12] when Christ says to Julian, "Wilt thou see how much I love her, that thou might rejoice with me in the love that I have in her and she in me?"[13] In the love Christ has for Mary, Julian recognizes how much Christ loves each and every human being, for he told her, "From eternity he knew he would die for love."[14]

There is no doubt that when the divine embodies flesh, there will be growing edges. Jesus experienced these throughout his short life.

His relationships—from Mary to John the Baptist, the disciples, to the religious authorities, and the Romans—they were complicated and/or fraught. He was not of this world, but he put on our flesh so that we would know that this is not all there is.

Jesus becomes hope incarnate in our moments of despair. He becomes the source of confidence when times are out of joint and we have lost our reason. He becomes mercy when we stray and cheat ourselves from that which is good. He becomes grace and showers us with it when we do not deserve it. He becomes love so that he we might clothe ourselves with it. The way death and life, grief and joy, dance nonstop with each other is guaranteed in this life of ours, but when we think we have reached our limit, as Mary surely did, Christ becomes the wonder that returns us to love, a love that was there since eternity. Amen.

---

12. Veronic Mary Rolf, *Julian's Gospel: Illuminating the Life & Revelations of Julian of Norwich* (Maryknoll, NY: Orbis Books, 2013), 378.

13. Ibid. (25:6–10.203).

14. Ibid., 377.

TIME TO BE OF A NEW MIND

The Very Rev. Randolph Marshall Hollerith
Third Sunday after the Epiphany, January 24, 2021

Today's readings are all about repentance, about turning from the old ways and embracing God's ways, about admitting our sin and finding new life. As Brian Maas writes in *The Christian Century*, repentance is "the heart of the message of John the Baptist, arrested as the passage from Mark (for today) begins (1:14–20). It is the first command of Jesus's preaching as he bursts upon the stage in Galilee. . . . It is the collective response of the people of Nineveh as they hear Jonah's reluctant proclamation in the streets of their city. And it is God's response to the Ninevites' decisive reaction to that proclamation. There's no escaping that throughout the day's text: there's a whole lotta repenting going on."[15]

When we think of Jonah, most of us don't get much beyond what we learned as kids—that Jonah was swallowed by a whale (the actual translation is big fish). But the story of Jonah is a story about judgment, repentance, and mercy. Jonah was commanded by God to go to Nineveh, the heart of the hated Assyrian Empire, and cry out against their wickedness. He was to proclaim God's judgment against them and demand they repent. But Jonah doesn't want to go, not because he is afraid for his own safety, but because he doesn't want to give the Ninevites a chance to repent, he wants to see them punished for their evil ways. As a result, he flees from God and is swallowed by that whale. When he is finally spit back on shore, he does as God commands, goes to Nineveh, and delivers God's word to them: "Forty days more, and Nineveh shall be overthrown" (Jon. 3:4). When the Ninevites do in fact repent, Jonah is furious because in his mind evil should be punished and the righteous rewarded. Bad things should happen to bad people and good things should happen to good people. Jonah understands God's judgment, what he can't wrap his head around is the extent of God's mercy.

---

15. Brian Maas, "Repentance at the Heart," *The Christian Century*, January 22, 2021.

In our lesson from Mark for this morning, Jesus arrived in Galilee and proclaimed, "The time is fulfilled, and the kingdom of God has come near; repent, and believe in the good news" (Mark 1:15). John the Baptist had been arrested, and Jesus was carrying on John's message. However, in this lesson the Greek word for repent is not the same as the repentance commanded of the Ninevites, it isn't about turning from one's wicked ways. The word Mark uses for repent is "metanoia," which means "to be of a new mind." Here Jesus is telling his followers that God's kingdom is coming, and they need to be transformed by God's love, they need to be of a new mind and leave behind the old. This metanoia is demonstrated by Simon and Andrew as they put down their nets, set aside their fishing boats. and become followers of Jesus.

I can't think of better lessons on this particular Sunday in January, four days after the inauguration of a new president, as our nation once again renews itself as it does every four years. Like the Ninevites, God wants us to turn from our wicked ways. Like Jonah, God wants us to understand that God's love and mercy are bigger than we can imagine. And like the disciples, we need to be of a new mind.

Friends, I think it is time for all of us to take a long hard look at ourselves, our behaviors, our values, our way of life, and repent. We need to be of a new mind, to listen to Jesus's call to all of us to take up the work of his kingdom, to live as people of faith. As Bishop Curry says, "To be a person of faith is to be the one who says, Why not? It is to refuse to accept and acquiesce to the way things often are. It is to pray and work for the way things could be."[16]

It is time to be of a new mind and realize that racism can't be rooted out of our society until each of us is willing to root it out of ourselves. It is time to be of a new mind and realize that if we don't defend truth, whether we like that truth or not, then we will be destroyed by lies. It is time to be of a new mind and confront the fact that our democracy cannot survive if we do not repent of our selfishness and greed and find ways to better share our national prosperity with all our citizens. It is time to be of a new mind and stop taking our democracy for granted, assuming that it will always be here. It is

16. Curry, *Love Is the Way*, 118.

time to be of a new mind and realize that patriotism doesn't mean America first, but as Steven B. Smith reminds us, "Patriotism teaches that real loyalty to our country involves virtues like civility, law abidingness, respect for others, responsibility, love of honor, courage and leadership."[17] It is time to be of a new mind and realize that when it comes to people we dislike, people we disagree with, people we dismiss—we need to learn as Jonah did that God in fact loves the people we hate. It is time to be of a new mind and offer compassion to the people whose experiences differ from ours, to set aside our fears in order to understand the fears of others, to silence our own egos long enough to understand and value the stories of others and not just our own.

Friends, we have been through so much in the past year. We are tired, worn out from the confinement of the pandemic, the grief of seeing so many people die from this virus, the stress of our national turmoil. It would be easy now to sit back and think that with a new year, a new administration, and a new vaccine, that life will get back to normal. But our God isn't calling us back to normal. The kingdom that Jesus proclaimed, the good news that he announced to our world two millennia ago, is breaking forth still, and we are supposed to be about the work of that kingdom. We are being called, just as Simon and Andrew were. Now is our opportunity to repent of our sins, learn from our mistakes, and get back to the work of kingdom building. The love that Jesus proclaimed is needed now more than ever. We must be bearers of that love, proclaimers of that love, living examples of that love.

As Bishop Curry writes in his book, *Love Is the Way*:

My job is to plant seeds of love, and to keep on planting, even— or especially—when bad weather comes. It's folly to think I can know the grand plan, how my small action fits into the larger whole. All I can do is check myself, again and again: Do my actions look like love? If they are truly loving, then they are part of the grand movement of love in the world, which is the movement of God in the world. In the church, I have reminded

---

17. Steven B. Smith, "The Two Enemies of Patriotism," *The Wall Street Journal*, January 23, 2021.

us that we are part of the movement that Jesus began, the Jesus Movement. And if that is so, we are part of a greater whole. And that means it doesn't all depend on us. . . . None of us can know where our witness to love might lead—what light we might bring to the world. Our job is to do our job, and to let God do God's job.[18]

Amen.

---

18. Curry, *Love Is the Way*, 199.

REPAIRERS OF THE BREACH IN 2021

The Rev. Canon Jan Naylor Cope
Fourth Sunday after the Epiphany, January 31, 2021

Today's gospel lesson depicts the inauguration of Jesus's public ministry. We know in the Gospel of Mark, things move along very quickly. They're often short on detail, and the action is always urgent. The first chapter of Mark is no exception. In the twenty verses that precede what you just heard this morning, Jesus is baptized in the River Jordan by John, proclaimed by God as God's own Son with whom God is well pleased. The Holy Spirit descends upon Jesus. He's driven into the wilderness where he is tempted. He recruits four disciples. That's in the first twenty verses!

As we pick it up today, Jesus and the disciples go to Capernaum to the synagogue and Jesus teaches. We hear very quickly that there's something different about him. The gospel writer makes it clear that there is authority in what Jesus has to offer that sets him apart. If that's not enough—after the people are reportedly astonished by that—Jesus, with a few words, calls out an unclean spirit in an unnamed man (Mark 1:21–28). The Holy Spirit drives out an unclean spirit, evil or otherwise, that is no match for what Jesus has to offer. Jesus quickly marries word and deed in his ministry, and his fame spreads throughout the Galilee. I think it's fair to say that Jesus makes quite a splash with his first appearance in the synagogue.

I was thinking and praying about that passage and remembered another time in this very Cathedral when someone fresh out of the gate made quite a splash, as well—although it wasn't intended to be so, and it turned out in a slightly different way. I'm remembering August of 2016 when Dean Randy Hollerith, for his very first Sunday, prepared to step up in this extraordinary pulpit to offer us a word. Now, a few days before the service, the Head Verger Torry Thomas and I met with Randy to walk him through the service so it would be familiar to him before Sunday came.

There was something Randy said when we were walking through the service that occasioned my telling him, "You know, on occasion, there are people who show up in the service who may not be totally well and will disrupt a service. But I don't want you to worry about that, new dean, because we have a protocol for that. If something happens, just know that we're on it. But, of course, it's rare and it won't happen." I'll never forget it: Randy said, "Oh, I come from an urban parish in Richmond. I'm accustomed to that." Sort of, been there, done that.

So, the great day comes with our new dean. He steps up into this pulpit and he just gets out, "Good morning. It's a joy to . . ." when three protestors show up out of nowhere and start making a ruckus. I couldn't believe it! In my mind, I'm thinking, are you kidding me? They weren't really that disruptive. Truthfully, they were really very peaceful. They had homemade signs that were small—I couldn't quite read what was on them—and they were singing a song. Thankfully, Randy didn't miss a beat. He picked right back up, and he showed all of us what grace and generosity look like under stress, and that has marked his ministry with us ever since.

But what particularly stays with me is the sermon he preached that day. You'll recall, in August of 2016, our country was terribly divided. We were in a very ugly presidential election, and things were getting unsettled all across the country. It was a tough time. Randy, on that day, chose the scripture passage from Isaiah 58 that was appointed for the day that calls us to be repairers of the breach. He made the important point that we were broken and that we were called to heal that which is broken in our own lives and broken in the lives of those around us. That this Cathedral would commit itself to being repairers of the breach; that we were called to be healers, reconcilers, peacemakers, seekers of justice, and bridge builders. It was a powerful message four-plus years ago. It's an urgent message today. I don't need to tell you how broken all of us are. Our country is broken. It's hurting, it's anxious, afraid, and many are quite angry. Never has this message been more important than it is today.

Our scriptures today offer us a glimpse and a reminder of a way forward. The passage from Deuteronomy (18:15–20) speaks to listening for the true prophet that's been offered—God's words of authority—that there will be false prophets, but we're not to be led astray. Jesus speaks shortly before the passage you heard today that the kingdom of God has come and that we are to repent, to be of a new mind, to be of a new purpose. The question for us is, who are we following? Who are we listening to? Whose are we?

As much as we all admire and respect our dean Randy Hollerith—and we do—he and we are clear. He's not the savior of this Cathedral. Jesus is. As much as I love my denomination, the Episcopal Church, we have our problems, too. As much as we admire and respect our presiding bishop Michael Curry—and we do—he and we are clear: he's not the savior of the Episcopal Church. Jesus is. As we look at our country that is so broken, it's important that we remember that no administration, no president, no group of elected officials, current or past, is the savior of our country.

Yes, they're responsible to lead us and represent us, but it's incumbent upon We the People to bring us together with God's help. As Christians, we follow Jesus. I think in this time when people are examining our Constitution to ensure our rights, that it's incumbent upon us to dust off the Decalogue—the Ten Commandments—to get our grounding and our bearings on what God and Jesus lift up as the core foundation of who we are and whose we are. The Ten Commandments make clear that there shall only be one God, no other gods before God. God is God, and we are not.

We are called not to steal, not to kill, not to bear false witness, not to lie, not to covet. You see, the Mosaic Law is grounded in those commandments. They show us what it means to be in right relationship with God and with one another. Jesus goes on to interpret and teach us what it means to follow him. He was an observant Jew. The Mosaic Law was his grounding, as it is ours. The largest body of Jesus's teaching in scripture comes in the Sermon on the Mount, beginning at the fifth chapter of the Gospel of Matthew. He teaches us much in that; he also says this, you have heard it said, "An eye for an eye and a tooth for a tooth." But I say to you, turn the other cheek, go the extra mile, love your enemies, and pray for those who persecute you.

Jesus never said it was going to be easy. He said it was essential. That if we were to bring about the kingdom of God in our time, those are our guideposts. Those are the goals that we try to bring about as best we can, one with another, with God's help. I know this is a challenging time. I know that we are broken. We are hurting and we are worried. Remember, also, that Jesus said he would never leave us or forsake us; that he would be with us always. We stand on that promise. We are not alone in this enterprise, and with God's help, we can do this together.

We're in the closing days of the season of Epiphany where we remember the light that came into the world and the darkness did not overcome it. It can't overcome it.

My brothers and sisters, look for the true light, follow the light and be the light.

We can do this with God's help. Amen.

ONE MOMENT CAN CHANGE EVERYTHING

The Rev. Canon Leonard L. Hamlin Sr.
Last Sunday after the Epiphany, February 14, 2021

I come this morning, humbled, yet grateful for this moment to be able to connect with my colleagues here and those who are joining us from your living rooms, your offices, and perhaps in many of the other places that have now been transformed from ordinary to extraordinary, from common to sacred.

Yet, as I come this morning—in my preparations I've wrestled with this subject, as all preachers do—what would I say? But preaching is not just subject. It is also tone. What would I say that would hit the right note that many of us, as we know, recognize that the church would make a certain sound? Because even in hitting the note from the resonance of that sound, there's vibration that comes. And I'm praying on this morning that we might be mindful of all that comes from a moment like this.

But I was also reminded that preaching is never without context. Perhaps it may be attempted without regard for context, but one of the challenges and charges for any preacher is to hear, to see, and to seek God within the contexts that are often recalled by us, experienced by us, faced by us, and in many moments, weighing upon us. And even through the contexts that are not clear in the future, that are calling to us on this Valentine's Day, in this month of Black history and on the heels of a week filled with conversations, exchanges, and questions, I found myself asking the primary question that I encourage all of us to ask.

I know it is a question that, like me, many of you have felt called to ask in many situations. It's a very simple question—"God, where are you in the midst of this?" This is a critical question for those journeying along the road of faith. It is *the* question we are more inclined to ask when moments are dark and difficulties of life are present. Perhaps it's an easy question for me to ask, as I consider the unique history being shared this month, because it is a question that has been intertwined in my experience, in the African American experience, in the faith journey of those who have come before me. It is one that has been asked over and over—"God, where are you?" It is also raised by those who have experienced life on the margins or who have been knocked down by life circumstances, whether momentary or lasting. At some point we have all asked—"God, where are you?" After being awakened by the question, we often find ourselves standing in the intersection where divinity and humanity meet. And we also ask a question that in this moment, perhaps, is best expressed by a spiritual that has been echoing through generations, as I hear the voice even today of one who would cry out, "Lord, how come me here?"[19]

I have often found myself in situations where I've asked, "God, where are you?" And then I've asked the question, "Lord, why am I in this moment?" It is in this intersection, this well-traversed intersection of life, where divinity is meeting humanity, that the preacher's task is to bring forth from the past the flame that will light the path going forward and not just hold the ashes of the difficult circumstances. Well, I was reminded by my good friend, Reverend Dr. Paul Smith, this week that memory is one of God's great gifts to the human spirit.[20] Today, I reached back hoping to grab the flame and not just pick up ashes. And I invite you to reach back with me and perhaps some of your memories that we might light the path forward and not just hold on to the ashes of difficult circumstances. I had to go seeking and asking this week. I had to ask, like many of you who are connected in this moment, "God, where are you? And Lord, how come we here?"

I have been asking in the face of hundreds of years of racial discrimination, prejudice, and injustice. I have been asking, "Lord, where are you?" while the burdens are still present, while I deal with this problem of the present past. I've had to go seeking and asking amid listening to the political posturing of recent days and the partisan divisions that will shape the future and the lives of adults and children in this land and perhaps around the world. I've wondered about the future and what the future will hold. I've had to go seeking and asking while witnessing the relational burdens of friends and colleagues reaching for one another, all the while working to show love for one another. I've had to go seeking and asking while trying to hold family together and fighting off the overwhelming feelings and concerns associated with the effects of all of the viral, economic, and racial pandemics, all seemingly showing up at the same time.

There are moments when it feels like everything is crashing together. I've lived long enough to experience emotional and spiritual

---

19. African American spiritual.

20. Paul Smith, personal conversation.

crashes. But I also know the literal pain of a physical crash. There are degrees of crashes, but I've experienced and focus in on the degree of a crash where you are left feeling trapped. I know that experience both physical and literal and in the spiritual. I know what it is to be trapped in circumstances, to feel it and to experience it. It is an overwhelming feeling to be trapped by circumstances and encounters.

It was now forty years ago that I was trapped after a physical crash. And in order to get out, the first responders had to use a tool called the jaws of life. These big cutters can cut away doors and give access to those who are hurting and suffering and in need of care. Well, my charge and my assignment as the preacher, my history and my faith, my family, and my foundation, reminded me that we all have a tool that we can use today. It is a tool that is able to help us cut through what is keeping us trapped. It is a tool that can be used to cut us out of what has trapped us, hurt us, and even separated us. It is a tool that, when used appropriately, can lift us, and as Howard Thurman would conclude, is "designed to be life affirming and not life denying."[21]

I invite you, no matter where you are, to join me for just a moment. You wonder what that tool is. It's simply the Bible. That tool is the gospel that has been read before you. It is that tool that can help us in our steps moving forward. It is the written word that sheds light on the living word. It is the passage that has been placed before us today. And we all have a tool that we can use. If we are not using it on ourselves, we can use it to help someone else in a difficult moment.

And so here today, I grabbed my Bible. And I hope you're joining me, whether you're on your couch or in your kitchens, no matter where you are, that you got this tool available to you and are prepared to use it, not just for yourself, but for those who may be hurting and who are around you in this moment of confusion and chaos. It is here in Mark's gospel (9:2–9).

We're invited to go up into the mountain with Jesus, Peter, James, and John. I invite you to do some climbing with me for just a moment. And I know there are times we all don't feel like climbing. We don't feel like moving because I want to just stay right where I am, because I want it to be delivered to me or brought down to me and made convenient for me. But in order to get what God is revealing, there are times where

---

21. Howard Thurman, *Essential Writings*, Modern Spiritual Masters Series (Maryknoll, NY: Orbis Books, 2006), 18.

he invites us to climb above the difficult, climb above the tough, climb above all that is going on, so that we can see beyond the problematic and the painful. So, I invite you to get a better view because it is true that your view expands the higher that you climb. And so, no matter where you are, there's an invitation before each of us. There's an invitation out of the gospel. There's an invitation that is living in the spirit to climb just a little bit higher than where we've been. Whether you're with family, whether you're with friends. No matter who you are in relationship with, there is a time that we're called to climb, that we might be in his presence and really live in the presence of one another.

After climbing in this text, Peter, James, and John reached a certain point where high up on this mountain it is recorded that Jesus was transfigured. His appearance was transformed and changed. His clothes were altered. Here, his presence was powerful. As Peter, James, and John stood in that moment in that space, Elijah and Moses showed up, and a divine conversation broke out. It was in that moment of being overwhelmed that once again, in all of his enthusiasm and perhaps his character, Peter shouted out to Jesus, "Rabbi, it is good for us to be here; let us make three dwellings, one for you, one for Moses, and one for Elijah" (Mark 9:5). Mark records that Peter did not know what to say for he was terrified. It was at that moment that a cloud shadowed them, and a voice rang out and declared, "This is my son, the beloved; listen to him!" (Mark 9:7).

What happened to Peter is a mistake that happens to us. This was a divine moment where Jesus was speaking, but instead of listening, he wanted to busy himself. Sometimes we're in such a hurry to do that, we forget that it's important to just be. Jesus was being transformed in order that they would listen and that they, and we, who are hearing today, would be transformed. It is not just about his transformation. It is about our transformation. They were still wrestling with who Jesus was. While at the same time, they may have been wrestling with who they knew themselves to be. I would often tell my former congregation to not concern yourself with what people say about you. Concern yourself with what God is saying to you, because folk are going to talk about you, no matter what you do. And there are times that when we are walking in his likeness, people will give him something to talk about.

In certain moments, we say, "Don't just sit there, do something." But I say this morning, it is also true that there are times that in order to find our way, in order to see our way, in order to acknowledge the way, the truth, and the life, we need to say, "Don't just do something. Sit there." Peter wanted to do work with his hands when he had not first done the work of his heart. The acknowledgment and the celebration of human doings should never be a good substitute for the acknowledgment and celebration of human beings. And sometimes our human doings are just substitutes for what it really means to be human beings. There's a difference between doing and being. Just because we are doing doesn't mean that we're truly being. We have made significant progress in celebrating our doings, but limited progress in celebrating our being.

When I think of all who are listening, acknowledging the week that has gone by, and recognizing the witness of faith that has been lifted during this Black History Month . . . when I think of those who have gone before me, the presence of love that is being talked about on Valentine's Day . . . there has always been a searching for God and a reaching for one another. There are moments where we must reach back and grab the flame and not pick up the ashes. I reached back this morning and grabbed the flame. And I hear this morning those who kept reaching as they would seek out and create sacred space when they were denied space. I reached back and I still hear the voices of those as they would lift, "It's me, it's me, it's me, oh, Lord. Standing in the need of prayer. Not my mother, not my father, but it's me, oh, Lord. Standing in the need of prayer."[22] I reached back, and I still hear the voices, and in this place echoing around, I can feel their presence as they would under the cover of night and in divine corners and perhaps even in prayer closets steal away to Jesus. Even though many would cry out, "Sometimes I feel like a motherless child," and declare, "Nobody knows the trouble I've seen."[23] Somehow through the mysterious and miraculous and powerful perspective of faith that was available to them, they would declare, "I don't feel no ways tired."[24]

Well, today my back is straightening up a little bit. In this moment, my head is lifted a little bit higher because I'm standing in his presence. You're in his presence in your home. You're in his presence with the family and neighbors that are around you. And today, you ought to be able to move just a little bit more and move a little bit further by saying,

---

22. African American spiritual.

23. African American spiritual.

24. African American spiritual.

"I don't feel no ways tired," because faith should not limit what we see or who we have been created to be.[25] Faith should help expand what we see and give us the confidence in our being. Faith should steady our steps as we seek to move out into places that some would call difficult, as we seek to walk on water, as we seek to walk in this journey called life.

I remind you, and I lift today noted African American preacher and justice leader Vernon Johns. He preached a sermon years ago at the Hampton University's Minister's Conference and titled it, "Human Destiny." As part of that sermon, he said, as he gave witness, "Now, you know, your definition of home enlarges as you travel. If a man were to ask me in Baltimore, 'Where do you live?' I would say 1134 McCulloh Street. If he asked me that same question in New York, 'Where do you live?' I would say in Baltimore. If he asked me in Canada, 'Where do you live?' I would look back at him and I would say in the United States of America. If he asks me while I traveled into Europe, 'Where do you live?' I would say in America." He went on to say that you see your definition of home enlarges as you move out. And so, he says, "If my little grandchild heard that I had passed on and asked what happened to granddad, I would like for my granddaughter to say, that which drew him out of the boundless deep, turned home again."[26]

And, you know, as I get older and I stand with him today, I'd like to say, as someone has said, I'd like to think God is my home. So, I invite you to step out of where you are, and God would be your home. I think of my father on this day, I think of my parents today. I'm thankful for an aunt who is turning ninety-seven this year, who I know it is her faith that has kept her, her faith that has held her through difficult situations. And growing up, I remember my father being alone in the kitchen while I was doing homework out in the dining room. He would often sing about the old rugged cross. But I remember today how he would get there and in his old, great baritone voice, remembering his father, grandfather, those who had come before him, the legacy passed from generation to generation. And I didn't plan on this, but he would say:

[Singing] "Tis the old ship of Zion. Tis the old ship of Zion. Tis the old ship of Zion. Get on board. Get on board."[27]

---

25. African American spiritual.

26. Paraphrased from Henry H. Mitchell, "Black Preaching" (Philadelphia: J. B. Lippincott, 1970), 99.

27. African American spiritual.

5

Hope on the Horizon

THE COST OF LOVE

The Very Rev. Randolph Marshall Hollerith
Second Sunday in Lent, February 28, 2021

In our gospel for this morning (Mark 8:31–38), Peter was looking for a quick fix and an instant answer to his people's political problems. He was under the false assumption that to end the Roman occupation of Israel, all you had to do was find the promised Messiah, fire up the crowds, mix in a little armed revolt, and the Jewish people could be free. Now, Peter knew that Jesus was the Messiah. In the verses just before our reading for today, he says as much, and he is the first of the disciples to do so. But Peter's idea of Messiah and the reality of Jesus were very different. Peter was sure the Messiah would be a great general and leader, a charismatic figure who would rally the Jewish people, lead an insurrection, and toss out the hated Roman invaders. What he learns and cannot stomach in our lesson for this morning is that Jesus the Messiah hasn't come to lead them into battle and wage war, rather he has come to lay down his own life, to suffer and die, in order to walk the way of love.

When Jesus announces this fundamentally different understanding of Messiah to his disciples, Peter pulls him aside and rebukes him. It's understandable. Put yourself in Peter's shoes. As the Rev. Dr. Jon Burnham points out, "Imagine that your country has been invaded and is being ruled by godless men. Sense, now, that the tension is mounting, and you are about to go into battle. That you are about to conduct a coup d'état. That you (and the other disciples) are going to attempt to overthrow this government by a sudden violent strike. That the odds are stacked against you, but you have a very strong belief that God is on your side," because the Messiah has come, and his name is Jesus.[1]

---

1. Sermon by the Rev. Dr. Jon Burnham, Pastor, St. John's Presbyterian Church, Houston, Texas, March 8, 2009.

When Peter pulls Jesus aside and challenges him with this vision of military might and political power, Jesus knows that the temptation to earthly power the devil plagued him with for forty days and forty nights in the wilderness has come back to plague him in the words of Peter. Turning on his friend, Jesus says to him, "Get behind me, Satan! . . . For you are setting your mind not on divine things but on human things" (Matt. 16:22). Jesus goes on to tell Peter and the other disciples that not only must the Son of Man suffer and die, but if they want to follow him, then they too will need to pick up their crosses and willingly suffer for the way of love. Because those who want to save their life will lose it, and those who lose their life for the sake of the gospel, will save it.

This is a powerful passage. It is in fact the center point of Mark's gospel, and from this moment on Jesus turns his face toward Jerusalem and the cross. So, let's take a deeper look and ask, what does Jesus mean when he says, "the Son of Man must undergo great suffering and . . . be killed" (Mark 8:31)? There is a theory that's been widespread in the church for centuries that says—Jesus must suffer and die because God needs someone to pay the debt for our sins. It's called "substitutionary atonement" and it goes something like this: we rang up a big debt of sin with God, a debt we couldn't repay, and so God sent his son to be killed in our place as the substitute sacrifice for our sins. In short, Jesus comes to die to pay our debts to God.

The truth is, I've never liked this theory very much. Because, if our God is the God of love, as scripture tells us, then love doesn't need payment in order to forgive. Love doesn't demand suffering and death in order to forgive. On the contrary, love forgives despite everything, freely, completely, and without strings attached. No, when Jesus told his disciples that he must suffer and die, what he pointed out for them was that his way of love—his way of peaceful, open-handed, truth-telling, sickness-healing, justice-seeking, poor-protecting love—this kingdom of love that he came to reveal to us—was not something the powerful could abide; it threatened their very existence, and so they killed him for it. Jesus's suffering and death were not to be the price paid to forgive sins; they were the cost of love.

On this Sunday when we give thanks for the work and legacy of Historically Black Colleges and Universities, I can think of no finer examples of what I am talking about then the men and women who came out of so many of these institutions and walked Jesus's way of love in their struggle for civil rights. Medgar Evers out of Alcorn State, Mordecai Johnson and Howard Thurman out of Howard University, Septima Clark out of Benedict College, Martin Luther King Jr. out of Morehouse College, Thurgood Marshall out of Lincoln University in Pennsylvania, and John Lewis out of American Baptist College in Nashville, just to name the tip of the iceberg. Individuals determined to change the world, to fight for justice, to end oppression, not through violence and hatred, but through nonviolent protest and love. And just like Jesus, some of them paid with their lives.

One of the books I have enjoyed reading the most during these days of pandemic has been Jon Meacham's *His Truth Is Marching On: John Lewis and the Power of Hope.* It's a powerful book that tells the story of a remarkable man who lived in hope and dedicated his life to the struggle for justice. Among other things, it tells the story of how a young John Lewis was trained by James Lawson in the ways of nonviolence. The same James Lawson who later drafted a statement of principles for the Student Nonviolent Coordinating Committee, or SNCC, that said in part:

> Nonviolence as it grows from Judaic-Christian traditions seeks a social order of justice permeated by love. . . . Through nonviolence, courage displaces fear; love transforms hate. Acceptance dissipates prejudice; hope ends despair. Peace dominates war; faith reconciles doubt. Mutual regard cancels enmity. Justice for all overthrows injustice. . . . Love is the central motif of nonviolence. Love is the force by which God binds man to Himself and man to man. Such love goes to the extreme; it remains loving and forgiving even in the midst of hostility. It matches the capacity of evil to inflict suffering with an even more enduring capacity to absorb evil, all the while persisting in love.[2]

Lawson taught Lewis that the bigotry, discrimination, and hatred experienced by so many African Americans then, and unfortunately still to this day, could only be defeated by love, Christ-like love. As John Lewis

---

2. Jon Meacham, *His Truth Is Marching On: John Lewis and the Power of Hope* (New York: Random House, 2020), 126.

would later say, "Hate is too heavy a burden to bear. If you start hating people, you have to decide who you are going to hate tomorrow, who you are going to hate next week? Just love everybody. Or as King said, 'just love the hell out of everybody, it's the better way. It's the best way.'"[3]

My friends, we need Jesus's way of love now more than ever. We've seen too much violence, anger, and hatred in the past year. The world needs a better way, and we are the ones being asked to take up our crosses and follow Jesus. We are being asked to take up our own sufferings, our own hurts, our own struggles, and in spite of them to walk the way of love. To carry them with us as we set about working for justice, peace, and the dignity of every human being. Just as the disciples were being asked by Jesus to lose their lives, their lives of "petty jealousies and fear and suspicion and competition and anxiety and arrogance and pride and greed and envy and anger and vengeance," as Dr. Robert Pace writes, because their lives focused too much on these things. So our lives focus too much on these things as well. We are called instead to turn our attention to divine things—love of God, love of neighbor, forgiveness.[4] Jesus came to show us that this is the only way. It may mean that we must lose something of our own lives to do it, but we will find Christ's life in the process. And, when all is said and done, that is the only life worth living. Amen.

---

3. Ibid., 118.

4. The Rev. Dr. Robert Pace, "Losing Our Lives for Good," Sermon, St. Andrew's Episcopal Church, Amarillo, Texas, February 25, 2018.

REJOICE AND REMEMBER

THE REV. CANON ROSEMARIE LOGAN DUNCAN
Fourth Sunday in Lent, March 14, 2021

Today we are in the middle of our annual Lenten journey. This Fourth Sunday of Lent is often referred to as Laetare Sunday, from the Latin word meaning rejoice. We are invited to rejoice and to enter more deeply into the mystery of God's grace, mercy, and love.

Our gospel contains one of the most quoted citations used on banners, on books, on posters, and bumper stickers, John 3:16, "For God so loved the world that he gave his only Son, so that everyone who believes in him may not perish but may have eternal life." We rejoice because this single verse reminds us that the heart of the gospel is God's love and our belief. But there's more to today's gospel than that. Our reading opens with words that seem somehow out of place, as we have been dropped in the middle of a conversation. To understand our gospel pericope, it is good to place it within the wider context of John 3. In the beginning verses of this chapter, Nicodemus, the Pharisee, approached Jesus at night. Nicodemus acknowledged Jesus as someone who had come from God because of all the miraculous signs he performed. Jesus gets to the heart of the matter by responding with: ". . . no one can see the kingdom of God without being born from above" (John 3:3).

Nicodemus, thinking literally and physically, cannot process or make sense of these words. Jesus continues the conversation, teaching Nicodemus about the need to be born of the Spirit, but Nicodemus is still perplexed. Jesus laments that Nicodemus cannot seem to grasp such a heavenly concept and then recalls the moment in our first lesson from the book of Numbers which Nicodemus would have known to illustrate his point. Jesus draws a parallel between the way that Moses lifted up the serpent on a pole to heal the Israelites and the way that he too, as the Son of Man, will be lifted up. For Jesus, both images—the serpent and the cross—are reminders of the saving action of God.

And in looking upon Jesus, we too, like the Israelites, must face our own sin and trust in God's provision. Without that, we cannot see Jesus for who he truly is. We must look up. In this gospel, John suggests that what keeps us from looking up is our preference to live in the shadows. We hide behind the things we trust—power, greed, pride, authority, security, comfort—instead of putting our full trust in God. Leaving the shadows, stepping out of darkness means being seen for all that we are, most notably, those aspects we'd prefer to hide. And isn't that what Lent demands of us? If we want to live into the life God promises for us, then we need to look at our lives directly, seeing the good and bad—the pain and the hope mingled together. We have to, at some point, face our own sin—our own mistakes—our own brokenness. It has been suggested that our hearts must be broken first for the word of God to fall in the cracks.[5] God didn't send his Son to the world to condemn or judge the world. Instead, he came as the light of the world to save us, as our gospel proclaims.

So much of life seems like an ongoing task of finding the light in the darkness. I know that's how this last year has felt. On Thursday, the world noted the one-year anniversary of the World Health Organization's official declaration of the COVID-19 pandemic and the associated shutdowns, including this Cathedral building.

There is something to be said for noting anniversaries; they are important as they anchor the human experience, provide meaning and context to events that impact the individual, families, communities, nations, and importantly, people of faith. Marking important moments of our past allows us to claim times that bind and unite us together with one another and to God. We can experience a variety of emotions, and when we are our best selves, we have the capacity to reflect, grieve, celebrate, remember, recommit, and hopefully learn to be better.

We have lived in a pandemic state for a year, and in the process we have lost over five hundred thirty-two thousand of our fellow sisters, brothers, and siblings in this country. None of us imagined how long and how painful this time would be. And with the backdrop of a health crisis, a new generation has been exposed to the reality that institutional and societal structures of inequality—racial, political, economic, cultural, and more—continue to keep us separated one from another. We continue to look for the light in our darkness even as the hope of multiple vaccines is dampened by disparities in access and distribution. Fractures that we as a nation have tried to bury are now more visible—brought into the light.

These issues are not new. The denial of equal rights connects us to another anniversary of the past week, that of the fifty-sixth anniversary of Bloody Sunday—March 7, 1965, when civil rights marchers were brutally

---

5. Ellen F. Davis, *Getting Involved with God: Rediscovering the Old Testament* (Cambridge, MA: Cowley Publications, 2001), 169.

beaten by law enforcement officers on Selma's Edmund Pettus Bridge. The day became a turning point in the fight for voting rights. Footage of the march broadcast across the country helped galvanize support for passage of the Voting Rights Act of 1965. This year's commemoration was the first without John Lewis, who up to his death, encouraged us all to engage in good trouble, necessary trouble when faced with injustice anywhere. For what we don't learn from our past, we are destined to repeat.

And yesterday, many took to the streets remembering the senseless death of Breonna Taylor, whose life was tragically cut short, as they called for justice, accountability, and continued reform between law enforcement and communities.

While each of these anniversaries has touched us this year to different degrees, the most personal anniversary for me is that of losing Bishop Barbara Clementine Harris who joined the saints a year ago yesterday. The first female bishop of the Anglican communion, Bishop Harris served as suffragan bishop of the Diocese of Massachusetts from 1989 to 2002 and assisting bishop here in the Diocese of Washington from 2003 to 2007. Active in the civil rights movement of the 1960s, she registered voters in Mississippi and participated in a portion of the fifty-mile march from Selma to Montgomery.[6] Bishop Harris was a self-proclaimed advocate for "the least, the lost and the left out." Sounds a lot like what we are called to as followers of Jesus. She wrote, "If we can believe that Jesus, who died, rose again from the dead . . . then we can, in peace, give over those who have died—known and unknown—to a loving, compassionate and ever-merciful God who has prepared for us a better home than this Good Friday world."[7]

In all that has happened over this year, the words of our gospel still ring true: "For God so loved the world that he gave his only Son, so that everyone who believes in him may not perish but may have eternal life." The work of these last weeks of our Lenten journey is acceptance of God's love for us—God's divine presence in our lives. Today we are called to behold what God has done, is doing, and will do for you and me in the cross of Christ. On this Fourth Sunday in Lent when we are to rejoice, let us open our hearts and listen to the promises of our loving God. Amen.

---

6. Barbara C. Harris with Kelly Brown Douglas, *HALLELUJAH, ANYHOW! A Memoir* (New York: Church Publishing, 2018), 52.

7. Tracy J. Sukraw, "Barbara C. Harris: Remembering an Irrepressible 'First' and Tireless Advocate for Justice," Diocese of Massachusetts News, Episcopal Diocese of Massachusetts, March 14, 2020, *www.diomass.org*.

REAL LOVE

The Rev. Canon Rosemarie Logan Duncan
Maundy Thursday, April 1, 2021

Our liturgy this night is one of endings and beginnings. What began on Ash Wednesday is brought to a close here. What begins tonight does not end until the resurrection of Easter. We began our journey remembering our mortal nature marked as a reminder of who and whose we are. We begin tonight invited to remember the story of a meal shared, feet washed, and of the ultimate gift of love. Why then is remembering so important?

To remember is to bring something to mind, to look back on something in the past—sometimes deliberate; sometimes spontaneous—it can be an event, information, feeling, or experience. Remembering has the power to take the past and bring it forward into the present moment—the power to provide identity and purpose. And in remembering the past, our present lives can be forever changed. Tonight, we remember—for that is what we are called to do as God's people this Maundy Thursday.

Each of our readings contains this very theme of remembrance. In the first reading from Exodus, we hear the instructions given to the people of Israel gathering for the Passover meal that ends with this instruction: "This day shall be a day of remembrance for you. You shall celebrate it as a festival to the Lord; throughout your generations you shall observe it as a perpetual ordinance" (Exod. 12:14).

In our reading from Paul's first letter to the Corinthians, we hear how, on the night he was betrayed, Jesus gathered his disciples around the table, offered his body and blood, and said, "Do this in remembrance of me" (1 Cor. 11:24). But the message in our gospel is the reason we refer to this day as Maundy Thursday. "Maundy," which comes from the Latin word *mandatum*, meaning "mandate" or "commandment." In our gospel, Jesus washes feet and commands love in remembrance. This is his new commandment: "Love one another; even as I have loved you, you also must love one another" (cf. John 13:34).

Tonight we also remember that this is the second Maundy Thursday we have experienced in this extended time of COVID-19. As we gathered last year, we could not have imagined how very similar we were to the disciples on the night that Jesus gathered them together. Like them, we faced an uncertain time, a frightening time, a time marked by physical separation, isolation, suffering, and yes, death.

The uncertainty of our experience is something that the disciples would come to understand as well. From our gospel, we understand that Jesus knew things were about to change in his life and the lives of his disciples. Taking the form of a servant, washing their feet, Jesus calls them to something new and yes, rather shocking—calls them to an act of humility out of love. He was also teaching them about vulnerability; about opening self to receive the life of another. After Peter's protest, Jesus says, "You do not know now what I am doing, but later you will understand. . . . Unless I wash you, you have no share with me" (John 13:7–8).

Jesus's actions are punctuated with a sense of urgency. From the opening sentence from our gospel—"Jesus knew that his hour had come to depart from this world and go to the Father. Having loved his own who were in the world, he loved them to the end" (John 13:1)—Jesus loved them to the fullest extent possible; loved them with every fiber of his being, even to suffering death on the cross. Such love is total and unconditional.

The love Jesus exercises with the disciples is a reconciling love. They don't fully understand what he is doing in this moment. They can't grasp the significance of the Last Supper or his washing of their feet or what he means with this new commandment. But their eyes will be opened to the true meaning and significance of his words and actions soon enough. The love Jesus asks the disciples to exercise is the love he exercised toward them—a love that breathes new life into relationships that are broken. A love that not only repairs and restores, but also heals, transforms, and strengthens.

As he shared a last meal and took the role of a servant, Jesus showed his disciples how to remain in relationship with him, with each other, and with those he came to serve even after he would no longer be with them. A new normal was about to begin. They would be on their own without him, sent out to look at others the way Jesus looks at them.

Jesus taught the disciples the lesson they needed to know and a lesson that we have also learned: that relationships aren't based on proximity. If anything, we have learned to reach across the miles to connect and to even have moments of joy in the midst of our separation. Our ability to remain connected, though, is all about love. Jesus taught that evening that love is the unifying agent—a love that has no limits or bounds.

What we have learned this year in our separation is the deep desire and longing for intimacy and closeness with others and with God. We've come to see that feet have been washed in new ways of service throughout the world. Strangely enough, it took a pandemic to remind us of what really matters, of what is really essential in our lives—essential to our faith.

If we remember nothing else, we know that we are always united by bonds of faith, hope, and love, for there is no social distancing with Jesus.

This night we remember what Jesus wanted his disciples to understand—that real love, and real faith, and real discipleship mean one thing and one thing alone: it means servanthood rooted in love. Just as Jesus had told them earlier, "I am among you as one who serves" (Luke 22:27), he now puts these words into action. Even for us, over two thousand years later, nothing has really changed about what real love is and how Jesus calls us to demonstrate it to others. Indeed, if we want to know what it means to follow Jesus, the mandate is clear. It means being willing to serve others with the open heart of love. And when we learn to serve, we learn to live.

As we continue our journey to the cross, may we remember this night the great gift of love received and the command to share it. For by this, everyone will know that we are his disciples. Amen.

RESURRECTION BEGINS WHILE IT'S STILL DARK

The Rt. Rev. Mariann Edgar Budde
Easter Day, April 4, 2021

Then Peter began to speak to them: "I truly understand that God shows no partiality, but in every nation anyone who fears him and does what is right is acceptable to him." (Acts 10:34)

But by the grace of God I am what I am, and his grace toward me has not been in vain. On the contrary, I worked harder than any of them—though it was not I, but the grace of God that is with me. Whether then it was I or they, so we proclaim and so you have come to believe. (1 Cor. 15:10-11)

Early on the first day of the week, while it was still dark, Mary Magdalene came to the tomb and saw that the stone had been removed from the tomb. (John 20:1)

Given all that you are holding in your heart right now and all that is happening in our world, it might help to know, or remember, that resurrection is a process, not an event, and it begins while it is still dark.

The first stirrings of new life of hope and possibility are hidden from us, like the first sprouts from a seed that haven't yet broken through the soil, or the healing that's taking place while we're still in pain. We may not feel anything at first. Think of Mary rising early that first Easter morning, if she slept at all, and walking toward Jesus's tomb with no expectation that there would be anything other than the somber work of grief waiting for her there. That's how resurrection begins, below the surface of our awareness.

We often speak of Mary as the first witness to the Resurrection, which she was, but she was more than a witness. Walking toward the empty tomb while it was still dark, Mary was as much a part of the first resurrection as Jesus rising from the dead. Mary was rising, too.

Rest assured that God will summon us as well, wake us up in the middle of the night, if need be, and propel us forward before we realize that anything has changed. God doesn't want us to miss the opportunity to choose life again.

Movement is key in resurrection. Sometimes our bodies know what to do before our minds can take in what's happening. Both Jesus and Mary were moving forward. "Don't hold onto me, Mary," he said when they met in the garden (John 20:17). There was no looking back for him, no standing still. A friend said to me recently, "I will go anywhere as long as it's forward." That is the stirring of resurrection.

In the third chapter of the Gospel of John, Jesus says that we can only speak of what we know and testify to what we have seen. If we are to speak of resurrection, we need to experience it. I've been thinking all week about what I can say, from experience, about resurrection. This is still a work in progress, but here goes.

First, let me say what I can about the context, our human condition.

We live in a world of profound contradictions—intense beauty and harsh, unforgiving natural phenomenon, a seemingly natural order of things and mind-boggling chaos. Within every human being, there lies the full range of human possibility—our highest aspirations and our most base behavior, not to mention all that is mediocre and merely boring.

As human beings, we are capable of exquisite artistic expressions, brilliant scientific discovery, and breathtaking physical accomplishment, *and* of petty mean-spiritedness, unspeakable cruelty, and horrific acts of war. We are both self-centered and altruistic, stingy and generous, anxious and brave. We like to think of ourselves as agents of our own destiny, yet we are susceptible to forces of social manipulation that prey on our insecurities and inspire crowd behavior that later bring us shame. We are both sinner and saint; we can be hopelessly lost and miraculously found.

There is more suffering in this world than any heart should hold. None of us is spared suffering, some of which we bring on ourselves, and far too much that we inflict on others through personal and systemic patterns of what scripture calls sin—all the ways we fail one another, ourselves, and God.

Into this wondrous, confusing, beautiful, and broken world, God comes to us. To those called to follow him, God comes in the person of Jesus. As he came as a human being over two thousand years ago, who, as the author of Acts (10:38) describes, "went around doing good," he comes to us now, as the Risen Christ. He comes in solidarity and judgment. He comes with forgiveness, exhortation, unconditional love, bringing gifts of resilience and mercy.

Jesus doesn't take away our suffering. I wish he did, but he doesn't. Instead, he holds it with us, and goes down with us, when we are forced down, even to the point of death—our physical death, yes, but also all the other deaths we experience as we live.

But then, while it is still dark, we find ourselves rising and moving forward.

We may not realize what's happening at first, but gradually it dawns on us that something is different, something is happening. It's as if we're being carried for a time, or led, or invited to walk through a door that we didn't know was there. It feels disorienting and unfamiliar at first. Sometimes we resist because we've grown accustomed to the dark. But whatever it is that's stirring in us beckons us on and we go. There is some sorrow involved and a part of us doesn't want to, for a whole host of reasons. But there's this energy propelling us forward on a new road. It's not an easy road, because life is never easy. But it's life, there for us to choose and to live.

My first experiences of what theologians call this "cruciform" reality of death and resurrection were small and deeply personal. Like all of you, I've known the death of a dream, the death of relationships, the loss of some physical capabilities that I treasured, and losses of other kinds. Once amid devastating grief, I stumbled into a church at Easter and heard a sermon on little deaths and little resurrections, which the preacher described as practice for the ultimate resurrection that awaits us all. It was all rather corny, truth be told, but for the first time in months, I found myself willing to believe that I could live again. Amazingly so, a new life slowly emerged, and I found myself moving slowly toward it.

It wasn't the first time I had experienced a kind of resurrection, nor the last. You'd think it would get easier with experience, but each loss is a fresh one, and each journey through the dark is just as dark as the last. But it does become familiar. More than that, it becomes a way of life and of looking at the world, through the lens of the cross and resurrection.

This pattern of cross and resurrection as a way of life is important for us to hold onto now when we are on the precipice of so much societal stirring and suffering all around. For resurrection is not an individual journey; it is communal. As important as our individual resurrection experiences are, resurrection's goal is what Jesus called the kingdom of God and what Dr. Martin Luther King Jr. called the Beloved Community—a world aligned with God's dream, God's love, God's justice for all humankind.

Just as we have a part to play in our own rising, we do in bringing about the kingdom of God and creating Beloved Community. We realize this whenever we find or place ourselves, like Jesus, in situations of sorrow and suffering, of brokenness and injustice, and when we accept that suffering as the cost of love and societal transformation.

Resurrection flows through us when we show up in places that seem beyond hope, where it's still dark and we cannot see. Resurrection occurs when, stirred by a power that is not ours, we find ourselves walking toward a new horizon alongside other people, toward the dream God has for us all.

No one knew the promise of communal suffering and resurrection better than Dr. Martin Luther King Jr. who was assassinated fifty-three years ago today, April 4, 1968. What a poignant contrast to have our Easter celebration on the same day of that searing memory, and a fitting one after a year of so much loss. I can't stop thinking about King and the last week of his life that began in this pulpit and ended with a bullet on the balcony of the Lorraine Hotel.

King believed in the power of what he called "redemptive suffering," suffering, like that of Jesus, for love and justice. He walked in faith toward the dream not only given to him, but all who long for freedom, human decency, and the opportunity to realize their God-given potential. He continued toward that dream when darkness returned again and again, which it did with vengeance in the last year of his life. He wasn't a perfect man, we know that, but he never seemed to veer from the path of sacrificial love and redemptive suffering. He believed in it for himself, for his own people, and incredibly enough, in his generous heart, for everyone else. He never gave up on love.

King's faith, while communal, was also deeply personal. One of the last requests he made before he died was for singer Mahalia Jackson to sing his favorite song at that night's prayer meeting:

> Precious, Lord, take my hand.
> Lead me on. Help me stand.
> I am weak, I am tired, I am worn.
> Through the dark, through the night.
> Lead me on, to the light.
> Take my hand, precious Lord, lead me home.[8]

---

8. "Precious Lord, Take My Hand." George N. Allen (1812–1871), arr. Roy Ringwald (1910–1995). Joyce Merman. Copyright 1968, Shawnee Press. Reprinted under One License #A-709283.

God calls each one of us to walk toward the dawn, while it's still dark, trusting that it will not always be night. God beckons us to rise for ourselves and for others, in fulfillment of God's dream. As followers of Jesus, we are called to his way, a life of sacrificial, healing love.

So, take heart this Easter morning, no matter where you are on the resurrection road. Christ is Risen and so have you. God is God, and by the grace of God you are who you are, called by Jesus to walk toward the light even while it's still dark.

HOPE ON THE HORIZON

The Rev. Canon Jan Naylor Cope
Second Sunday of Easter, April 11, 2021

One week ago, we gathered in a joyful celebration of our Lord's resurrection. We boldly and joyfully proclaimed that he is Risen. The Lord is Risen indeed! Here we are, one week later, the Second Sunday of Easter, and like Thomas, we haven't seen Jesus. But do we believe and do we live our lives as if we do? "To believe"—taken from a Greek root meaning "to give one's heart to." It's more than just feelings. It's about ourselves, all of us, that we give our heart to the belief that Christ lives. Jesus lives.

As we reflect on where we find ourselves today, I think it's important to reflect on where we've been, acknowledge where we are, and turn an eye toward hope on the horizon or possibly hope that is even at our doorstep—if we stay open and look for it. One year ago, Presiding Bishop Michael Curry preached an Easter sermon that was roughly two or three weeks after the entire global community locked down because of a global COVID pandemic. On that Easter Sunday, he said, "It may not look like it. It may not smell like it. It may not even really feel like it, but it's Easter, anyway." Who could have imagined a year ago, the year that we experienced together: a year of lament—the longest year of lament and loss that I think any of us have ever experienced.

Yet, Easter is here, anyway. Last Sunday, Bishop Mariann, in a very thoughtful sermon, reminded us that Easter and resurrection are a process, not a moment. It always begins in the dark. Over the course of a year, we've experienced, yes, the pandemic and loss from COVID, but it also laid bare, in plain sight, the pandemic of racism and social injustice. We have much kingdom work to do. Our gospel lesson today (John 20:19–31) gives us a glimpse of how we go about that. Of course, the gospel lesson appointed for today is always the gospel lesson for the Second Sunday of Easter. It's familiar to all of us. Unfortunately, it tends to get shorthanded into the story about doubting Thomas. If we look at it carefully, it's less about Thomas's doubts or anyone else's and much more about Jesus's grace and generosity. Jesus met the disciples and Thomas and you and me right where we are. In the past year, a metaphor for us might've been where we find the disciples: locked behind closed doors, full of fear.

Into that fear, Jesus offers the words: peace, forgiveness. "Peace be with you. As the Father has sent me, so I send you." Then he breathes the Holy Spirit on all gathered to go out empowered by that Holy Spirit to do the work God had given them to do. So, too, we have the Holy Spirit in Jesus's presence in our midst, to go out to do the kingdom work we've been sent to do. But we understand that that's going to be a process and not a singular event.

In a recent interview on "On Being," Krista Tippett was in conversation with a clinical psychiatrist and professor at the University of Massachusetts Medical School, Christine Runyan.[9]

They talked about what's happened over the course of the past year: that we have a nervous system—all of us—that immediately responds to threat. When a global pandemic is announced, our nervous systems kick in immediately with stress responses commonly known as fight or flight. Part of the problem is that those stressors have remained with us. As a result, we have experienced things like loss of memory, a drop in productivity, maybe even a few of us have been crankier than one might expect us to be normally, along with isolation and depression. All have been hallmarks of this experience and time together. So, if you felt any of those things, know that you're in good company. We want it to be over, but it's not yet. Dr. Runyan said that we're trying to grieve a trauma that's ongoing.

I can't tell you how many people have reached out to the Cathedral to ask us if we're going to have some national service of grief around COVID. We all want it to be over and it's not yet. But hope is on the horizon. How are we preparing ourselves to step out when it is safe for us to do so? How do we open up those locked doors that have held us in fear? In a recent column in *The New York Times*, David Brooks talked about his own experience of this. He made the observation that when we are engaged in something larger than ourselves, our lives have meaning and purpose. We begin to see those moments of hope and resurrection, if you will.[10]

---

9. Krista Tippet, interview with Christine Runyan, "What's Happening in Our Nervous Systems," *On Being*, March 16, 2021. *https://onbeing.org/programs/christine-runyan-whats-happening-in-our-nervous-systems.*

10. David Brooks, "How Covid Can Change Your Personality," opinion, *New York Times,* April 1, 2021), *www.nytimes.com.*

Isn't that true of all of us? For me, resurrection came into full blossom last Sunday. Easter Sunday in the afternoon. The Cathedral has been shut for over a year. We've been broadcasting online as we are today, but for the first time we offered what we called curbside communion. We had two different communion opportunities available. On the north side of the Cathedral, we had walk-up communion. On the south side of the Cathedral, people drove up and received communion. I was on the north side of curbside communion, where people walked up. Much like we read in scripture with the post-Resurrection experiences, at first, with all of our masks and not seeing people for a year, it was a little difficult to identify and recognize people—much like Mary in the garden with Jesus. She didn't recognize the resurrected Christ until he called her by her name, Mary. With some of you all masked up, it was when I heard your voice and you called me by name, Jan, that I could truly see you and know you and rejoice.

For others, it was when you came up close. Just as Cleopas and his companion didn't recognize Jesus until the breaking of bread, it was when you held out your hands and we shared the body of Christ, the bread of heaven, new life, one with another, and our eyes met, that we could truly see one another, know one another and see new life and new possibility. For my friends and colleagues on the drive-through side, they had their own experiences, including the Hollis family who got in the car and drove five hundred miles from Greenville, South Carolina, to be with us in person and to receive the bread of life.

My brothers and sisters, hope is not just on the horizon, it's on our doorstep, if we but look for it. We have work to do: holy, important work to do. It's time for us to unlock those doors and in safe and small and still masked steps be in community and be about the Lord's work. As Henri Nouwen famously put it, "The great mystery of God's revelation in Christ is that he not only came, lived, died, and rose among us, but that he continues to come, to live, to die, and to rise in our midst."[11]

He lives. You asked me how I know he lives? He lives within my heart.[12] May we show forth in our lives what we profess by our faith. Amen.

---

11. Quoted in *Forward Day by Day*, Forward Movement, Cincinnati, OH, May 15, 2011, 16.

12. Alfred H. Ackley, *He Lives*. Copyright 1990, Belwin Mills/Alfred. Reprinted under One License #A-709283.

LIFE LAID DOWN

The Rev. Patrick L. Keyser
Fourth Sunday of Easter, April 25, 2021

Jesus said, "I am the good shepherd. The good shepherd lays down his life for the sheep." (John 10:11)

A few weeks ago, we welcomed our choristers back to the Cathedral Close. Many of you know that when our building is open for public worship, our boy and girl choristers provide musical leadership on most Sundays of the year. Though we have been able to include some solo performances by our choristers during Sunday worship at various times in the past few months, I must say it has been such a blessing to welcome them back in person and once again hear them make beautiful music as they sing together masked and distanced outside in the Cathedral Garth. I have the great joy of serving as the chaplain to the choristers, which means I have the pleasure of meeting with both the boys and the girls every week to check in with them and see how they are doing. I consider it one of the most joyful aspects of my ministry here.

Seeing them again has certainly brought me much joy these past few weeks, and I know the return to in-person activity and the opportunity to be together with their peers has been good for the kids as well. Spending time with them has reminded me of the particular challenges of being a kid in these pandemic times. It seems most children were able to quickly adapt to the technological changes required for a virtual world, but that does not mean it was an environment in which most were able to thrive. Navigating teenage years is already challenging on its own. The particular stresses of the pandemic—isolation from friends, lack of opportunities for in-person socialization with peers, missed rites of passage both small and great—all these and many more have made this year so difficult and stressful for children.

As I've been considering the challenges children face during this pandemic and praying that we are starting to turn a corner, we have been confronted with further news of children suffering, suffering in ways tied up with the evil forces of racism and violence that infect our country. Suffering that many of us might wish to avoid or ignore altogether. Ten days ago, body cam footage was released showing a police officer shooting and killing thirteen-year-old Adam Toledo in an alley in the West End of Chicago. He was thirteen years old. I was shaken when I first heard the news. I immediately thought of the kids I work with, several of whom are the same age. At thirteen, a kid should be enjoying being a kid—having fun, spending time with friends, learning about themselves, discovering their passions and hopes for life. The killing of a thirteen-year-old child ought to shake us in a particular way.

Two weeks ago, more tragic news reached us that yet another Black person was killed by the police. Daunte Wright, just twenty years old himself, was killed by a police officer who allegedly attempted to use her taser but fired her gun instead, shooting and killing him. Daunte Wright was a father. He had a two-year-old son. Several photos of him holding his young child have been widely shared in recent days. They show a young man filled with pride, beaming as he holds his precious son. In a recent interview Daunte Wright's mother reminded us that "he had a two-year-old son that's not going to be able to play basketball with him."[13] A young man killed; a child left without a father.

As individuals around the country and indeed around the world awaited the verdict in the case of the man charged with murdering George Floyd, a photo from a few years ago was widely shared that showed George Floyd sitting with his daughter in the front seat of his car.[14] Amid all the media attention on the trial, that photo grabbed my attention and added such a depth of humanity to it all. Like Daunte Wright's son, that young girl will grow up without her father. The world will forever know the name George Floyd, but she won't have the opportunity to grow up with and be guided by her father. That was taken away from her, as it has been for too many others.

George Floyd's death on May 25, 2020 sparked a wave of protests against police brutality and the killing of Black and Brown people across this country and indeed the world, in what became one of the largest movements for social change in this country's history. Almost eleven months later, a jury issued its verdict this past Tuesday [April 20, 2021], and Derek Chauvin, a former police officer, was found guilty of all three

---

13. Denise Lavoie, "Daunte Wright: Doting Dad, Ballplayer, Slain by Police," Associated Press, April 14, 2021. *https://apnews.com/article/daunte-wright-shooting-minnesota f70fb7fc4c 205740507b7ec53d7315f0.*

14. Clint Smith, "George Floyd Was Also a Father," *The Atlantic*, April 21, 2021. *https:// www.theatlantic.com/ideas/archive/2021/04/george-floyd-was-also-father/618663/.*

charges of murder and manslaughter. We pray that George Floyd's family begins to find some peace. Some might want to see this verdict as a victory, but that word feels hopelessly inadequate, even inappropriate. It was a basic form of accountability. For a case that included clear video footage of the entire event including the over nine minutes in which Chauvin knelt on George Floyd's neck slowly taking his life away; for a case that had so appalled the world that it caused millions of people to rise up in protest; for a case such as this still so many found themselves on Tuesday afternoon incredibly nervous and fearful as they awaited the verdict—it was but a beginning on a path toward justice. The danger of this moment, particularly for those of us who are White, is to see it as a sign that lasting change has come and that there is no further work to be done. The danger of this moment is to believe that in the conviction of one man, there is no longer a problem in this country. What then are we to do, especially those of us who claim the Christian faith and seek to faithfully follow Jesus?

The scriptures meet us this morning offering words of comfort and challenge. The past three weeks have presented us with gospel narratives that tell of Jesus appearing to his friends after his resurrection. On this Fourth Sunday of Easter our focus, though still rooted in the Resurrection, shifts as we hear Jesus identify himself as the good shepherd. This image is a familiar and comforting one for so many, an image that conveys such tenderness and intimacy. The good shepherd knows his own, and his own know him. They know his voice and follow him. The good shepherd leads and protects his sheep. Our psalm this morning, one of the most beloved passages of scripture, reinforces this sense of intimacy and protection: "The Lord is my shepherd; I shall not be in want. He makes me lie down in green pastures and leads me beside still waters . . . though I walk through the valley of the shadow of death, I shall fear no evil; for you are with me; your rod and your staff, they comfort me" (cf. Ps. 23:1–2, 4). Here at the Cathedral our smallest chapel is dedicated to the good shepherd and features a beautiful image of Jesus gently and lovingly cradling a lamb.

The image of the good shepherd can be a source of great comfort, but we must also consider what at first might seem like a basic question—what makes the good shepherd good? The text offers us a clear answer: "I am the good shepherd. The good shepherd lays down his life for the sheep. . . . For this reason the Father loves me, because

I lay down my life in order to take it up again" (John 10:11,17). Unlike the hired hand, who when seeing the wolf coming leaves the sheep and runs away, the good shepherd does not flee or abandon the sheep. The good shepherd lays down his life so that he may take it up again—new life rising out of death. That is the power of resurrection.

This scriptural expression "to lay down one's life" is unique to the Gospel of John and the letters of John. We find it again, in fact, in our reading from 1 John. The author of that letter proclaims that we know love because Jesus "laid down his life for us" (1 John 3:16). Jesus's laying down of his life is the greatest example of love—an example that not only allows us to know and see love, but also invites us to action showing us that "we ought to lay down our lives for one another" (1 John 3:16). Here is a call to imitate Jesus in a very real, and indeed a very costly way, to lay down our lives for one another, just as the good shepherd laid down his life for us. This call to imitate Jesus is a call to authenticity in the way we live as Christians, as people who seek to follow Jesus. The writer of 1 John goes on to ask us, "How does God's love abide in anyone who has the world's goods and sees a brother or sister in need and yet refuses help?" (1 John 3:17). It is a plea for harmony between our beliefs and our behavior. We who believe that Jesus is indeed the good shepherd who laid down his life for us so that we might have life and have it abundantly must follow him in that way and lay down our lives for one another. This is the dynamic of a resurrection life, of a way of being that really believes that in laying down, in letting things die that need to die, new life will spring forth.

This dynamic is, I believe, one we must live every day of our lives as we daily die to sin in all its various forms. It is foundational for the Christian life. But here, in this moment, God calls us as individuals, particularly those of us who are White, and as church to a particular form of this dynamic, of laying down so that new life might emerge. The murder of George Floyd revealed to so many White folks what was already so very clear to our siblings of color: racism and injustice still deeply infect this land. Millions rose up in the days following George Floyd's death. The reality that we must face is that the racism within us, the racism within our society will not be healed in a week, a month, a year, perhaps not even in a lifetime. It will be not healed by a guilty verdict in one case. The path ahead is one of long-term commitment. This is no time to become complacent. It is no time to feel that the work is done, for that is so obviously not the case. It is a time to heed the words of the author of 1 John who tells us, "Little children, let us love, not in word or speech, but in truth and action" (1 John :18). It is a time to continue to lay down those things that need to be cast down, within ourselves, within our church, within our society, to allow God to bring forth new life.

Last May, a few days after George Floyd's death, I met with our girl choristers on Zoom. One of the head choristers, at the time a rising high school senior, addressed her friends and colleagues with words I simply won't and can't forget. She told them, "I need you to be as angry about this next week, next month, next year as you are right now. I need you to be in this with me for the long term." That is our call as people of faith seeking to faithfully follow Jesus. It is a call to lay down our lives for one another, to allow what needs to be given up to be given up, so that new life can emerge, in ourselves and in this country—so that children are no longer killed, so that children are no longer forced to grow up without a parent, so that Black and Brown bodies are no longer killed by the police. Jesus the good shepherd, who laid down his life for us and revealed to us the costly yet lifegiving way of love, shows us the way. Let us continue on so that all God's children might have life and have it abundantly.

GOD IS LOVE!

THE REV. DANA COLLEY CORSELLO
Fifth Sunday of Easter, May 2, 2021

When I was applying to attend seminary, I was asked to write an essay describing how a particular bible verse or chapter influenced my call to ministry. Well, as one who didn't grow up in the church and had only a cursory knowledge of children's bible stories, I was a bit stumped. I asked my mother what her favorite verse was and instead of just telling me, she found her Bible and opened it to 1 John, chapter 4. I will never forget it; it was as if she were offering me a glimpse of a secretive spiritual truth hidden in one of the Gnostic gospels. She said, pointing, "Look, everything you need to know is in that sentence. God is love."

This memory remains indelible because both my parents rejected organized religion and all its trappings as soon as they could. They were raised in fundamentalist denominations smack dab on the buckle of the Texas Bible belt during the forties and fifties. I can say with confidence that my mother's instinctive beliefs about who God was did not mesh with what the church was teaching. Religion, in her mind, had to be more than mere personal salvation and a puritanical obsession with the petty sins of others. Fear of going to hell did not inspire her to be more loving, forgiving, or compassionate. She had been born a child of God; her factory settings had attuned her to John's truth that "fear has to do with punishment" (1 John 4:18)—and that faith came from neither. What she discovered late in her life was that "against the lovelessness of fear, the gospel actually proclaims the fearlessness of love."[15] No longer did my mother have to placate God out of fear, or wallow in guilt when the thought of a sin might be coming on. After decades of searching and pining, she found a God of her own understanding and it was a God of love.

With stunning brevity, the author of 1 John tells us who God is and by definition who God is not. God's chosen self-definition is love, and divine love in the New Testament is expressed by the Greek word *agape*. God's love is utterly gratuitous, extravagant, it is pure—an offering that

---

15. William L. Self, Commentary on 1 John 4:7–21, *Feasting on the Word*, Fifth Sunday of Easter, Year B, 471.

expects nothing in return, which means it is spontaneous and unmotivated, and there is nothing we can do to earn it or be withheld from it. *It just is.* Sounds like grace, doesn't it?

What is so fascinating about this passage in 1 John, and something I realized when preparing this sermon, is that for years I misinterpreted it or, at best, was a lazy reader. I assumed its theology was the same as what Jesus commands in the gospels: "[Y]ou shall love the Lord your God with all your heart, and with all your soul, and with all your mind. . . . The second is this, 'You shall love your neighbor as yourself" (Mark 12:30–31)—and in that order. But 1 John, chapter 4 begins with this mandate in verse 7, "Beloved, let us love one another." He does not write, "Beloved, let us love God." "The complexity of this concept, then, indicates that perfect love is not the love of human beings for God, but the love of human beings for each other."[16] As you know, it's much harder to love one's enemy or anyone for whom we feel has no claim on us than it is to love a mysterious, cosmic, and unseen God.

And of course, underlying this scripture are the two great parallel commandments: love of God and love of neighbor. These two are intractably linked—it is impossible to obey the first without obeying the second.

Beloveds, my soul friends, we are mandated to love the "other" simply because that is what God does. You see, I have had this all wrong. For years now, I have concluded my prayers by saying, "Christ Jesus, help us or help me to love you more" when I should have been praying, "help us to love one another more."

I think though that the breathtaking beauty of this passage really hinges on verse 19: "We love because he first loved us." We love because he first loved us! Think about that: God's love birthed us into being. This love manifests as the Spirit, which quickens us into holy beings. Because we are birthed into love by love Incarnate, we become children of love, worthy of all love. It is important to note that this verse, "We love because God first loved us" does not mean, "We love others; therefore, God must love us." For John, "Human love is always derivative of the source: God's love."[17]

---

16. Cary W. Charles, Commentary on 1 John 4:7–21, *Feasting on the Word*, Fifth Sunday of Easter, Year B, 469.

17. Ibid.

And this is exactly why I struggle with the doctrine of original sin. If the divine image of God and God's love is coded into our factory settings, why then should we, in our purest essence as newborns, be stained with sin and all its wretchedness? How can an innocent child be birthed from sin when the Bible tells us that we are birthed from love? I love the story that the Celtic theologian, John Philip Newell, tells of the fourth-century Celtic monk Pelagius who was "convinced that when we hold a child immediately after its birth, when we feel the softness and smell the sweetness of the baby's skin, when we look into that baby's eyes, we are seeing a being from a deeper place. We are seeing and smelling God. Pelagius believed that what is deepest in us is 'of God not opposed to God.'"[18] Friends, you might have guessed that I am more of a Pelagian than an Augustinian and, of course, an Episcopalian because I can explore these questions and not be labeled a heretic! I know that we are born into a sinful world, and I do not question our capacity for sin as human beings. But I do not think that we possess a "sin" gene as part of our DNA. I think my mother had it right: we are born from love into love, not from sin and shame.

And as John tells us in the tenth verse, this is exactly why God gifted us with the ultimate sign of love—Jesus, the living love of God given in the flesh to human beings to save us from ourselves. 1 John describes Jesus as the atoning sacrifice for our sins. Well, as you might imagine, I am not a big fan of "substitutionary atonement" theory either. I won't go into the nitty-gritty of why, since the dean did so beautifully during his February 28 sermon. But allow me to share his argument, and I quote, ". . . if our God is the God of Love . . . then love doesn't need payment in order to forgive. Love doesn't demand suffering and death in order to forgive. On the contrary, love forgives [in spite of] everything, freely, completely, and without strings attached. . . . Jesus's suffering and death were not to be the price paid to forgive sins; they were the cost of love."[19] End quote.

The one thing we cannot do is claim to love God while letting the dry rot of hatred or indifference toward the "other" consume us. "Those

---

18. John Philip Newell, *Sacred Earth, Sacred Soul: A Celtic Guide to Listening to Our Souls and Saving the World* (New York: HarperOne, Forthcoming 2021), 22–43. I have also heard JP Newell tell this story numerous times in person!

19. See page 168.

who say, 'I love God,' and hate their brothers or sisters, are liars; for those who do not love a brother or sister whom they have seen, cannot love God whom they have not seen" (1 John 4:20).

The filmmaker Tyler Perry astounded viewers in a moving speech during last Sunday's [April 25, 2021] Academy Awards ceremony when he accepted the Humanitarian Award. He addressed the very essence of the twentieth verse of 1 John, chapter 4. He began:

> You know, when I set out to help someone, it is my intention to do just that. I'm not trying to do anything other than meet somebody at their humanity. One time I was walking to my car and I see this woman coming up out of the corner of my eye and I think she's homeless, let me give her some money. I reach in my pocket and I'm about to give her the money and she says: "Excuse me, sir, do you have any shoes?"
>
> This stopped me cold because I remember being home-less and having one pair of shoes and they were bent over at the heel. I take her into the studio. So as we're standing there [in] wardrobe and we find her these shoes and I help her put them on and I'm waiting for her to look up and all this time she's looking down. She finally looks up and she's got tears in her eyes. She says: "Thank you, Jesus. My feet are off the ground."
>
> In that moment I recall her saying to me, "I thought you would hate me for asking," but I'm thinking, how could I hate you when I used to be you?

Perry then spoke about his mother who grew up in the Jim Crow South grieving the murder of Emmett Till and the civil rights boys and the four little girls who died in the Birmingham church bombing:

> My mother taught me to refuse hate. She taught me to refuse blanket judgment. I refuse to hate someone because they are Mexican or because they are Black or White, or LGBTQ. I refuse to hate someone because they are a police officer. I refuse to hate someone because they are Asian.

Perry then dedicated his award to, quote:

> Anyone who wants to stand in the middle where the healing happens. Anyone who wants to meet me in the middle, to

refuse hate, to refuse blanket judgment and to help lift someone's feet off the ground, this one's for you, too.[20]

WOW! Just wow!

It was Howard Thurman who wrote that "Hatred destroys the core of the life of the hater. Hatred bears deadly and bitter fruit. It is blind and non-discriminating and cannot be controlled once it is set in motion."[21] Please, my beloveds, let us practice love. While our love will always be flawed, we must not hold back because of our fears and inadequacies. Act lovingly, even if imperfectly. Remember, there is no fear in love, because God's perfect love casts out all fear.

And to proclaim anything less than the heart of the universe as being love is to betray the gospel. This one's for all of us. God is love! God is love! God is love! Alleluia! Alleluia! Alleluia! Amen.

---

20. Tyler Perry, Humanitarian Award Acceptance Speech, Academy Awards, April 25, 2021.

21. Howard Thurman, *Jesus and the Disinherited* (Boston: Beacon Press, 1976), 76.

THERE IS WORK TO BE DONE

The Rev. Canon Leonard L. Hamlin Sr.
Seventh Sunday of Easter, May 16, 2021

This morning, I want to tell you one thing: there's work to be done. As I reflect upon the prayer that I have just prayed, I'm not able to account for the number of times I have prayed that prayer in similar or even identical form. And every moment that I've stood to preach in recent months, I have asked that God would bless us, keep us, cover us. But most of all, fill us for all the places that He would send to us.

I am not certain how closely or intently you may have been listening. Maybe you missed it because you dismissed it. There may have been some who characterized the prayer as the mere moment of expected formality preceding the preaching occasion. We may not be in the same place, yet you were close enough to hear me praying.

Through the use of technology and the amazing machinery, we find ourselves sharing this digital space. Those who have turned on and tuned in were both in earshot of the prayer and in position to eavesdrop on the prayer that was being lifted to God, but at the same time, being offered in order to join us closer to God. For some, you heard the words but missed the message. For others, the prayer was an opportunity to step more deeply into the moment. It was a recognition of our being present and the realization of God's presence. The prayer was a petition, a spirit-filled push, a pull, and even a press to open what has been mistakenly closed, or close what may not need to have been opened. Even with a few words, the prayer is a time of learning, listening, relating, and connecting ourselves with God, and even to those who are around us. It is a time when we struggle to find the right words. And a moment when we are challenged to grow, to transform, and even to love.

Time and time again, I have heard generations before me and have been in fellowship with others on this faith journey who, when thinking about prayer, have declared that there's power in prayer. I have heard others join in their response by lifting that wonderful line that says prayer changes things. I have heard others who even reminded me, who said even when prayer doesn't immediately change things, it will, pray, change you in order that you may change things. In the most difficult of times, the darkest of circumstances and struggling situations, I have been told that prayer is all you need. I did not always understand what was being communicated and the truth that was being shared, as words can every so often be insufficient natural tools to express limitless realities.

As a boy who grew up sitting in prayer meeting after prayer meeting, taken there by parents, by loved ones, I was there on Wednesday nights, Saturday nights, other nights during the week. There, time and time again, I would sit in the corner and listen to the elders of the day, or even those who were convicted by the experiences in the moments, witnessing those who were carrying their struggles and their burdens of life, raise up when they would sing prior to their praying on bended knee,

> Sweet hour of prayer! Sweet hour of prayer!
> That calls me from a world of care
> And bids me at my Father's throne
> Make all my wants and wishes known
> In seasons of distress and grief
> My soul has often found relief
> And oft escaped the tempter's snare
> By thy return, sweet hour of prayer![22]

I lift that this morning, not because I've heard those words, but I lift that because I believe those words.

When we think this morning—pastor, Christian leader, and missionary, as well as writer, Arthur Tappan Pierson stated when reflecting upon prayer, he said, "There has never been a spiritual awakening in any country or locality that did not begin in united prayer."[23] It was Mother Teresa who stated, "Prayer enlarges the heart until it is capable of containing God's gift of Himself."[24] Theologian, philosopher, and Bishop of Hippo, more familiar to many, known as St. Augustine, stated, "Pray as though everything depended upon God and work as though everything depended on you."[25] Austin O'Malley, noted author, here wrote,

---

22. William W. Walford, "Sweet Hour of Prayer" (1845).

23. Quoted in J. Edwin Orr, "Prayer and Revival," from a lecture at a Prayer Congress in Dallas. *http://www.jedwinorr.com/resources/articles/prayandrevival.pdf*.

24. Sally Joann Hughes, *From the Heart: Bible Studies* (Meadville, PA: Christian Faith Publishing, 2020).

25. Johnny Hunt, *My Daily Devotional Prayer Book—Volume 2* (Nashville: Thomas Nelson, 2011), 243.

"Practical prayer is harder on the soles of your shoes than on the knees of your trousers."[26] An unknown author is credited with stating, "Do not make prayer a monologue, make it a conversation."

I could go on, but the text lifted from the New Testament this morning (John 17:6–19) comes out of a prayer and a conversation that Jesus was having with God. The disciples were close enough to hear the words and eavesdrop on the divine conversation that Jesus was having with the Father, as they were gathered in the Garden of Gethsemane. These words that were written, the passage that was read, and the reading that has been provided, are part of a larger discourse referred to as the "Farewell Discourse" or the "Last Supper Discourse" given by Jesus to his disciples. It began in the proceeding verses and chapters, around the table, and moved out into the Garden of Gethsemane where we meet Jesus in prayer. We know this moment is filled with tension. It is filled with anxiety. It is even overcome by questioning, and the questioning of the disciples who were attempting to make sense of Jesus's words. Jesus knows he will be arrested. He knows he will be beaten. He knows he will be ridiculed and crucified, but he knows he will be resurrected and will ascend to the Father. But throughout the evening, they listened as they heard all of his words.

And I remind you that he took them to a place that was not just a place of pretty flowers, though we refer to it as a garden. It is not the garden that we think about, where everything is in bloom. Or a garden where it's just peaceful. But the Garden of Gethsemane was a place where planting and harvesting and producing took place. It was a workspace at that time. Even in translation of Gethsemane, it's called here the Valley of Fatness or, here, the Fertile Valley. And many of us know that it is translated as "the olive press" or "the oil press." It was a place where they took raw material and they turned it into something of value. He took them to the garden where they would be able to think about the work around them, so that maybe they might embrace the work that needed to be done within them.

But throughout the evening, they would hear Jesus tell them time and words, one after the other, "to love one another, as I have loved you. Don't let your hearts be troubled. Believe in God, believe also in me. The one who believes in me will also do the works that I do. And even

26. Marcia Ford, *Traditions of the Ancients: Vintage Faith Practices for the 21st Century* (Nashville: B&H Publishing Group, 2006), 137.

in fact, will do greater works than I have done." They heard him say, "I will ask the Father and He will give you another Comforter." They heard him say, "I am the true vine. And I have said these things to keep you from stumbling, but the hour has come" (John 14, paraphrased).

And here in the gospel reading at the end of Jesus's discourse, we find Jesus praying and the commentators, as well as preachers, over the years and throughout generations, have reflected upon this section of John. And have noted that throughout the years, the relationship of Jesus and his disciples to the world has often been complicated. The disciples were selected from the world, are recognized to be in the world. We are told that they are hated by the world, and yet they are not of the world. Jesus prays that his disciples be protected from the evil one who is working in the world. But pointedly, he asks the Father that they, the disciples, not be taken out of the world. It is in the closing words of this discourse that we can hear Jesus say, "As you have sent me into the world, so I have sent them into the world. And for their sakes I sanctify myself, so that they also may be sanctified in truth" (John 17:18).

Jesus sends the disciples into the world to continue his mission. In a moment when there is anxiety; in a moment where there's overwhelming wondering about the future; in a time that is similar to this time where there's still classism, economic deprivation, Jesus's prayer could have been focused on isolating them. But Jesus focused on sending them. Jesus prays that they would be set apart.

We've heard the word "sanctification," and I don't have enough time to get into all that goes on and how we twist that to sometimes our own advantages and self-purposes. But I remind you, sanctification is simply being set apart for a purpose. A purpose that could only be achieved as they were sent. And we've got to be careful that we do not separate the sanctification from the sending. So that if someone declares the desire to be holy as God is holy, that there is a purpose in the holiness that can only be achieved as part of the sending. The ministry would call for them to connect with others, to engage with others, to welcome the stranger, to love their neighbor, to proclaim the good news to the poor, to continue the work as they would proclaim freedom for the prisoners, to recover sight to the blind, and to set the oppressed free. There was work to be done. But let me remind you, I've been told that this kind of work cannot be done by proxy.

Ministry cannot be done by proxy. There are some responsibilities where proxy may work well, but it's not discipleship. You can serve on a board and by proxy cast your vote. You can hold an office and give someone the authority by proxy. You can vote on an issue, but you cannot maintain a fruitful relationship by proxy. Anyone who is married or is in a deep relationship, you realize that a marriage and a relationship do not work well by proxy. There can be no substitute for personal service in this life and in the life of a believer.

Jesus is sending them into the world, so that the world would have what it may be missing. He was sending them into the world in order that there would be light in a dark place, salt in unsavory places, power where there's weakness, selflessness where there is selfishness, love where there is hate. The prayer and their experience were preparing them to receive the promise of the Spirit for a purpose.

God is calling us this morning to climb higher heights, to let down our nets, to cast out into the deep, to walk even on water. Now, some of that may sound ridiculous to some of you, but faith in God will sometimes call us to embrace the ridiculous, in order that someone would be able to see the miraculous.

God has been stirring things up over this past year. As we look out around us, there is something that will happen when we stir each other. And when things get stirred up in order that we would not remain in the same place. And so, I remind you throughout the generations. Preacher after preacher has reminded you the importance of how the eagle stirs her nest. That even in making the nest, the eagle makes that nest in the bottom of the nest, with thorns and sharp objects down at the bottom, and then covers them with all sorts of feathers and soft bedding, in order that when they're young, the eaglets can rest on that soft material. But as they begin to grow, there's a certain time that will come where the eagle starts to remove what is soft when they could not get comfortable. And those thorns start to pop up. Those sharp objects start to remove some comfortable places and sooner or later the eaglets even have to get uncomfortable so that they can say, "I need to move out of here."

Well, I don't know, God, what you've been doing, but over this past year, we've been stirred in a way that we've been pushed out of our nest. And I've heard people talk about being in a rush to get back to a comfortable place. But God's given us the ability and stirred us, so that we would use the wings that we have been given through his prayer to climb to higher heights, to go where we've never gone before, to do what we need to do. And so, the nest has been stirred. And the question that we've got to ask today, as we hear him send us: "Will we do the work that needs to be done?"

> Because somebody prayed for me
> Had me on their mind
> Took the time and prayed for me
> I'm so glad he prayed
> I'm so glad he prayed
> I'm so glad he prayed
> For me.[27]

---

27. Dorothy Norward, Alvin Darling, "Somebody Prayed for Me" (1994).

WE NEED A REVOLUTION

THE MOST REV. MICHAEL B. CURRY
Day of Pentecost, May 23, 2021

Good morning. It is a particular joy to be with you this morning, to be able to be here at the Washington National Cathedral. I thank Bishop Budde and Dean Hollerith, and all of the clergy and the staff, and the congregation, the musicians, the acolytes, and all of us who gather because of the miracle of technology that makes it possible for the Spirit to reach us near and far away.

Like many of you, this has been my church while I was at home, and I would watch and worship and pray with you here. I would sneak around the church and make presiding bishop visits here and there, but I would never tell them that I was coming. It has been a blessing and a privilege to continue to worship God, even in the time of pandemic. I count it a blessing and a privilege to be here this day.

Allow me to offer a text. It's Pentecost Sunday, the Day of Pentecost. From the Acts of the Apostles, chapter one: before Pentecost happened, Jesus said to his disciples, "You will receive power. You will receive power when the Holy Spirit is come upon you. And you will be my witnesses in Jerusalem, in Judea, in Samaria, to the ends of the earth" (cf. Acts 1:8). In first-century Palestine, and in the twenty-first-century world of a global pandemic, you will receive power and you will be my witnesses.

Professor Judy Fentress-Williams of Virginia Seminary offers wonderful commentary on the Bible, which I've started reading through as part of my personal devotion. I sort of fast-forward around because it goes from Genesis to Revelation. When I was working on this message, I fast-forwarded to the Acts of the Apostles and the Day of Pentecost. I came across these words from Professor Fentress-Williams, "The gift of the Holy Spirit is God's ongoing presence and power. And the book of Acts offers an account of how the Spirit empowers and supports this newly birthed revolutionary movement."[28]

Pentecost is about a revolution. It is not about mere moral reform. It is not about tinkering at the edges. It is about transforming an old order into a new order. But do not despair, I know the evidence is not in yet.

---

28. Judy Fentress-Williams, *Holy Imagination: A Literary and Theological Introduction to the Whole Bible*, Kindle ed. (Nashville: Abington Press, 2021).

It looks like the old order is still around, but do not despair. I remember when I was in college, Gil Scott-Heron said it this way, "The revolution will not be televised."[29] It will not always be obvious for eyes to see, but it is real. There is a revolution—a Jesus movement revolution—a revolution of love, a revolution of compassion and goodness and justice and right, and human decency and kindness. Oh, there is a revolution. And Pentecost is about the birth of that revolution, to transform this world and creation from the nightmare it often is into the dream that God has intended. since God said, "Let there be anything."

Jesus told his disciples, there's going to be a revolution before they could see it and maybe before they could believe it. But he said, "Don't worry about that now. The revolution will not be televised, but you will receive power: power when the Holy Spirit comes upon you, and you will be my witnesses in Jerusalem, in Judea and Samaria and to the ends of the earth and to the end of time. You will be my witnesses because the Spirit is going to give birth to a revolution." And Lord knows, we need a revolution.

When I was a little boy, growing up in Saint Philip's Church in Buffalo, New York, I remember being in Sunday school, probably second or third grade, and we had a wonderful, really remarkable Sunday school teacher who could tell Bible stories and hold the attention of second and third graders. I'll tell you one that I remember. I remember the Day of Pentecost; in the old prayer book it was Whitsunday. But I remember it was the Day of Pentecost, or we were near it, and she brought a cake to class. It was a birthday cake and she had candles on it. We got to light the candles, and then we sang "Happy Birthday" to the church, because Pentecost is the birthday of the church. You know, that was a good teaching, that at age sixty-eight, I still remember that.

But it's occurred to me that that's only the beginning. Pentecost is about something more. That's where Professor Fentress-Williams is right. Pentecost is about the birth of a revolutionary movement. A Jesus Movement—a movement of people whose lives were centered on this Jesus of Nazareth, and his teachings, his example, his spirit, to the point that his way of love becomes their way of life. When that happens, there's going to be a revolution.

---

29. Gil Scott-Heron, lyrics and music, "The Revolution Will Not Be Televised" (1970). *https://www.loc.gov/static/programs/national-recording-preservation-board/documents/The RevolutionWillNotBeTelevised.pdf.*

I realized that when I went back to the text. Take a look at Acts, chapter two, and then Luke, chapter one. Remember that Luke is part one and the Acts of the Apostles is part two, both written by Luke, by the same person. In Luke, chapter one, you have the story of an angel visiting a young woman named Mary. And the angel says, "You're going have a baby, Mary, and his name's going to be Jesus. He's going to be great. He's going to be a world changer." Mary responded, "How can this be? I'm a virgin, I'm a young woman. How is this possible?" And the angel said, "Don't worry about that, Mary, the revolution will not be televised. The Holy Spirit will overshadow you."

Then fast forward now to the Acts of the Apostles, chapter two. It says on the Jewish Feast of Pentecost that the followers of Jesus had sort of gathered in that upper room. The Spirit came with wind and fire, and all sorts of Lord knows what. It was like the world was being created, like it was a big bang because a new world was coming into being. They began to speak, and they began to tell the good news about Jesus. They began to tell of God's glorious deeds in the life of this Jesus of Nazareth. Folk from all over the Greco-Roman world surrounding, if you will, Jerusalem, were there for the Pilgrim Feast, and they spoke different languages, but everybody heard and everybody understood! Like Mary, they asked, "How is this possible? We don't speak the same language. We're different people. We're different ethnic groups, different variations on religious traditions. Maybe even different political parties. Maybe even different nationalities. Maybe even every different set you can think. How is it possible that we all hear?" Once again, the same Holy Spirit that birthed Jesus in the life of Mary so that she would give birth, the same Jesus was now born, if you will, by Spirit in their midst.

I figured this out. Or better yet, I didn't figure it out, Phillips Brooks figured this out for me. Phillips Brooks, a great bishop and preacher, probably one of the greatest preachers in the history of Christianity in America, and certainly in our church history, wrote a poem, that hymn, "O Little Town of Bethlehem / How still we see thee lie." Look at or listen to one of the verses: "*O holy Child of Bethlehem / Descend to us, we pray / Cast out our sin.*" Cast out our selfishness! Cast out our self-centeredness! Cast out our egocentricity! Cast out our power politics! Cast out our greed! Cast out our indifference! Cast out our injustice! Cast out our bigotry! Cast out our prejudice! "*Cast out our sin and enter in / Be born in us today.*"

On Pentecost Day, the Spirit gave birth to Jesus in the lives of human beings, and they were changed and they, in time, changed the world. Because when this Jesus is born in us, when Christmas happens in Michael Curry, when Christmas happens in you, then Pentecost, stay with me now—I want you to know, I went to seminary—Pentecost becomes the extension of the incarnation. I think I'm on solid theological ground there. When that happens, a new world is coming into being. A new reality. Because the Jesus who is born is the Jesus who said, "Blessed are the poor. Blessed are the poor in spirit." The Jesus who is born in us, is the Jesus who said, "Blessed are those who are persecuted because they love somebody." Because they just tried to do right. The Jesus who is born in us, is the Jesus who said, "Love your enemies. Bless those who curse you. Pray for those who despise you." The Jesus born in us, is the one who said, "Do unto others, as you would have them do unto you." The Jesus born in us, is the one who said, "As you did it to the least of these who are members of my family, you have done it unto me. Love the Lord, your God. Love your neighbor. Love yourself." When that Jesus is born in us, and in our communities, and in our world, there's going to be a revolution.

That's what happened on that first Pentecost. There were folk from all around: Parthians and Medes, Elamites, and residents of Mesopotamia, Judea, Cappadocia, Pontus, Asia, Phrygia, Pamphylia, Egypt, parts of Libya, Cyrene, Rome, Jews, and Proselytes, Cretans, and Arabians. All of them suddenly became more than themselves, as individual collections of self-interest. Suddenly a new community got born! Suddenly a new family got born!

But it was more than that. The walls that divided the differences that hurt came down like the walls of Jericho when Joshua fought the battle. If you read this story, oh, if you read this story, it is utterly remarkable that when this Jesus became the center of their lives, when the Spirit gave birth to Jesus, the life of Jesus in their lives, his way of love became their way of life and the Acts of the Apostles said that they made poverty history. Acts, chapter four says there was not a needy person among them, because they shared everything they had. My sisters, my brothers, my siblings, if we would share in our country and our communities, if we would share in our world, then no child would go to bed hungry. Jesus was right.

In their time they set folk free. Paul and Cyrus, preaching in Philippi, saw a woman who was a slave and they ministered in her life and set her free. Any time they became more than individual collections of self-interest, they became something resembling God's beloved community, the human family of God, to the point that the Apostle Paul would write of them. Listen to this: this is before the Emancipation Proclamation. This is before civil rights legislation. It's before voting rights. This is before the Magna Carta. This is before the French Revolution. This is before all of our advances. This is before the Universal Declaration of Human Rights. Before all of that, Paul would write of these people who were birthed by the presence of Jesus in their lives. He says, "All who have been baptized into Christ, have put on Christ. There is no longer slave or free; there is no longer male nor female; there is no longer Jew or Gentile" (cf. Gal. 3:27–28). They became more than they could have ever become on their own. They became God's beloved community, the human family of God.

But there's more than that. Paul says in Romans, chapter eight, that the whole creation yearns and groans for the revealing of the children of God, that God's world might be God's World. That the entire world, all of us, all of God's children, might become God's human family, God's family of humanity and all creation. And my friends, when that happens, it's a revolution.

I was probably sixteen or seventeen. I was getting ready to go off to college. I was in the car with my daddy, and he said something to me that he had said to us growing up. He said, "When you get to college, you treat every girl the way you want somebody else to treat your sister." I remember thinking, "Man, you have just ruined all the dreams I had for college." But I knew what he meant. He said, "Treat every girl the way you want somebody else to treat your own sister because that girl is your sister. Treat every boy the way you want somebody else to treat your brother because he is your brother. Treat every woman like she's your mother, because she is. Treat every man like he's your father, because he is. Treat them like you want your own family to be treated because they are your family. Show them the same love, honor, care, dignity, and respect that you would want for your own. Do unto others, as you would have them do unto you." This is not rocket science, but it is world changing. He said, "If we did that, if we did that, then every child would have access to quality education. If we did that, then there would be justice and equality for everybody in this land and around the world. If we did that, we would learn how to lay down our swords and shield down by the riverside. And study war no more." We need a revolution.

I was supposed to be here last year for Pentecost and was going to preach. It still wasn't appropriate for me to travel yet so I did a sermon from my home in Raleigh. I had composed a wonderful sermon. I don't remember what it was about because I never preached it. During the time that I basically composed it and the time the Day of Pentecost came—all in the same week—we saw George Floyd murdered before our eyes. I couldn't preach the same sermon. I remembered talking with Bishop Budde and Dean Hollerith on the phone, trying to figure out what to do. Pentecost in the time of a pandemic, in a world where a man is murdered, it doesn't just change a sermon. It demands change of who we are and of the world. Then coming here this week, Pentecost again, we learned of the killing of Ronald Greene in Louisiana, in which his family was lied to by officials of the government. They were told that he died in an accident. He didn't die in a car accident. He was in the hands of law enforcement and fortunately, somebody leaked the tapes. So here we are, Pentecost again. Let no one tell you we don't need a revolution.

The old ways are not working. They do not work. We need a revolution. A Jesus Movement revolution. A revolution of the Spirit and of love. But be not dismayed. "But be not dismayed," like the old song says. "*Whate'er betide, God will take care.*" If we heed this Jesus and his way of love, which is bigger than any religion. Let me be clear. The way of love is ecumenical and interfaith. It is not the province of anybody, right? Because my Bible says, I believe it says in 1 John, chapter four, "Our beloved, let us love one another. Because love is of God; and those who love are born of God and know God. Those who do not love, do not know God. Why? Because God is love" (cf. verses 7–8). Love is ecumenical. Love is interfaith. Love is bipartisan. Love is multiethnic. Love embraces and includes us all because the source and the origin of love is not any of us. The source and the origin of love is God. When we live in love, we live in God, and the God who created this world the first time can make a new creation.

Let me bring this to a conclusion. A few years ago, I was listening to public radio on a Sunday afternoon, probably in the summer. I suspect I was on vacation. There came a broadcast about a man named Norman Gershman, who had recently published a photographic essay and published a documentary on the Muslims of Albania. The title of the documentary film was *God's House*. God's house. God's world. In the documentary, he told of the small community of Muslims in Albania during the Second World War. You may recall that during that time, Europe was engulfed in darkness as armies of the Third Reich marched through Sudetenland, Austria, Czechoslovakia, Poland, Holland, Belgium, France, eventually all of Europe, save England alone. As Nazi armies advanced toward the small country of Albania, messages were sent by couriers to the Albanian foreign ministry. "You are to identify all Jews living in Albania, provide their addresses and any contact information." It so happened that the foreign minister of Albania was a Muslim, a member of this small community. And in the spirit of Harriet Tubman, he organized an underground railroad, if you will. He sent out word to the small—I want you all to hear me—to the small Muslim community in Albania. It said, "The Jewish people are to be your people. They must live in your homes. They must sleep in your beds. They must eat at your tables. You are to treat them as members of your own family, for that is who they are." And the Muslim community of Albania saved two thousand Jews from the Holocaust.

My sisters, my brothers, my siblings. This is a revolution. A revolution of love; a revolution of goodness; a revolution of kindness; a revolution of compassion; a revolution that happens when the Spirit gives birth to Jesus in our lives.

> There's a sweet, sweet Spirit in this place,
> And I know [it is] the Spirit of the Lord . . .
> Sweet Holy Spirit, Sweet heavenly Dove
> Stay right here with us, filling us with Your love.
> And for these blessings we lift our hearts in praise;
> Without a doubt we'll know that we have been revived,
> When we shall leave this place.[30]

God love you. God bless you. And may God hold us all in those almighty hands of love.

---

30. Doris Akers, "Sweet, Sweet Spirit." Copyright 1962. Renewed 1990 by Manna Music, Inc. (ASCAP) (1962). *Lift Every Voice and Sing II*, #120.

CONTRIBUTORS

Mariann Edgar Budde is the ninth Episcopal bishop of Washington.

Jan Naylor Cope is the provost of Washington National Cathedral.

Dana Colley Corsello is the canon vicar of Washington National Cathedral.

Michael Bruce Curry is the twenty-seventh presiding bishop and primate of the Episcopal Church.

Kelly Brown Douglas is the dean of the Episcopal Divinity School at Union Theological Seminary and canon theologian of Washington National Cathedral.

Rosemarie Logan Duncan is the canon for worship at Washington National Cathedral.

Leonard L. Hamlin Sr. is the canon missioner and minister of equity and inclusion at Washington National Cathedral.

Randolph Marshall Hollerith is the eleventh dean of Washington National Cathedral.

Patrick L. Keyser is the priest associate at Washington National Cathedral.

Jon Meacham is the Rogers chair in the American presidency and co-chair of the Project on Unity and American Democracy at Vanderbilt University, and canon historian of Washington National Cathedral.

ABOUT THE EDITOR

Photo credit: Danielle E. Thomas, Washington National Cathedral

Jan Naylor Cope is an Episcopal priest serving as provost of Washington National Cathedral. She is a frequent guest preacher and speaker nationally and internationally and an adjunct professor of advanced preaching at Wesley Theological Seminary. Her meditations have been included in *The Pilgrim Way of Lent: Reflections from Washington National Cathedral* and *The Bible Challenge* (Forward Movement Publications). She and her husband, John, live in Washington, DC.

DISCARD